AMERICAN WOMEN
CONSERVATIONISTS

AMERICAN WOMEN CONSERVATIONISTS

Twelve Profiles

by Madelyn Holmes

McFarland & Company, Inc., Publishers
Jefferson, North Carolina, and London

Excerpts from *Earth Horizon* by Mary Austin copyright © 1932 by Mary Austin, © renewed 1960 by School of American Research. Reprinted by permission of Houghton Mifflin Company. All rights reserved. *Silent Spring* by Rachel Carson copyright © 1962 by Rachel Carson. *The Sea Around Us* by Rachel Carson copyright © 1950, 1951 by Rachel L. Carson. *The Edge of the Sea* by Rachel Carson copyright © 1955 by Rachel L. Carson; copyright renewed 1983 by Roger Christie. *Under the Sea Wind* by Rachel Carson copyright © 1941 by Rachel L. Carson. Used by permission. *The Everglades: River of Grass* 50th Anniversary Edition copyright © 1997 by Marjory Stoneman Douglas. Used by permission of Pineapple Press, Inc. *Marjory Stoneman Douglas: Voice of the River* copyright © 1987 by John Rothchild. Used by permission of Pineapple Press, Inc. *Beyond Black Bear Lake* by Anne LaBastille copyright © 1987 by Anne LaBastille. Used by permission of W.W. Norton & Company, Inc. Excerpts from *Loving and Leaving the Good Life*, *The Maple Sugar Book*, and *Simple Food for the Good Life* are copyright © 1992, 1950, and 1980 (respectively) by Helen Nearing. Reprinted with permission from Chelsea Green Publishing Company, White River Junction, Vermont, and the Goodlife Center, Harborside, Maine.

LIBRARY OF CONGRESS CATALOGUING-IN-PUBLICATION DATA

Holmes, Madelyn, 1945–
    American women conservationists : twelve profiles / by
Madelyn Holmes.
      p.   cm.
    Includes bibliographical references and index.

    ISBN 0-7864-1783-8 (softcover : 50# alkaline paper) ∞

    1. Conservationists—United States—Biography.   2. Women
conservationists—United States—Biography.   I. Title.
QH26.H66   2004
333.72'092'273—dc22   2004002809

British Library cataloguing data are available

Front cover: Rosalie Edge with a red-tailed hawk, early 1940s, Hawk Mountain Sanctuary *(photograph by Maurice Brown,* © *Hawk Mountain Sanctuary Archives).* Background ©2004 Comstock. *Back cover: (top)* Marjory Douglas *(Florida State Archives);* Mary Austin, 1921 *(photograph by E.O. Hoppé, Huntington Library, San Marino, California).*

Manufactured in the United States of America

McFarland & Company, Inc., Publishers
  Box 611, Jefferson, North Carolina 28640
  www.mcfarlandpub.com

Contents

Preface

As an historian by profession, I naturally turn to the past to find personal inspiration, and the historical figures whose lives and writings form the core of *American Women Conservationists* have served as my most recent sources of inspiration. They are six women with a cause—the conservation of the natural environment of the United States. Mary Austin, Florence Merriam Bailey, Rosalie Edge, Marjory Stoneman Douglas, Helen Nearing, and Rachel Carson believed that this land was their land, and that they would devote their lives to preserving the flora and fauna for future generations of Americans. These women were passionate, persistent, and powerful writers. In a final chapter of the book, I have included brief portraits of six post–World War II conservationists: Faith McNulty, Ann Zwinger, Sue Hubbell, Anne LaBastille, Mollie Beattie, and Terry Tempest Williams, women who have followed in the footsteps of the historical six.

My own concern with conservation issues goes back to the early 1970s when, as a graduate student in agricultural economics in New Jersey, I decided to focus my attention on land use planning in suburban areas. I interviewed market gardeners in the New York City region—farmers who were searching for creative ways to maintain their farms instead of selling out to housing or shopping-mall developers. The people I found had decided to open roadside markets and pick-your-own operations in order to keep their land rural.

This interest in rural land preservation turned international in scope when I moved to Denmark and interviewed farmers in the greater Copenhagen region. The Danish solution was a governmental policy of *fredninger*—translated into English as land preservation. These *fredet* areas were either publicly or privately owned and maintained, but the government

1

ensured their preservation by enforcing certain land use restrictions and underpinning its commitment with payments to private owners.

When I returned to live again in the United States in the mid–1980s, I got a job as an historian at the National Park Service in Salem, Massachusetts, reorienting my perspective to U.S. preservation policies. To my mind, the American system of national parks that started off with the establishment of Yellowstone National Park in 1872 is one of the high marks in the history of how we the people have tried to conserve our land for future generations. Several of the women in *American Women Conservationists* furthered the growth of the National Park Service with their own important initiatives.

The women conservationists who have inspired me and whom I feature in this book may not be everyone's choices. In the first chapter of the book I have tried to answer the question: Why focus especial attention on these six historical women? My explanation is straightforward in that I sought out women who had made a major contribution through writing and whose ideas were pivotal to the development of thought about the natural environment in the United States. In chapter 7, I present my reasons for selecting the particular six contemporary conservationists— women who share fields of interest or ways of living with at least one of the historical antecedents. These women represent only a small sample of possible candidates, but their writings represent a broad spectrum of conservation concerns: preservation of deserts and old-growth forests, wildlife protection, wetlands maintenance, self-sufficient sustainable ways of producing food, and pollution control.

A note about the word "conservationist." In modern usage, we tend to limit the word "conservation" to the protection of natural resources and attach it to concepts of best use and planning. Here, I am referring to its original definition: "keeping in a safe or entire state." That is exactly what these women in *American Women Conservationists* advocated. Each believed that the natural environment of the United States should be preserved in whole units, as living ecosystems.

Rachel Carson, whose words awakened the public to think ecologically, has pinpointed the purpose for writing about these great people in history. In the twenty-first century the very definition of the word "civilized" is a topic for discussion. If we want to be considered a civilized society, we will need to heed the warnings of these women conservationists about protecting our natural endowment. According to the author of *Silent Spring*, "the question is whether any civilization can wage relentless war on life without destroying itself, and without losing the right to be called civilized" (p. 95).

These women knew how to live environmentally sound lives, and they offer role models to all of us. Their eloquent observations of nature have encouraged me to be more attuned to my surroundings—to find value in the rich diversity of natural life. Reading what they wrote and discovering the conditions under which they worked have enriched my life. I hope their stories will enrich yours.

Most of the archival research for this book took place at the Library of Congress, where I was able to uncover the major writings by almost all the women conservationists I have featured. For only two—Rosalie Edge and Mollie Beattie—did I need to search for supplementary resources. Nancy Keeler at Hawk Mountain Sanctuary in Kempton, Pennsylvania, furnished me with Rosalie Edge's unpublished autobiography, and Harvard University's Frances Loeb Library supplied a copy of Edge's booklet *Our Nation's Forests*. Prudence Doherty, archivist at the University of Vermont Special Collections, not only suggested that I include Mollie Beattie but also was instrumental in tracking down her writings.

Field research for this book led me into wilderness areas and national parks from Florida to Washington State, Maine, Utah, New York, Maryland, Virginia, Massachusetts, California and home to Vermont. Although we hiked or canoed through all kinds of weather and over any type of terrain, my husband Lewis was an intrepid companion, and for explorations through Olympic National Park, Redwood National Park, and Joshua Tree National Park, I appreciated the additional accompaniment of daughter Amanda and son-in-law Nicolas.

I am grateful to the following for providing illustrations: Huntington Library, San Marino, CA; Hawk Mountain Sanctuary, Kempton, PA; Florida State Archives, Tallahassee, FL; Smith College Archives, Northampton, MA; and Beinecke Rare Book Library, Yale University, New Haven, CT. I also am grateful to Pantheon Books, New York, for permission to quote from two books by Terry Tempest Williams: *Refuge* and *An Unspoken Hunger*.

Introduction

Deserts were boring—driving past mile upon mile of sand without even enough signs, marking gas stations or restaurants, to be able to play alphabet, my favorite car game. That's my memory from a California childhood, sitting in the back seat of an unairconditioned Chevy driving through the Mojave Desert, impatiently counting the minutes until we would see something. Years later, I read the graphic descriptions of desert plants and animals in Mary Austin's book *The Land of Little Rain*, published in 1903, and I realized what I had missed.

When I heard that my in-laws had retired to Naples, Florida, I was thrilled. The Everglades, teeming with exotic flora and fauna, would be only an hour or two away. But after reading Marjory Stoneman Douglas's classic book *The Everglades: River of Grass*, I became aware that the massive drainage projects that had made southern Florida habitable for my in-laws had irreparably disturbed the natural web of life in this wetlands region.

Similarly, today, when a friend suggests getting up at six in the morning to go birding, I remember early twentieth-century personal revelations about bird life by Florence Merriam Bailey, who offered readers an appreciation of animals as an antidote to hunters who viewed animal killing as a sport. Or when I hear about destruction of ancient forests in the Pacific Northwest, I am reminded of Rosalie Edge and her militant struggles in the 1930s to establish Olympic National Park, knowing that old-growth forests were essential to the well-being of the ecosystem.

And when I consider moving out of my ninth-floor apartment to live a life more in tune with nature, I think of Helen Nearing, who with husband Scott Nearing lived the "good life" on subsistence farms in Vermont and Maine. But when I watch herbicide companies sponsoring prime-time

5

television shows, I realize that Rachel Carson's dire warnings of forty years ago about the environmental hazards from toxic chemicals that confront us daily have gone unheeded.

Today, a host of other American women—Faith McNulty, Ann Zwinger, Sue Hubbell, Anne LaBastille, Mollie Beattie, and Terry Tempest Williams—are continuing where these pioneer conservationists left off.

What each of these women contributed was very important. Their ideas have been pivotal in bringing about a fundamental change in the ways that we interact with the natural environment, and their writings have led the American public to view their land through new lenses. In respect to thinking about wildlife protection, wetlands maintenance, preservation of arid lands and forests, organic gardening, and environmental pollution, these women were trailblazers. Feathers are more beautiful on live birds than atop a woman's hat; swamps have value when left undrained; deserts are no longer considered to be wastelands; the price index for timber is not the sole gauge of a tree's worth; a mountain slope can be more than an awesome ski run; and harmful insects and weeds can be controlled biologically rather than chemically.

My aim in writing this book is to make these American women conservationists household names, as they deserve to be, but some of my reasons for choosing these particular women are predictable and some are personal choices. I was looking at the outset for conservationists who had made a major contribution through writing. So that if a woman had led campaigns or had headed organizations but had not devoted a significant proportion of her life's work to writing about nature, I did not seriously consider her name.

This predilection for writers is partly personal. For several years I taught writing at The George Washington University in Washington, D.C., and I used anthologies of nature writings as sourcebooks for my classes. Invariably, very few women turned up in these collections. Yet, I knew that American women, especially from the middle of the nineteenth century, had entered the writing profession in not inconsequential numbers. Surely, women who loved plants and animals, who lived in rural areas, and who set their stories, poems, and books in every region of the country had written something about nature worthy of being anthologized.

Only two of my subjects, desert writer Mary Austin and environmentalist Rachel Carson, appeared in any of the books I had used in teaching. The others were chosen for biodiversity, to cover a range of issues from wildlife protection to the conservation of wetlands, forests, and mountains. Not surprisingly, there was considerable overlapping, for lovers of nature did not confine themselves to writing about only one type of fauna, flora, or terrain.

Among women who concentrated their attention on animals, women birders were by far the most numerous. I chose Florence Bailey as my subject because of the stylistic appeal of her field guides, as well as for her collaborative lifestyle with Vernon Bailey, husband and fellow naturalist.

When selecting a spokesperson for old-growth forests, I sought leads in an encyclopedia of American forest history to find the name of Rosalie Edge. Having read her hard-hitting pamphlets, I concurred with a reporter in the Altoona, Pennsylvania, *Tribune*, who called her "this glorious Joan of Arc of conservation." There was no competition when picking a writer about wetlands. Marjory Douglas has been the voice of the Florida Everglades since 1947 when her best-selling book, *The Everglades: River of Grass*, was first issued.

No book on U.S. conservationists would be complete without a figure from the "back to the land" movement. Helen Nearing, who with husband Scott Nearing escaped in 1932 to the Green Mountains of Vermont and later to the coast of Maine, reported their experiments with environmentally sound farming replace in *Living the Good Life*.

I highlight the lives and writings of these particular women, but they represent only a few of the hundreds who, beside the more familiar names of Henry David Thoreau, George Perkins Marsh, John Muir, John Burroughs, Theodore Roosevelt, and Aldo Leopold, laid the foundation for our contemporary environmental consciousness.

Before 1890, when, according to historians, the U.S. frontier was "officially" closed, Americans had considered their land—the continental United States—to be an endless expanse of unlimited resources. And to immortalize the frontier mentality, Americans exterminated the buffalo and staked out homesteads on any territory they could lay claim to, regardless of its suitability for agriculture. At least two prophetic voices, writing in New England in the mid-nineteenth century, offered early warnings of the detrimental effects of this type of attitude toward the land of the United States. Henry David Thoreau in Massachusetts published his classic book *Walden* in 1854 and Vermonter George Perkins Marsh published his monumental treatise *Man and Nature* in 1864.

Female contemporaries of Thoreau and Marsh also wrote about nature and several introduced ideas of environmental conservation that would be developed more fully by women featured in this book. The most recognizable name from this early era is that of Susan Fenimore Cooper, daughter of one of the nation's first literary luminaries, James Fenimore

Cooper. Susan Cooper, who lived from 1813 to 1894, published *Rural Hours* in 1850 and continued to write about nature for more than forty years.

Her 1850 book describes the particular natural environment surrounding Otsego Lake, New York, in a town called Cooperstown that had been founded by her grandfather in 1786. It is based on entries in a journal she kept beginning about 1845 and depicts the happenings of nature during the course of one year. Although Susan Cooper was educated in New York and Paris, as a young woman of twenty she chose to return to Cooperstown, where she lived unmarried until her death at the age of 81. As a result, her writings are steeped in the local history, culture, flora and fauna of this region. After the success of *Rural Hours* she went on to write many books and articles, only some of which were about nature, and in 1868 she published a new edition of *Rural Hours* with an additional seventeen pages that she called "Later Hours." In this update she continues to share her intimate knowledge of the Otsego Lake landscape but also voices sentiments of the post–Civil War age, concerned that the railroad line in construction will destroy the valley's beautiful woods and that the village's new schoolhouse will teach children to aspire only for material prosperity and not for higher values in life.

In a series of three articles called "Otsego Leaves I, II, III," published in *Appletons' Journal* in 1878, Susan Cooper joined the ranks of literary ornithologists. With lyrical detail she offered readers a picture of bird life in her home village, discussing the families of robins who nested year after year under the eaves of her roof and the bird nursery in the hollow trunk of the venerable elm tree. She spoke out against the slaughter of small birds for hat adornments and even introduced an ecological argument, relating a decline in the number of birds to an increase in the population of unwanted insects. Near the end of her life in 1893, she published an article entitled "A Lament for the Birds" in *Harper's New Monthly Magazine* that bemoaned the decrease in the variety of bird species to be found on Lake Otsego, noting in particular the less frequent appearances of white pelican, white swan, and wild pigeons.

The following generation of women naturalists continued to write about birds but also became collectors of flora and fauna, taking part as amateur biologists in the more general nineteenth-century fascination with collecting objects of nature. In the regions where they lived, Mary Treat, Martha Maxwell, Annie Trumbull Slosson, and Katharine Dooris Sharp opened readers' eyes to the local environment as important popularizers of nature and early proponents of conservation.

Mary Treat (1830 to 1923) wrote about observations of nature from her backyard in Vineland, New Jersey, and published a best-selling book in 1885 entitled *Home Studies in Nature*. Her interests centered around insects and spiders and she became a specialist in carnivorous plants.

Martha Maxwell (1831 to 1881) gained a national reputation as a taxidermist, known for mounting spectacular displays of Colorado's flora and fauna. The wild animals in her collection appeared especially lifelike, molded in plaster but covered with their own skins and presented in scenes as part of natural landscapes. In 1873 she founded the Rocky Mountain Museum in Boulder, Colorado, and in 1876 she took her exhibit to the Centennial in Philadelphia where she was the star attraction of the Colorado pavilion.

Annie Trumbull Slosson (1838 to 1926) was a collector of insects, especially prizewinning mounted butterflies, who donated her 35,000-specimen collection to the American Museum of Natural History in New York City. In 1892 she was one of the founding members of the New York Entomological Society and wrote numerous articles about her collecting methods in Florida, Pennsylvania, Connecticut, and New Hampshire for journals of entomology.

Katharine Dooris Sharp (1846 to 1935) was a botanist who contributed a vast collection of floral specimens to the State Herbarium of Ohio. As a writer and poet, she advocated conservation of Mother Nature and proposed that a tract of land be protected in every neighborhood.

Olive Thorne Miller (1831 to 1918) continued the tradition of American nature writing that Susan Cooper had initiated, perhaps more than the collectors, focusing her attention on birds. She was extremely prolific, an author primarily of books for children in which she tried to instill her own love of nature. She started birding in Prospect Park in Brooklyn in the mid–1870s when she moved there with her husband and four children, and she published her most influential book for adults, *Bird-Ways*, in 1885. Mrs. Miller lectured against killing birds for women's hats and spoke out against pillaging of natural environments, which she believed should be preserved as refuges from the world of strife and crime. In one sense, what Susan Cooper began Olive Thorne Miller developed with her more detailed descriptions of birdlife. In turn, Miller's attitudes and writings exerted a profound influence on Florence Bailey within the succeeding generation.

It was not until the 1890s that Americans, both men and women, began to write in a noticeably different tone expressing a new consciousness about the need for conservation of the natural environment of the United States. Attitudes and actions toward the land appeared to shift gears, with changes occurring in what can be identified as three broad time periods: from 1890 to 1930, from the 1930s to 1962, and from 1962 to the present. The six historical women included in this book were opinion-molders. In their writings they espoused sentiments that have taken decades to gain widespread, public acceptance. They wrote about ecology—the interconnectedness of all forms of life—in whatever realm of nature was their focus: deserts, wildlife, forests, wetlands, mountains, or oceans. They were lonely voices, but they were not alone.

1890 to 1930

The book begins with Mary Austin and Florence Merriam Bailey, who made their most significant contributions to conserving the U.S. environment from 1890 to 1930. Each was clearly ahead of her time in the ideas she espoused; what they wrote informs our thinking today. Austin saw beauty in the natural world of the desert—in its plants, animals, landforms—and wrote stories about inhabitants who lived in accordance with nature's ways. Bailey made public her observations about bird life, assuming that a public educated about species' habits would not want to destroy animals.

During the early years of the twentieth century, when writers and policymakers started thinking seriously about protecting the natural environment of the United States, these women's voices were overshadowed by three names who held center stage: Theodore Roosevelt, John Muir, and John Burroughs.

Both before and after his eight-year tenure in the White House, Theodore Roosevelt wrote books about wildlife, travel, history, and his personal experiences as a hunter and North Dakota rancher. In speeches and executive orders as president of the United States from 1901 to 1909, he laid out the fundamentals of a national conservation policy that has underpinned succeeding twentieth-century governmental actions.

During his presidency he increased by millions of acres the public landholdings of the federal government. He added to national forests, working hand-in-hand with Gifford Pinchot whose public management policies instituted regulated use of forest reserves. Roosevelt created wildlife refuges and also utilized the Antiquities Act of 1906 to preserve eighteen national monuments that formed the basis for future national parks. For example, Olympic National Park in the state of Washington, created in 1938 with the active support of Rosalie Edge (see chapter 3), was established on land that had at its core one of his designated national monuments.

In Theodore Roosevelt's policies we see the beginnings of a governmental role in conservation, based on saving remnants of land that had been overlooked in the rapid settlement of the country. The two best-known nature writers of the period, John Muir and John Burroughs, wrote inspiring essays that helped to forge a conservation mentality in the American public. Together with Mary Austin and Florence Bailey among others, they introduced into the twentieth century a new attitude, a post-frontier way of approaching the interaction between Americans and their land.

John Muir, who started the Sierra Club in 1892, left his strongest legacy in the words he wrote about the mountains of California and, in particular, the Yosemite Valley. From Muir, who expressed spiritual emotions from climbing a mountain or a tree in a storm, a direct path leads to writers of today who also describe exultation in experiences of wilderness.

The nature writer from New York State, John Burroughs, whom Florence Merriam Bailey invited to Smith College to lead students on bird walks (see chapter 2), is most remembered for his appreciation of the intimate details of less dramatic nature in the Hudson River Valley. His philosophy of enjoyment of nature led him to a lifelong love of the simple things in life.

1930 to 1962

Rosalie Edge, Marjory Stoneman Douglas, and Helen Nearing, who wrote their most influential works during this time period, expressed ideas that were out of sync with their historical era. Edge struggled to preserve old-growth forests, writing about the less obvious uses of forests when the public wanted to enjoy "natural" products made from wood, such as redwood furniture and wooden toys. Douglas warned against draining the Everglades during a time when man was convinced he could engineer himself around any inconvenience in nature. Helen Nearing, vegetarian and organic farmer, advocated environmentally sound methods of growing and eating food when high-yield scientific agriculture was dominated by artificial fertilizers, pesticides, and chemically controlled production.

During this period in U.S. conservation history, environmental problems moved for a time into the forefront of governmental policymaking. In the wake of the agricultural depression and under the impact of the Dust Bowl disaster of the 1930s, the federal government, steered by Franklin Delano Roosevelt's New Deal, tried out a host of new solutions. Land use planning, soil rehabilitation, and civil engineering projects allowed people to presume that they could control nature, an attitude not seriously debated until the publication of *Silent Spring* by Rachel Carson in 1962.

At the same time as New Dealers were trying to tame nature, however, the Roosevelt administration continued to expand landholdings in national parks, an effort in which many women played crucial roles. Rosalie Edge's forceful advocacy for Olympic National Park is detailed in chapter 3 and Marjory Douglas's importance to the founding of Everglades National Park is described in chapter 4.

From 1930 to 1962, however, it was not only women conservationists who were formulating an ecological way of thinking about people's relationship with the natural environment. A number of men in the 1930s published important books decrying how Americans had destroyed their land. Russell Lord's *Behold Our Land*, Paul Sears's *Deserts on the March*, and Stuart Chase's *Rich Land Poor Land: A Study of Waste in the Natural Resources of America* were several that found large numbers of readers. The loud cries to stop the despoliation continued into the 1940s, climaxing in 1948 with the publication of two books: *Our Plundered Planet* by Fairfield Osborn and *Road to Survival* by William Vogt.

The male writer from this period whose words have continued to affect contemporary American perceptions of nature most strongly is Aldo Leopold and especially his book, *A Sand County Almanac* (published in 1949). In his lifetime, he changed his own attitude about the role of wildlife, beginning his career in 1909 as a forester and game manager employed by the U.S. Forest Service in New Mexico, motivated to exterminate predator animals. By the time he published *Game Management* in 1933, he had determined that saving native fauna could best be accomplished by setting aside areas in national forests preserved in a natural state with no logging or road building allowed, but with lawful hunting and fishing.

But Aldo Leopold's name today is most closely associated with his ideas about wilderness. In 1935, he bought eighty acres of land in Wisconsin, where he had become the first professor of wildlife management in the United States. In the first part of *A Sand County Almanac*, Leopold guides readers through nature's happenings during twelve months of life on this land, and in the third part of the book presents his environmental philosophy. In spelling out a "land ethic," he contends that "despoliation of land is not only inexpedient but wrong," and if people are to live ethically with nature they must respect "the biotic community that includes soils, waters, plants, and animals."

1962 to the Present

In the third time period, the contemporary era that was launched when Rachel Carson published *Silent Spring* in 1962, concern about preserving the natural environment in the United States became a popular movement. Contemporary conservationists Faith McNulty, Ann Zwinger, Sue Hubbell, Anne LaBastille, Mollie Beattie, and Terry Tempest Williams have been important voices of this new era, writing in concert with Edward Abbey, Wallace Stegner, John McPhee, Peter Matthiessen, and Edwin Way Teale, among scores of others.

In addition, many women today have joined the ranks of environmental experts, participating in scientific studies of flora and fauna, writing seminal books on animal behavior, or fighting legal battles to protect natural habitats of endangered species. Biologists have written about the perfidious mating habits of birds and have made strides in interpreting how animals communicate with each other. Ethologists have welcomed evidence of animal intelligence and aptitudes for learning. Protectors of wildlife have started breeding programs in captivity and then have reintroduced nearly extinct animals back into the wilderness.

Women continue to start their own organizations to protest egregious outrages against nature, but are also active at all levels in national, regional, and local environmental groups. In earlier decades of the twentieth century, women provided the Audubon Society with the core of its membership, participated actively in the Sierra Club, and joined animal protection organizations. In the 1970s, they started animal rights groups and assumed leadership positions in the National Wildlife Federation and the World Wildlife Fund.

In governmental organizations as well, women have been employed not only in entry-level positions as scientists and administrators but also have held some of the most important posts, such as secretary of the United States Department of the Interior, director of the U.S. Fish and Wildlife Service, director of the National Science Foundation, and as superintendents of several national parks. From her position as First Lady in the mid–1960s, Lady Bird Johnson launched a national campaign to "beautify" local communities by educating the public about the relation of the natural environment to the health and welfare of the whole society.

Originally, my intention in writing this book was to disseminate these women's important and prophetic ideas about the environment to a wide audience. But as I began to read their writings, I realized that each of these women had much to say about how people can live their lives in collaboration with nature. So that a book purportedly about non-human living things is, in actuality, as much concerned with human lives as with the lives of plants and animals.

Mary Austin was most impressed by Native Americans who arranged their existences in partnership with the natural conditions of the California desert and adjusted their housing, eating, and livelihood habits to fit in with their environment. Florence Bailey arranged her life to combine marriage with observing bird life and emphasized in her writings the domestic lives of animals. Rosalie Edge argued forcibly for the preservation of old-growth trees and, in fact, of all living creatures, going so far as rescuing peregrine falcons from a New York City hotel window to publicize her concern for predator animals. Marjory Douglas campaigned to stop human beings' upstaging of nature in a relentless drive to inhabit the wetlands of Florida. At an age when most people were content to sit in front of a television set, she was overbooked as a podium speaker. Helen Nearing not only wrote about the need to live a life in tune with nature, but together with her husband worked out a way of living that put their philosophy into everyday practice. Rachel Carson, critical of the artificial world of man's creation, focused her own attention on the wonders and realities of the universe, finding "reserves of strength in the contemplation of the beauty of the migration of the birds, the ebb and flow of the tides, the folded bud ready for spring" (*Sense of Wonder*, p. 29).

All of the women in chapters 1 through 6 of this book are historical figures, although two died as recently as the 1990s. Their writings, their ideas, and their lives have spurred on new generations of women conservationists in the United States. In chapter 7, the chronicle of women conservationists is brought up-to-date with briefer biographies of six women who have raised their voices and their pens in the struggle to preserve this American land from the 1960s to the present.

The book is structured as a series of cultural biographies, with full chapters devoted to each of the six historical conservationists and one composite chapter about the lives and writings of the contemporary American women. In each chapter the woman's own words tell her story, and the reader is exposed to the main tenets of her environmental thinking and literary contribution.

The order of presentation is chronological, beginning with Mary Austin and concluding with Rachel Carson. Chapter 7, with profiles of six contemporary women conservationists, opens with the oldest, Faith McNulty, and closes with the youngest, Terry Tempest Williams.

These women not only raised their pens on behalf of conservation of the American landscape but also wrote about strategies for living exemplary, environmentally sound lives. They pointed the way towards the future, directions that if we refuse to follow may lead to the destruction of the landscape as we know it—"This Land ... from California to the New York Island."

1

Mary Austin
(1868–1934)

If one is inclined to wonder at first how so many dwellers came to be in the loneliest land that ever came out of God's hands, what they do there and why stay, one does not wonder so much after having lived there. None other than this long brown land lays such a hold on the affections. The rainbow hills, the tender bluish mists, the luminous radiance of the spring, have the lotus charm [The Land of Little Rain, *p. 6*].

Mary Austin had never planned to write about the desert landscape, but as a young woman growing up on the fertile plains of Illinois she had a premonition that writing would be her vocation and that the natural world would be her subject matter. When she moved to California with her family in 1888, twenty-year-old Mary Hunter's only formal preparation was a science degree from Blackburn College in Carlinville, Illinois. Yet nature had endowed her with a keen sense of observation, an attraction to things wild, and an uncanny talent to depict what others might dismiss as empty space in colorful, mysterious, and even alluring language.

Her fourteen descriptive sketches of the California desert, published originally by Houghton Mifflin in 1903 as *The Land of Little Rain*, introduced this heretofore unfamiliar environment to the reading public. She followed up this book with others also set in the desert lands of California, most notably *The Flock* about herding sheep and *Lost Borders*, a medley of stories about people who inhabit the desert.

Even though she escaped from this environment, which at the same time attracted and repelled her, her writings about this landscape launched her career. When she visited London literati in the decade before World

17

War I, H.G. Wells called her the most intelligent woman in America. She went on to publish more than thirty books, novels with feminist themes or books about indigenous culture in the southwest United States, which were other lifelong interests. But it was her early writings about the desert—the rich, prose descriptions of adaptations by all forms of life—that established her as an American conservationist.

Mary Hunter, in true nineteenth-century style, was led to the desert by her husband, Stafford Wallace Austin. She didn't want to go to the Owens Valley in Inyo County in eastern California when he took a job there in 1892. Neither did she want to stay. Nevertheless, she did stay except for several health- or job-induced absences until 1906, when she left her husband and the desert permanently to make a home in the artist's colony of Carmel, California.

Childhood

The natural environment where Mary Hunter spent the first one-third of her life, a small agricultural town in southwestern Illinois, was a stark contrast to the California desert environment that she enshrined in her writings. Her childhood home in the Midwest was situated in the Mississippi River Valley on a wet plain menaced by fetid air that brought with it the feared autumn fever, in direct opposition to "the land of little rain" as she named the desert environment. The town where she was born on September 9, 1868, had already established a solid, middle-class Protestant society, far different from the not-yet-formed community of California homesteaders.

Carlinville, Illinois, located not far from the state capital in Springfield nor from the closest big city, St. Louis, had gone through its pioneering stage in the early 1800s. The town's population was overwhelmingly of English background with smaller enclaves of German and Irish immigrant families. Mary's heritage was first-generation English on her father's side, for George Hunter had emigrated from Yorkshire as a young man. On her mother's side, the family heritage was more mixed and had laid down longer roots in the United States, having moved into Illinois shortly after statehood in 1818. One branch of her extensive local relatives counted themselves among Carlinville's first families, and this connection made the annual Old Settlers' Picnic a childhood tradition.

Mary Austin insists in her autobiography, titled *Earth Horizon*, that all nature was "beautiful and interesting" and that she was not partial to the outdoors environment of her childhood. Yet the description of her backyard when the family lived on a farm in the outskirts of Carlinville is especially poignant:

> I remember the orchard with great clumps of frail spring-beauties coming through the sod; the smell of budding sassafras on the winds of March, and the sheets of blue violets about rotting tree-trunks in the woodlot. I remember the tree toads musically trilling, the katydids in the hickory tree by the pump.... I more than recall the hot honey-scent of red clover, and the heavy, low flying bumble-bees; long walks in winter over the snow with Father, and the discovery of green fronds of fern and leafy wild blackberry vines under the edge of February thaws.... [I]n the spring there were blossoming haws and wild crab-apples, with bluebells under them—there is no wonder in the world like a wild crab tree coming rosily out between tiny bracts of green—and blazing crimson sumach in the fall [*Earth Horizon*, pp. 48, 65].

Mary's parents, George Hunter and Susanna Savilla Graham, were married in 1861. Her father, who exerted by far the stronger influence over the child, was short-lived unfortunately and died in 1878 when Mary was only ten years old. But Mary retained many of the interests and attitudes of her father throughout her own lifetime.

George Hunter had immigrated to the United States when he was not yet twenty, traveling by ship with his brother to New Orleans and then up the Mississippi River to St. Louis. He had been attracted to farming but studied for a law degree, so that he actually made his living as an attorney. When the Civil War broke out, he was one of the first to sign up in the Seventh Illinois Regiment and rose to the position of captain in the Union Army. However, his health was irreparably damaged during his three-year stint in the war, and her father's ill health cast a dark shadow over her childhood memories.

The strongest bond between father and child grew up around their shared fondness for books. Carlinville, Illinois, was, in Mary Austin's words, the "western edge of American culture" and George Hunter, a relatively recent arrival to the United States, retained a lifelong love for Old World culture. He brought home a copy of *Alice in Wonderland* for her from the town library, along with a library card in her own name, and introduced Mary to the children's magazine *St. Nicholas*. One of her fondest memories of her father was "sitting on Pa's desk when he worked—he often wrote papers there to read at the Grange or the Horticultural Society" (*Earth Horizon*, p. 70).

In contrast to her father, Mary always portrayed the role that her mother played in her life in a negative light. In her autobiography, she emphasizes how she felt unwanted, overlooked, and even unloved by her mother. Susanna Graham was married when she was eighteen and gave birth to seven children, only three of whom lived to adulthood. After her husband died, she worked as a nurse and continued to participate in the local Methodist Church and the Women's Christian Temperance Union (WCTU).

Mary's childhood family consisted of an older brother, James, born in 1866, a younger sister, Jennie, born in 1870, and a younger brother, George, born in 1877. Mary's closest sibling and, as she expressed it, her "most beloved person," was Jennie. Unfortunately, shortly after their father died, Jennie caught diphtheria and died as well at the tender age of eight.

Perhaps it is from the story of her education rather than from family history that we can begin to understand how the child, Mary Hunter, developed into the conservationist writer, Mary Austin. Mary Hunter was a precocious child and had taught herself to read before her parents had formally enrolled her in the town's public school when she was five and a half. She learned to read words out of her older brother's primer. "[S]he demanded to be told what it said. When stories were read her, she was never happy until she got the page in hand and stared hard at it" (*Earth Horizon*, p. 47).

Her ability to read caused a disturbing incident when she finally started first grade. The teacher did not believe that she could read and made her sit in the front of the class wearing a dunce cap, because "little girls who tell fibs in school must wear the dunce cap" (p. 60). However, when the school principal walked into the classroom, he embarrassed the teacher by asking Mary to read aloud from a *McGuffey Reader*. After she had proven to the teacher that she was not lying and really could read, the principal moved her into the next grade level. Even though young Mary Hunter was continually promoted in school beyond the class for her chronological age, she nevertheless remembered her years at the town school only as the "stultification of young intelligence" (*Earth Horizon*, p. 58).

Yet her intellectual growth, love of books, and early forays into the writing profession progressed throughout her childhood years. Her family knew that she wanted to be a writer of books when she grew up, because she had announced her intention by the age of seven. The first piece of writing that she describes in her autobiography is an illustrated poem, and among her friends and family she was always the designated storyteller. She was imaginative and remembered "sitting in the midst of a haymow, of a hot summer's afternoon, or around the rim of the old rock quarry" regaling the other children with outrageous adventure stories (*Earth Horizon*, p. 72).

Her first major piece of writing, composed at the age of ten or eleven but since lost, was called "Play to be Sung." Young Mary Hunter, growing up in a small Midwestern town, had never had the opportunity to attend a performance of an opera, but as an imaginative child she created a two-scene play, written in rhyming verse. She set her opera in a seventeenth-century castle complete with a lady, her lover and two sword-fighting gentlemen.

When Mary was twelve years old, her sources of education expanded beyond the confines of the town's public school. New neighbors introduced to Carlinville the Chautauqua Literary and Scientific Circle, an adult education movement that was sweeping the country with "book learning." For Mary, the Chautauqua movement exposed her to new realms of knowledge, and the course that made the longest-lasting impression was the one she took in geology.

For this course, she purchased the first book that was exclusively her own. It was called *Old Red Sandstone* by Hugh Miller and she remembered reading it outside, sitting in her favorite cherry tree and reveling at how "the familiar landscape of Rinaker's Hill, the Branch, the old rock quarry, unfolded to the dimensions of a geological map" (*Earth Horizon*, p. 104). This book would not have been compelling reading for most twelve-year-olds, but Mary Hunter, burgeoning conservationist, was already marking out her own path as a writer. She continued throughout her teens to write poetry and to read "inordinantly," but it was not until she had completed the requisite public school curriculum that she was able to venture into the larger world of ideas.

Her higher education, however, took an irregular path. Like her brother before her, Mary enrolled at Blackburn College, a small Presbyterian college located in Carlinville. The college had originally been established to train young men for the Presbyterian ministry, but by the 1880s it had broadened its mission considerably. Unfortunately, after only a few months of college study, Mary's ill health forced her to curtail her studies and to limit herself to a few courses in art.

Then, because training to become a teacher seemed the only possible productive education for a young woman, she transferred to the State Normal School in Bloomington, Illinois. She lasted there for only five months before suffering a nervous breakdown, which she blamed on the normal school curriculum. The emphasis on pedagogical methods stifled her intellectual development, and she could not conform to the regimentation of the normal school's routines.

Eventually, she did return to Blackburn College and spent two full years there, graduating in 1888. She studied science, served as literary editor of the college journal, and was elected class poet. Even though she had decided on a literary career for herself before entering college, she chose to study science rather than English because she needed the laboratories and the instructors to expand her knowledge base. Her most specific memories of college courses were the direct observations, science experiments and, in particular, a course on "adaptations of flowers and insects" taught by Charles Robertson. She also took Latin, political economy, psychology, logic, natural theology, and history. Her favorite scholarly subject, folklore, which became her lifelong passion, was not a part of the college curriculum in the late nineteenth century.

During her final semester at college, she and several other women students started a secret society. All nine members pledged to do something purposeful with their educations. Mary Hunter had decided "to teach, preferably natural sciences, and then to write novels and other books" (*Earth Horizon*, p. 175). When she arrived in California soon after graduation, that is precisely the future career that she pursued.

Years in California

Mary Hunter traveled to California with her mother and younger brother during the summer of 1888, taking up residence with her older brother, Jim, at a homestead in the south central part of the state in the vicinity of Bakersfield. After one year of trial and errors, attempting to farm in a region where there was no water, Mary moved to Mountain View Dairy. There she was employed as a schoolteacher, while the rest of the family moved to a small farm in a more settled area only three miles from the city of Bakersfield. During this time she met Stafford Wallace Austin, her future husband.

The man she married in May 1891 was a young college graduate and also a newcomer to California. His family had lived in Hawaii for generations and could trace their roots there to missionary days. The family had once owned a plantation in the Hawaiian Islands, and Wallace's father was a circuit judge.

Shortly after the wedding, Wallace Austin's older brother offered him a business opportunity in the Inyo Valley to help start up an irrigation project. Even though this original project failed, forcing the couple into debt, they stayed in this remote, desert region of California for fourteen years. The couple's only child, Ruth, was born with an inherited brain defect in 1892, and although they cared for her at home until adolescence, when Mary left her husband in 1906 she placed Ruth in permanent institutional care.

Mary eventually took up schoolteaching as did her husband, and at the same time got her start as a writer. The first story she published was in *Overland* magazine in the early 1890s, and she went on to sell several others to *The Atlantic Monthly*, and to publications for children, such as *Youth's Companion* and *St. Nicholas*. By the end of the 1890s, Mary tried to relocate the family to Los Angeles and spent the academic year of 1899-1900 teaching at the Normal School there. However, after one year, she returned to her increasingly unstable marriage and resigned herself to life in the desert.

The specific desert region that Mary Austin wrote about is situated in central California, east of the Sierra Mountains. Her territory encompasses the desert environment of the Owens Valley and Death Valley and stretches from Mt. Whitney all the way to the Nevada border. Mary, writing in her autobiography, located the "land of little rain" in her inimitable style with more poetic than geographic precision: "[B]etween Owens Lake and the northern end of the Alabamas, clustered all that enchanted charm of the district which people who found themselves enmeshed in it sometimes cursed as they curse the beauty of women" (*Earth Horizon*, p. 253).

The Austins lived in several towns along the Owens River: Lone Pine, Bishop, and Independence. She also became well acquainted with the railroad center of Mojave, traveling there often by stagecoach. From Mojave, Mary could connect to a train to Bakersfield to visit her mother who lived there.

During the 1890s and into the turn of the century, this area still depended economically on exploiting the natural wealth of the land. The region was dotted with mines, and in some localities where water was available, land was used for farms, cattle ranches, and as pasture for itinerant flocks of sheep.

One hundred years later, two branches of the U.S. government—the National Park Service and the Army—vie for domination over this desolate land. They make strange neighbors. The 1994 California Desert Protection Act has preserved millions of acres as parkland and wilderness. Across the sand, the Army carries out tank-training maneuvers, tests bombs and helicopter gunships, and prepares troops for military encounters in the twenty-first century.

These two federal agencies are not the only ones to have laid claim to the "land of little rain." In the early twentieth century, the city of Los Angeles won permission to divert much of the water from the Owens River to a series of aqueducts to supplement the city's water supply. Today Owens Lake is no longer a body of water but a desiccated 100-square-mile lake bed.

When Mary Austin sat down to write a book about her impressions of the desert environment, she found it difficult to capture the correct tone. As she explained in her autobiography, she "had been trying to hit upon the key for it [the book] for a year or more, and found it at last in the rhythm of the twenty-mule teams that creaked in and out of the borax works, the rhythm of the lonely lives blown across the trails" (*Earth Horizon*, p. 296).

Her life, too, was one of these lonely lives. Although Mary Austin lived in the desert with her husband and with a mentally retarded daughter, she wrote of her own interactions with the environment. She loved desolate places—"a big, mysterious land, a lonely, inhospitable land, beautiful, terrible." She is charmed by "spring smiling" and even calls the unloved coyote "her friend."

In her autobiography she differentiates between her reactions and those of Wallace, her husband: "There was Mary's effort to interest Wallace in botany, always a consuming interest for her, which he was never able to carry to more than a collector's accent, the mere naming and classifying of kinds and orders, avoiding her concern with adaptations and local variations. ... [H]e escaped her inquiries as to the strange adjustments of desertness and drought and redivivamentes" (*Earth Horizon*, pp. 287–288).

It is never obvious when reading her stories whether she is reporting on her own adjustment or distancing herself by "creating" other characters. One story, however, recounted in her autobiography about adjusting to a desert sandstorm seems genuine and true to her character. Because Mary Austin and her husband were intellectuals, or at least shared an interest in books, her description of how they spent one evening while nearly buried under humps of sand offers an adaptation peculiarly human.

> On this particular evening, Carroll [British neighbor] and a visiting friend had lingered on their way back to camp, for supper and by that time, by a sudden veering of the wind, the trail had been blotted out. All of that night the four of us sat up in the tiny one-room shack, with the sand drifting in triangular heaps through every crevice, drinking hot tea from time to time against the icy cold, clustered around the one small lamp, wrapped in our shared bedclothes, reading aloud by turns Kipling's *Five Nations*, which Carroll's friend had brought new from the press [*Earth Horizon*, p. 254].

Mary Austin permanently left her life in the California desert in 1906. She wrote in her autobiography that she never wanted to return because the landscape she had known had been ruined. When officials from Los

Angeles had entered the Inyo Valley, buying up land to secure a water supply for the distant city, "she knew that the land of Inyo would be desolated, and the cruelty and deception smote her beyond belief" (*Earth Horizon*, p. 308).

She institutionalized her daughter Ruth, sold her house, and eventually divorced her husband. She moved to Carmel, California, where she became a member of the artistic community, which included Jack London, George Sterling, and Ambrose Bierce. After an extended trip to Europe, she settled part-time in Manhattan in 1912 but continued to spend a portion of every year in Carmel.

Mary Austin's Desert Books

To her, the central story of the desert is how living things, all species including humans, adjust to the environment. But not far beneath the surface lies her environmental philosophy. She wonders already in the second paragraph of her classic book, *The Land of Little Rain*, whether the desert land "that supports no man ... can be bitted and broken to that purpose" (p. 1).

Human beings, particularly white men, encounter difficulties adapting to a desert existence. In contrast, the indigenous peoples, who were the original human inhabitants of the desert, have worked out ways of living in tune with nature, respecting the land without attempting to alter it.

Mary Austin wrote about the desert's plants and animals not as a scientist but as a poet. Her written images capture the sensual qualities of the desert. She sees "a succession of color schemes more admirably managed than the transformation scene at the theatre.... One can never fix the precise moment when the rosy tint the field has from the wild almond passes into the inspiring blue of lupines" (p. 51). She smells "sage at sundown, burning sage from campoodies [Native American camps] and sheep camps, that travels on the thin blue wraiths of smoke; the kind of smell that gets into the hair and garments" (p. 59).

She also tells stories about the inhabitants: men and women who become part of the desert landscape. To locate raw material for these stories Mary Austin became a prospector herself, mining the desert for human resources. She gathered tales from neighbors' gossip, from people she encountered while hiking and riding, from the words of stagecoach drivers, and from her participation in community activities. She also sought out contacts with the Paiute Indians who lived in the region, and some of her most compelling stories concern the lives of Native American women whom she had known or about whom she had heard tales. Always in Mary Austin's writings, however, the richest source is herself—her responses, her immersion, her identity with the desert.

In *The Land of Little Rain*, she devotes major sections to desert plants. Yet, she often relates plant adjustments with human ones. "The solitariness of the life breeds in the men, as in the plants, a certain well-roundedness and sufficiency to its own ends" (p. 33). She draws attention to the mesquite plant, for instance, calling it "God's best thought in all this desertness."

> It grows in the open, is thorny, stocky, close grown, and iron-rooted. Long winds move in the draughty valleys, blown sand fills and fills about the lower branches, piling pyramidal dunes, from the top of which the mesquite twigs flourish greenly. Fifteen or twenty feet under the drift, where it seems no rain could penetrate, the main trunk grows, attaining often a yard's thickness, resistant as oak [p. 32].

Adaptation to an arid climate means laying down thick roots; as Mary Austin expresses it poetically, "the real brain of the plant is underground" (p. 4). To prevent evaporation, desert flora will grow silky hairs and exude viscid gum, but, because of arid conditions, a desert environment will not attract noxious weeds and there will be plenty of breathing space between plants.

In contrast to human settlement, Mary Austin considers animal adaptation to the desert to be a more natural phenomenon. Desert animals will work at night, collecting food and building their shelters, for in the heat of the desert sun the search for a shadowed spot may be a full-time occupation. She describes the alpine habitats of the wild sheep: "stony hollows where the bighorns cradle their young ... above the wolf's quest and the eagle's wont" (p. 79). And she points out the animals who are most at home in the desert. "Now and then one gets a hint of some small, brown creature, rat or mouse kind, that slips secretly among the rocks; no others adapt themselves to desertness of aridity or altitude so readily as these ground inhabiting, graminivorous species" (p. 79).

She devotes an entire essay to "the scavengers"—buzzards, vultures, ravens, and coyotes who are part of "the economy of nature" (p. 18). Here she introduces an ecological philosophy when she writes, "probably we never fully credit the interdependence of wild creatures.... The hawk follows the badger, the coyote the carrion crow, and from their aerial stations the buzzards watch each other" (p. 20). Only man, the "great blunderer," lies outside the natural scheme of desert life. Mary Austin reinforces her point: "There is no scavenger that eats tin cans, and no wild thing leaves a like disfigurement on the forest floor" (p. 22).

Several years later in 1909, Mary Austin published *Lost Borders** and turned her attention to the "strange adjustments" that people make who inhabit the desert. Her writing in this collection of short stories becomes psychological and even in the end philosophical, grappling in the final story, entitled "The Walking Woman," with the big question: What is valuable in life?

Before reaching that point, she offers her readers a range of human adaptations, selecting representative types of men and women: miners, prospectors, shepherds, wives, prostitutes, boarding-house keepers, doctors. In each story, there is no doubt that the desert plays a leading role, and because people behave differently in the desert the setting offers a storyteller full license to spin an imaginative tale. "Out there where the boundary of soul and sense is as faint as a trail in a sandstorm, I have seen things happen that I do not believe myself" (p. 156).

She asserts in "The Land," the introductory essay to *Lost Borders*, that "it is men who go mostly into the desert, who love it past all reasonableness…. Their women hate with implicitness the life like the land" (p. 159). Yet, in the subsequent thirteen stories, at least half feature a woman's adaptation to desert life. In several cases the adjustment is not especially negative or hateful, a reflection of Mary Austin's own response to living in the desert.

In two stories, "The Return of Mr. Wills" and "The House of Offence," she offers evidence of women making the best out of a situation that is not of their choosing. Neither story is especially positive, and the desert comes off as an ambivalent main character. Yet, in each one the author includes more than descriptions of adaptations to the desert, she also delves into the psychology of male/female relations.

Mrs. Wills is the wife of Mr. Wills, a clerk in a store, who is lured away from home by the prospect of a "lost mine." According to Mary Austin, "of all the ways in the West for a man to go to pieces this is the most insidious" (p. 182). The wife, whom she names only as Mrs. Wills, is left behind in a desert mining town with four children and no man to pay the grocery bills.

For a while, "she [Mrs. Wills] fell into the habit of sitting down to a cheap novel with the dishes unwashed, a sort of drugging of despair common among women of the camps" (p. 183). But she soon figures out how

---

Page numbers refer to the version of Lost Borders *published in* Stories from the Country of Lost Borders, *edited by Marjorie Pryse (New Brunswick, NJ: Rutgers University Press, 1987).*

to make the best of her situation. She and the older children find employment, and "as the slovenliness of despair fell away from her, … she filled out, grew stronger, had a spring in her walk" (p. 185).

However, the story does not have a happy ending, because Mr. Wills comes home and Mrs. Wills returns to novel reading. The only positive outcome could occur, according to the author, if the husband were to take leave again. Mary Austin leaves open this scenario as she describes the look on the face of Mrs. Wills, "with something like hope in her eye … that in time its [the desert] insatiable spirit will reach out and take Mr. Wills again" (p. 187).

Every mining town in the desert had a "house of offence." In Mary Austin's story, the "house of offence" is located across the backyard from a house belonging to Mr. and Mrs. Henby. The Henbys are a respectable, married couple; the husband is a blast foreman, and Mrs. Henby is content with tending her garden and cleaning the house. The story's plot revolves around the fact that even though the Henbys have been happily married for twenty years, they never have had a child.

Hard Mag, who is matron of the "house of offence," comes up with a self-serving remedy. She pleads with Mrs. Henby to adopt her ten-year-old daughter, Marietta. The child is about to be thrust back upon her mother, because an aunt who had raised her up to then had died. In a last-ditch effort to convince Mrs. Henby to take the child, Mag argues, "she'll spoil trade" (p. 251). In the end, the Henbys do adopt the child and Mag agrees to take her "house of offence" elsewhere.

In the story, the desert has the final word as the abandoned house burns down as soon as the "women of the house" depart. With a final flourish, Mary Austin concludes that "[i]t was allowed to burn quite out, which it did as quickly as the passions it had thrived upon…. The next year the Henbys took over the place where it had stood for a garden, and Henby made a swing under the cottonwood trees for his adopted daughter" (p. 254).

The characters Mary Austin is most enthusiastic about are indigenous Americans, who in her region belonged to either Paiute or Shoshone communities. Throughout her writing career, she maintained a fundamental belief that they alone among human beings had figured out how to live in harmony with nature. "The Shoshones live like their trees, with great spaces between, and in pairs and in family groups they set up wattled huts by the infrequent springs…. Their shelters are lightly built, for they travel much and far, following where deer feed and seeds ripen" (*The Land of Little Rain*, p. 33).

On every possible occasion in her writings, she details how Native

Americans in both their eating and working habits, as well as in housing and health arrangements, adjusted their existences to fit in with a desert environment. She describes how they use the bean from the mesquite plant to pound into a meal for making mush or cakes and asserts that "Desert Indians all eat chuckwallas, big black and white lizards that have delicate white flesh savored like chicken" (*The Land of Little Rain*, p. 35).

Mary Austin goes further in her writings than merely imparting knowledge about indigenous people's living conditions. She introduces readers to individual Paiute and Shoshone men and women, whom she portrays sympathetically and in some cases adulatorily. In *The Land of Little Rain*, she devotes one essay entitled "Shoshone Land" to Winnenap, the medicine man, and another essay to Seyavi, "The Basket Maker." In *Lost Borders*, she includes three stories about white men who love Indian women: "A Case of Conscience," "The Ploughed Lands," and "Agua Dulce."

Her descriptions of the three Paiute women in the love stories share many characteristics. They are sexually and emotionally faithful to the white men; are desert smart; grow fat quickly; and are undemanding to the point of self-sacrifice to meet the needs of their men. In the story "Agua Dulce," the loved one whose name is Catamenda goes so far as to deny herself drink and food, and although she is only seventeen years old is buried by her lover.

In contrast to Mary Austin's sympathetic depiction of Native American women, she portrays the white characters, Saunders in "A Case of Conscience" and Curly Gavin in "The Ploughed Lands," as men with moral shortcomings. Yet they are not entirely at fault, for, having grown up outside the desert, they have been conditioned by their own cultures. Their backgrounds left them incapable of adjusting humanely to a desert environment in which their indigenous women belonged.

Saunders comes across as a decidedly unsympathetic character, even though Austin does offer readers an Anglo-Saxon justification for his actions. The author explains, however disingenuously, that in attempting to return to England with his child and not its mother, Saunders is exercising a sense of responsibility for his offspring. But Austin ends the story with mother Turwhasé reclaiming her daughter.

> "My baby!" she said. "Give it to me!" Without a word Saunders held it out to her. The little dark arms went around her neck ...; the whole little body clung, the lines of the small face softened with a sigh of unutterable content. Turwhasé drew up her blanket and held it close. "Mine!" she said, fiercely. "Mine, not yours!" Saunders did not gainsay her; he drew out all the money he had and poured it in her bosom. Turwhasé

laughed. With a flirt of her blanket she scattered the coins on the ground; she turned with dignity and began to walk desertward [p. 173].

In "The Ploughed Lands," a story about Curly Gavin and Tiawa, the Paiute woman who loves him, the plot does not revolve around moral issues to the same extent as in "A Case of Conscience." Gavin, whom the author pictures as a white man with red curly hair and broad shoulders, gets lost in the desert, is rescued by Tiawa's father, and nursed back to health by Tiawa, who becomes infatuated with the young man. She guides him out of the Shoshone camp and the desert and into "The Ploughed Lands," where he belongs. During the journey, she tries continuously to attract his affection but fails completely until they reach cool air. Then, Curly Gavin "felt the grip of the desert loosen on him with the tension of a spring released" (p. 179), and he smiled at her and opened up his arms.

But Mary Austin's characters are not able to enjoy their fulfilled love, because in concluding the story the author returns each to his or her own kind. The white man cannot adapt to a desert environment that Tiawa cannot abandon.

In her portraits of Native Americans in *The Land of Little Rain*, Mary Austin reveals both her respect for and fascination with the lives of indigenous peoples. In the essay "Shoshone Land," she introduces Winnenap, who was born a Shoshone but who was captured in tribal wars and thereafter lived for fifteen years as a medicine man in a Paiute camp.

His occupation as a medicine man was a powerful one in the community but one also fraught with responsibility, as the person who in the end is subjected to punishment for unfortunate health disasters. After fifteen years of collecting, prescribing and administering natural medicinal herbs, Winnenap is sentenced to death, blamed for an outbreak of pneumonia. In discussing the sacrifice of Winnenap, Mary Austin remains ambiguously nonjudgmental. After describing in detail how he is killed by three men, she draws in vivid tones her image of Winnenap's heaven: "It will be tawny gold underfoot, walled up with jacinth and jasper, ribbed with chalcedony, and yet no hymn-book heaven, but the free air and free spaces of Shoshone Land" (*The Land of Little Rain*, p. 38).

Her portrait of Seyavi, the basketmaker, is not ambiguous; it is outright admiring. She praises her artistry, her mothering skills, and her endurance. In short, Seyavi is Mary Austin's exemplar of a human being who lives in harmony with her environment.

She sketches the outlines of Seyavi's life in "The Basket Maker," beginning when she was a singing and dancing young maiden, wreathed in her flower, "the white flower of twining (clematis)" (*The Land of Little*

Rain, p. 64). As happened to many Paiute women, Seyavi was widowed during the tribal wars and left with a young son to care for. The author describes how Seyavi and her son lived "very near to the bare core of things" (p. 61), eking out an existence in the caverns of Black Rock.

Later, it was as a maker of baskets that Seyavi managed to support herself and her son. She made "flaring, flat-bottomed bowls,... and for decoration a design in colored bark of the procession of plumed crests of the valley quail" (p. 63). And it is through this work that Seyavi's existence was connected with the desert. "The weaver and the warp lived next to the earth and were saturated with the same elements. Twice a year, in the time of white butterflies and again when young quail ran neck and neck in the chaparral, Seyavi cut willows for basketry by the creek.... But whenever Seyavi cut willows for baskets was always a golden time, and the soul of the weather went into the wood" (pp. 63, 64).

Mary Austin emphasizes throughout the essay Seyavi's pride, independence, and sense of accomplishment. She had never been tempted to remarry, and, at the end of her life, Seyavi sat wrapped in a blanket, gossiping with other women of the campoodie. She had grown fat and had lost her eyesight, but not her memory or her speech, and it was during that final stage when she shared her recollections about a desert life with the author.

The essay begins with a direct quote by Seyavi: "A man must have a woman, but a woman who has a child will do very well" (p. 61). The reader cannot be certain whether this is actually Seyavi speaking or whether it is Mary Austin expressing her own voice through Seyavi.

Mary Austin concludes *Lost Borders* with a story entitled "The Walking Woman," whose protagonist is not a Native American, raising even more ambiguity about the relation between "the woman" and Austin's own life and philosophy. The author paints a rather sketchy portrait of her title character, whom she names only as Mrs. Walker. Yet many features that she ascribes to the "walking woman" were also characteristics of Austin's life in the desert. For instance, both women came and went alone "unarmed and unoffended" among localities frequented by "rude and solitary men." Neither woman seemed especially concerned to maintain a pretense of ladylike behavior. Mrs. Walker roamed the region wrapped in a blanket and carrying a black bag. Mary Austin's physical appearance — long hair, large body — was often described as eccentric. Both women acquired "wisdom and information" about the desert environment and were well-versed in the whereabouts of water holes, trails, and physical markers. Each found mental comfort in the desert: "the large soundness of nature" was "sobering and healing" to both women. Mary Austin had suffered from recurring mental breakdowns; Mrs. Walker "had begun walking off an illness," and people gossiped about her possible state of insanity.

Yet the most significant connection between the two women was a shared philosophy of life, with the author mentioning her "unconscious throb of sympathy" with the "walking woman." Mary Austin describes how Mrs. Walker's affair with a Basque shepherd had combined into one intensive year all the essential experiences of life: love, work, and motherhood. She had met Filon Geraud, the shepherd, during a sandstorm and had struggled successfully, battling against the wind with him to keep a flock of sheep together. She had stayed by his side for six months until she was too pregnant "to keep the trail."

Austin concludes her story "The Walking Woman" with her own philosophy for living.

> She had walked off all sense of society-made values, and, knowing the best when the best came to her, was able to take it.... It was the naked thing the Walking Woman grasped, not dressed and tricked out, for instance, by prejudices in favor of certain occupations; and love, man love, taken as it came, not picked over and rejected if it carried no obligation of permanency; and a child, any way you get it, a child is good to have, say nature and the Walking Woman.... To work and to love and to bear children. *That* sounds easy enough. But the way we live establishes so many things of much more importance [pp. 261, 262].

Mary Austin's Native American Writings

In addition to Austin's important body of work about the desert environment, she harbored throughout her career a passionate interest in indigenous cultures, and from the outset was aware of the intimate connection that existed between the two fields. In the preface to a collection of Native American stories that she compiled for children in 1904, she wrote how indigenous people understand acts of nature in personal terms. "All his songs, his ceremonies, his daily speech, are full of the aspect of nature in terms of human endeavor" (*The Basket Woman*, p. vi).

Near the end of her life she founded a museum for Indian arts in Santa Fe, New Mexico, and published a book of Amerind poetry called *The American Rhythm*, culminating acts in a lifelong appreciation of the culture of Native American societies. Mary Austin marveled at what she called "aboriginal splendor": "[C]oncerned itself entirely with the principle of the conscious unity in all things, the gesture of a rhythmic beauty to interpret the significance of common things, the ploughing and watering and planting of the corn, the fine moralities of nature" (*Earth Horizon*, p. 362).

In her autobiography she describes her initial contacts with Native American women (referred to as *mahala*) when she lived as a wife and young mother in Lone Pine, California. One of the *mahala* who lived in a nearby campoodie (camp) nursed Austin's baby. And when her daughter, who turned out to be seriously retarded, did not begin to talk, the *mahala* fed her dried tongues from meadowlarks to induce her to speak. Mary Austin also participated in some Native American women's activities, such as seed gathering and trout fishing, and absorbed useful information about which wild plants were suitable for eating or for medicinal purposes. She responded especially positively to their attitudes about productive work and in particular basketmaking, which was a specialty of the Paiutes. She followed along as they gathered willow twigs and cedar roots and gradually was drawn into the life of the campoodie.

Mary Austin got to know intimately communities of Native Americans during the fourteen years that she lived in the California desert, and many individuals appear as characters in her short stories. "I lapped up Indians as part of the novelist's tormented and unremitting search for adequate concepts of life and society, and throve upon them" (*The American Rhythm*, p. 38). She also became an outspoken critic of the U.S. government's Indian policies, opposing, as she put it, "the colossal stupidities, the mean and cruel injustices" perpetuated by the government's Indian Bureau (*Earth Horizon*, p. 266).

By 1911, having moved away and distanced herself from everyday contacts with indigenous cultures, she wrote about Native Americans in another genre, composing a three-act drama called *The Arrow-Maker*. Mary Austin was herself interested in acting and, when she lived in the desert towns of Lone Pine and Independence, helped to form amateur theater groups. In fact, one of the few activities that she admits enjoying with her husband were their joint performances in Shakespearean plays.

The Arrow-Maker was produced at the New Theater in New York City in 1911. At first, the producer, George Platt, had insisted that she alter the folk play to make it more melodramatic. But she considered the play to be a ritualistic presentation of how Paiute society dealt with the dual themes of love and ambition and made sure that the production remained true to her intent. In the published version, the author adds a preface and notes about costumes and dances.

The play focuses around one character, Chisera, who is a medicine woman. Fifteen other characters, all from the same tribe as Chisera, dramatize a story that examines the role of a genius in society. As Austin explains in the preface, Chisera is a genius who is a woman, and the society decides how to use her "great gift" to their best advantage.

In the course of the play's three acts, Chisera confronts issues of love and jealousy, exploitation by an ambitious man, obligations to serve the community, and questions of loyalty to one's own society. *The Arrow-Maker* is a tragedy, and, in the final act, set in a mountain cave with starving and destitute Paiute women and children, Austin draws a portrait of a people defeated in a brutal tribal war.

The American Rhythm, Mary Austin's collection of Amerind poetry, was her most significant publication in the field of Native American culture. The author considers her book to be a "re-expression" of Amerindian songs, magic formulas, and tribal lays, not a translation. When the collection of poems first came out in 1923, the reading public did not rush out to buy the book. The second printing in 1930, at a time of growing interest in Native American societies, elicited a greater response, and Austin's poems since then have found entry into many anthologies of U.S. poetry.

The book includes a substantive introduction that discusses not only Amerind poetry but also offers Austin's reflections on the science of poetics in general. In this scholarly essay she attempts to convince readers to take indigenous poetry seriously, claiming that it displays a "superior sense perception" (p. 29). Mary Austin maintains that Amerind poetry was "Avery far from the academic notion of the 'simple lyric cry' of primitive man" (p. 33). Below, Austin's re-expression of the Paiute poem, "The Grass on the Mountain," provides evidence for her strongly held convictions.

> Oh, long long
> The snow has possessed the mountains.
> The deer have come down and the big-horn,
> They have followed the Sun to the south
> To feed on the mesquite pods and the bunch grass,
> Loud are the thunder drums
> In the tents of the mountains.
> Oh long long
> Have we eaten chia seeds
> And dried deer's flesh of the summer killing.
> We are wearied of our huts
> And the smoky smell of our garments.
> We are sick with the desire of the sun
> And the grass on the mountain.

But Mary Austin contends that words are only one component of "three-plied" Amerind poetry—that is, it consists of "movement and melody and words." And in her analysis she gives equal weight to the melody and dance aspects of the poetry. "When the expression is communal, the movement and instrumented rhythm may be a complexity rivaling the harmonic intricacies of a modern orchestra" (p. 46).

The rhythm of the poetry is the central ingredient and, in tracing the origins of Amerind poetic rhythm, she relates the poetry to the natural environment. The rhythm is steeped in the geographic features distinctive to the land of the United States and the ways that human beings have adapted their activities to living in this environment. She argues that the same sights and sounds that impacted indigenous peoples and were expressed in their poems were also important to American immigrants. "It was back to the foot pace on the new earth, ax stroke and paddle stroke" (p. 13). And she quotes from President Lincoln's Gettysburg Address as an example of new American oratory that "fell unconsciously into the stride of one walking a woodland path with an ax on his shoulder" (p. 16).

Not only does she insist that a direct and intimate connection exists between aboriginal verse and American poetry, but that "it is probably not too much to say that all verse forms which are found worthy the use of great poets are aboriginal, in the sense that they are developed from the soil native to the culture that perfected them" (p. 44). In particular, she finds that the poetry of Amy Lowell, Carl Sandburg, Vachel Lindsay, and Edgar Lee Masters are most closely linked to aboriginal rhythms and resonate with the American landscape, reflecting the essence of the natural environment in their writings.

Years in New Mexico

The other state in the country where Mary Austin is remembered as a writer and as a conservationist is in New Mexico. Years before she decided to live there year-round, she traveled there frequently, making short excursions as well as one extended trip, which provided the raw material for her book, *The Land of Journeys' Ending*, published in 1924. That same year she built a house, Casa Querida, in Santa Fe, New Mexico, where she remained until her death in 1934 at the age of 66. She chose the Southwest because as she put it, "I liked the feel of roots, of ordered growth and progression, continuity" (*Earth Horizon*, p. 349).

She moved to Santa Fe when she had already reached maturity as a writer and at a time in her life when she was more dependent on support

Mary Austin, 1921. Photograph by E.O. Hoppé. (Reproduced by permission of *The Huntington Library, San Marino, California*.)

from friends. During her ten-year residence there, she spent long periods suffering from debilitating illnesses but she also fostered a strong, supportive relationship with her niece, Mary Hunter. Mary Austin's community in New Mexico included writers and artists who shared her passions in life: Native American culture, Southwest nature, and Spanish colonial arts.

Long before 1924 she had befriended Mabel and Tony Luhan, whose house in Taos, New Mexico, functioned as an unofficial cultural center. She relished in Tony Luhan's Pueblo background and shared a genuine mutual affection with Mabel. In Santa Fe she met fellow Illinoisans, Frank and Alta Applegate. Alta reminded her of her sister Jennie, and Frank shared her interest in Spanish colonial arts. Other writers of distinction, such as D. H. Lawrence, Sinclair Lewis and Willa Cather, also were drawn to the region for longer or shorter periods of time.

After she moved to New Mexico permanently she continued to communicate with the public her observations about the natural environment, as well as about both the Native American and Spanish cultures of the Southwest. In 1927 she represented New Mexico at the Seven States Conference in an effort to stop the construction of Boulder Dam, but she was the only delegate from New Mexico in opposition.

She, together with Frank Applegate, created a revival of Spanish arts by establishing a permanent collection of folk literature, songs, furniture, and religious and cultural artifacts. She bought an old private chapel and Frank purchased an old house that he restored in the original style. They reinvigorated traditions, submerged for a century, by starting a Spanish market and fiesta.

But Mary Austin's name has been forever preserved in the memory of New Mexicans by the important role that she played in furthering the arts of Native Americans. She was a prime mover in the creation of a living museum for Indian art, which John D. Rockefeller funded. The museum housed a substantial collection of jewelry, blankets, embroideries, paintings, and pottery from not only the Pueblo peoples but also from Navajos and Apaches. In 1931 Mary Austin wrote a novel, *Starry Adventure*, about Native American lives in New Mexico.

Mary Austin's Legacy

She always maintained her early inclinations as a conservationist in the Owens Valley, and she always wrote with eloquence and passion about the natural environment. When she had completed *The Land of Little Rain*, publishers had asked her to write another book like that one. But she could not, she explained in her autobiography. "I had used up all I had in the first one.... I wrote what I lived, what I had observed and understood. Then I stopped" (*Earth Horizon*, p. 320).

As a personality, many of her contemporaries regarded Mary Austin as arrogant, self-contained, or even otherworldly. But in her writings she was able to instill a sense of understanding and love for the desert environment with words that resonate with conservationists today.

2

Florence Merriam Bailey
(1863–1948)

I have offered suggestions on how to observe in the field, hoping that the friendship thus acquired by seeing the songsters in their homes may urge the student to go on and gain for himself the delights of a deeper study of birds [Birds of Village and Field, *pp. iv, v*].

Florence Merriam Bailey was one of a multigenerational handful of American women, born in the nineteenth century during the Victorian age when women "stayed at home and didn't do anything," who wrote best-selling books about birds that launched a popular movement for the protection of birds. Olive Thorne Miller predated Bailey; Celia Leighton Thaxter, Mabel Osgood Wright, Gene Stratton-Porter, and Neltje Blanchan Doubleday wrote during Bailey's time period; Margaret Nice followed in the next generation. No one told them that it was unladylike to study birds, but many male writers called their books amateurish. Yet these women wrote as much as, if not more, than nature writers whose names are familiar today, such as Henry David Thoreau, John James Audubon, John Burroughs and John Muir.

Florence Merriam, born into the upstate New York Merriam family in 1863, was by nature a conservationist. It would have been surprising if she had not followed that path through life. Her father, although by profession a businessman and congressman, was a friend and correspondent with John Muir. Her brother, Clinton Hart Merriam, who was eight years her senior, was one of the most well-known naturalists of his generation: he started the United States Biological Survey and had easy access to Theodore Roosevelt when he was in the White House. Florence Merriam

38

even married into the profession. Vernon Bailey, her husband for 42 years, was employed as chief naturalist at the U.S. Biological Survey.

Childhood

But it was far more than her male relatives that created in Florence Merriam an innate connection with the natural environment. As a child growing up in the countryside in New York in the foothills of the Adirondack Mountains, she learned to recognize animals and plants as a matter of course. Living with nature was her way of life.

The Merriam estate was situated in Lewis County near the town of Leyden, approximately sixty miles northeast of Syracuse and twenty miles north of Rome. During Florence's childhood in the 1860s and 1870s, the family maintained a farm on their property, which was managed by a hired farmer. Nearby, other members of the Merriam family lived; her aunt Helen and her grandparents all owned estates in the vicinity. Even though Florence was not a robust child, she gained an intimate knowledge of her natural surroundings from walks with her father in the woods and by following her brother Hart in his collecting expeditions. Their father built Hart a three-story building to house his specimens.

Throughout her life, the plants and animals of this region remained her frames of reference. As a child, she learned the habits, songs, and identities of the birds who fed at the family's dining-room window. That knowledge of birds of New York State became part of Florence Merriam's background. As an adult, when she wrote about birds of Massachusetts, California, Oregon, Washington, D.C., Montana, New Mexico, Texas, Kentucky, North Dakota, she always alluded to her childhood experience.

In nineteenth-century New York, the rural gentry educated their children at their estates, so the Merriam children were tutored at home. Not until her brother Hart had left home to study medicine did Florence acquire any formal education. She was sent away for medical treatment to a doctor in Syracuse, and she attended public school while living with that physician's family. Later, she boarded at Mrs. Piatt's school in Utica, New York, in preparation for college.

She entered Smith College in Northampton, Massachusetts, in 1882 as a special student. Even though she studied at Smith for four years, receiving a certificate in 1886, she was not awarded a Bachelor of Arts degree until 1921. Florence Merriam's pre-college education had not prepared her to undertake a full course of study in college. Throughout her childhood, her frail health had often made it impossible to pursue rigorous study schedules. Therefore, at nineteen, she lacked many of the prerequisites for the advanced study of liberal arts subjects. During her four years at Smith, however, she concentrated in science, writing a senior thesis on evolution and launching her career as a nature writer with an article she wrote for the college's Science Association.

It was during her years at Smith that Florence Merriam realized that protecting birds would be her impassioned cause. In the 1880s, the latest rage in fashion were hats trimmed with bird feathers and in some cases whole birds. Because the 300 students at Smith College were fashion-conscious young women, Florence was surrounded by her favorite birds, displayed atop the hats of her classmates. She was so incensed that she activated a campaign on behalf of live birds. Together with Fanny Hardy from Maine, she founded the Smith College Audubon Society on March 17, 1886.

While still in college, her newspaper article "An Appeal to Women" was printed in the *Watertown Times* in New York, and, during fall 1886, she published 5 more newspaper articles on behalf of live birds and against their use as decorations on women's hats. With such titles as "French Milliners and Bird Murder," "Fashion and Law," and "A Plea for the Birds," the articles appeared in small-town newspapers in New York and New Hampshire, as well as in the *Evening Star* in Washington, D.C.

Organizing meetings, campaigning in the press, and distributing fact sheets on the widespread destruction of bird populations proved to be effective tactics. Milliners in Northampton, Massachusetts, were overwhelmed by orders from Smith College students, paying to have birds removed from their hats.

This initial success encouraged Florence Merriam and Fanny Hardy to introduce positive activities as well. They started leading bird walks, so that their classmates could share their enthusiasm for live birds. As Florence Merriam reported in *Audubon Magazine*, they wanted their classmates to experience field study: to "see how the birds look, what they have to say, how they spend their time, what sort of houses they build, and what are their family secrets."

Fanny Hardy had grown up in a family in Brewer, Maine, where she also had been exposed throughout childhood to the natural world. Her father, Manly Hardy, who was a successful fur trader, had amassed a collection of 3,300 birds. Fanny Hardy, using her married name Fanny Eckstorm, went on to write several natural history books, as well as historical and regional works about the environment of Maine.

The Smith College Audubon Society engaged John Burroughs, a distinguished writer and birder, to assist in its campaign to educate the student body about birding. Florence Merriam invited him to the campus, initiating an annual tradition of Burroughs-led bird walks that continued long after she had moved on.

In June 1886, Florence Merriam left Smith College and embarked on a career that she pursued for the rest of her life. In Harriet Kofalk's recent biography, *No Woman Tenderfoot: Florence Merriam Bailey, Pioneer Naturalist,* the author includes an excerpt from a letter that Florence wrote to her brother Hart when she decided on her career: "For what better form of philanthropic work could anyone choose, with my background, instincts and training, than to write of nature with birds as my text, to open closed eyes to the uplifting, ennobling influences of nature?" (*No Woman Tenderfoot,* p. 43).

Florence Merriam's Bird Guides

Florence Merriam's first book, *Birds Through an Opera-Glass,* was published in 1890 by Houghton Mifflin in Boston when she was twenty-seven years old. The book incorporates within the text a yearlong series of articles, "Hints to Audubon Workers: Fifty Common Birds and How to Know Them," that had been published in *Audubon Magazine,* starting in June 1887. For this book she added another twenty birds, as well as appendices to assist readers in classifying the birds they observe and references to encourage further field study.

Birds Through an Opera-Glass begins with the most familiar birds— robin, crow, and bluebird—with descriptions of their coloring and songs, as well as their nests and habits. The entries vary in length from half a page to five or six pages and often include illustrations as well as musical phrases to characterize specific birdsongs. This book, in contrast to those that followed, placed birds in the natural scenes where they are found and included personal reminiscences of birds Florence Merriam had observed at her childhood home in New York and at her college home in Massachusetts.

Many times throughout the text, she breaks into enthusiastic ecstasy, portraying with fervor her love for a particular bird. She writes about the "homely cheeriness" of the song sparrow: "When he throws up his head and sings the sweet song that gives him his name, you feel sure the world is worth living in" (p. 67). Or she calls the nest built by a golden-crowned thrush "a tiny palace of beauty" and describes the "slender gold form" of the American goldfinch as "fairy-like beauty."

At this early stage in her career, Florence Merriam sprinkled her prose with frequent quotes from more renowned nature writers. Observations from Thoreau, Audubon, Emerson, and her mentor John Burroughs appear throughout the book, as well as poetic passages by Shelley and Lowell.

The main thrust of the book is to assist the novice birder in identifying common birds. She provides general information about the families of perching birds and interrupts discussion of a specific bird to relate either its color, song, or bill to other birds previously described. In the midst of her entry on the warbling vireo, for example, she writes:

> Birds naturally group themselves by occupation, and, as a Darwinian corollary, by coloring. The sparrows spend most of their time on the ground searching for seeds, and are protected by their earth-colored suits; the woodpeckers live clinging to tree trunks, and many of them are disguised by their likeness to the bark; the flycatchers take their living from the insects that swarm in the air, and their dull colors serve as non-conductors of attention; while the vireos, who live on measure-worms and similar morsels, are so exclusively devoted to foliage that they might well be called leaf-birds [pp. 131–132].

While describing the habits of the nighthawk, she breaks the text to generalize about birds' bills which are "modified to suit the needs of the birds" (p. 169). In the nighthawk, for example, "the enormous fish-trap of the kingfisher is exchanged for—almost no bill at all, merely a hook and eye for a wide gaping mouth" (p. 170). She goes on to list "the woodpeckers' long strong bills for hammering and excavating; the sparrows' short stout cones for seed cracking; the vireos' long slender bills for holding worms; and the fly-catchers' bills hooked at the end for holding insects" (pp. 169–170).

In writing her first book, Florence Merriam used a technique to reach her audience that she later abandoned as she became more confident in her store of knowledge and more fluent as a writer. Throughout *Birds Through an Opera-Glass*, she inserts anecdotes of birding experiences from her childhood. In the entry on the blue jay, she describes a scene when she spotted a flock in the forests of the Adirondack Mountains.

> Coming down into the forest primeval, where the majestic hemlocks towered straight toward the sky, ... there we found the blue jays in their home. A flock of them lived together, feeding on wild berries and beech-nuts, sporting among the ferns and mosses, and drinking from the brook that babbled along near the trail.... But the memory of the spot is dreary. Unmoved by the beauty of the scene, to which the blue jays gave color and life; unawed by the *benedicite* of the hemlocks; betraying the trust of the friendly birds, the boy of the party crept into their very home and

shot down one after another of the family as they stood resistless before him. Today the pitiful lament of the brave old birds haunts me [p. 75].

She even chose to conclude her first book with a memory from childhood—enjoying the song of the hermit thrush on summer evenings at sunset. "The song of the hermit [would] stir us with its full richness and beauty, ... filling the cool evening air with its tremulous yearning and pathos, and gathering up into short waves of song the silent music of the sunset—nature's benison of peace" (p. 205).

In 1896 Houghton Mifflin published Florence Merriam's second book about birds, *A-Birding on a Bronco*. This was written very much in the same vein as the first one, with long, narrative passages about her experiences while observing bird life. *A-Birding on a Bronco* differed, however, in one major respect: the setting. She was writing about birding in southern California, where she lived on two occasions (spring 1889 and spring 1894) at her uncle's ranch, Twin Oaks in northern San Diego County.

Florence Merriam's health had been an ongoing concern since childhood. After leaving Smith College in 1886, she suffered from a series of ailments and traveled often to the western states for health cures. In 1894 Houghton Mifflin published *My Summer in a Mormon Village*, an account of her trip to Utah. *A-Birding on a Bronco* shared features with that book, combining travel and nature writing. Yet it lies more comfortably in the category of a birding book and is richly illustrated with drawings by Louis Agassiz Fuertes. This artist, whose portraits of birds have been compared favorably with those of Audubon's, was still a college student at Cornell University when he agreed to illustrate her book, his first in a long career as a bird illustrator.

The book's title, *A-Birding on a Bronco*, refers to her method of birdwatching while living in California. She rode a white horse named Canello, with whom she worked out a mutually compatible routine: while he grazed on alfalfa, she observed bird life. Nonetheless, she does mention that differences between horse and rider did occur, especially when Florence Merriam spotted an interesting bird to observe in a locality where the hot sun beat down through the brush and there was nothing for Canello to eat. And viewing particular features of birds was made more precarious when seated on a horse, as she did not exercise complete control over the binoculars. "When I was intently gazing through my glass at a rare bird, he would sometimes give a sudden kick at a horse-fly, bobbing the glass out of range just as I was making out the character of the wing-bars" (p. 4).

As in *Birds Through an Opera-Glass*, Florence Merriam interweaves information about bird habits, sightings, and songs with personal experiences. She relates a story of nightly battles between a nest of owls and a neighbor's dog and her own encounter with quicksand. In adventure-story style, she writes how once during a birding outing, when she was preoccupied with her search for chewinks, "suddenly Canello pricked up his ears and raised his head with a look of terror." She and the horse were trapped in mire, and only after she had dismounted and the bronco had strained and struggled did "he finally wrench himself out."

Also in 1896 *Forest and Stream* magazine ran a series of her articles entitled "How Birds Affect the Farm and Garden." It was this series that laid the foundation for her third book about birds, *Birds of Village and Field*, published by Houghton Mifflin in 1898.

This book, subtitled *A Bird Book for Beginners*, was considerably more authoritative and comprehensive than her previous ones. She reports on 212 birds, rather than the 70 she described in her first book. She also includes information gathered from other ornithologists, referring to specific studies of bird-life histories and nesting habits. At the same time, she curtails the number of personal anecdotes.

> I have written this book to make it possible ... to know the birds without shooting them. I have done this by borrowing only necessary statistics from the ornithologies, giving untechnical descriptions, and illustrated keys based on such colors and markings as any one can note in the field; for I have written for those who do not know a Crow or a Robin as well as for boys who would get a start in bird-work, and teachers who would prepare themselves for this increasingly popular branch of nature study [*Birds of Village and Field*, p. iv].

Even though the book is "untechnical," still the author prefaces each entry with the bird's Latin name, general physical characteristics, and its geographical distribution. The book is lavishly illustrated with hundreds of drawings of both whole birds as well as body parts, such as wings, bills, tails, or feet. More than 20, full-page plates by Ernest Seton Thompson, Louis Agassiz Fuertes, and John L. Ridgway also are included.

As in her first book, Florence Merriam mentions the bird's song in almost every entry. In this book the sounds are written phonetically and italicized, in contrast to actual musical notation in *Birds Through an Opera-Glass*. She describes "the clear, plaintive *pee'-ah-wee* of the sweet-voiced flycatcher" (p. 90) and writes of the bluebird that "as he sits on a branch lifting his wings, there is an elusive charm about his sad quavering *tru-al-ly, tru-al-ly*" (p. 44).

She discusses what is distinctive about each bird with more sophistication and depth than in her earlier works. For instance, in the entry on the ruffed grouse she not only states how its ground color allows it to adapt to its environment, but also how its form changes to adjust to climate change. "The bird does not go south in winter, but has to wade through the snow for its food; and to meet this necessity its toes, which in summer are bare and slender, in winter are fringed so that they serve admirably for snowshoes" (p. 35).

In *Birds of Village and Field*, she presents an argument on behalf of economic ornithology, explaining that "the relation of birds to insects is only just becoming known." She reinforces her point that "birds are the natural check to insects," by including numerous drawings of worms, beetles, grasshoppers, caterpillars and moths, which are "pests to the farmer but necessities of life to the bird." She explains: "Except in rare cases where individuals attack cultivated fruits and grains, our native birds preserve the balance of nature by destroying weeds that plague the farmer, and by checking the insects that destroy the produce of the agriculturist" (pp. xix, xx).

She pays particular attention to what birds eat in this book. In brief one-line summaries, she wraps up descriptions of families of birds by focusing on how their diets benefit agriculture. The blackbirds and orioles are "strikingly colored birds, most of which spend their days devouring insects," and the finches and sparrows are "a family which does equal public service by making way with vast amounts of weed seed" (p. 362).

Throughout the book she elaborates upon the balance of nature thesis, buffeting her remarks with data gleaned from economic ornithologists. But Florence Merriam never loses sight of her audience and her main purpose for writing birding books—to encourage the public to enjoy studying live birds in an ongoing campaign to protect bird life on this planet.

Ornithologists were recommending to fruit growers that they plant mulberry trees and elderberry bushes nearby cherry, apple, or peach orchards to protect marketable fruit and provide birds with their requisite nourishment. Florence Merriam translates this information for her lay reader, offering advice on ways to entice birds into homes and gardens. She suggests planting elder bushes to attract thrushes, "the quiet, brown, woodland choristers, the most famous of American songsters," into the garden in the fall (p. 358).

Similarly, to attract robins, she suggests planting a few mulberry trees around the house, because mulberries ripen at the same time as cherries. This is good news for fruit growers who can plant mulberries to salvage cherry harvests and for bird-lovers who can offer wild fruit for birds to eat. In addition to mulberries and elderberries, Florence Merriam, making use of information gathered from the results of stomach examinations of the robin, lists more than 30 wild fruits that birders could plant to attract birds to the garden.

Life in Washington, D.C.

Florence Merriam moved to Washington, D.C., in 1893, eventually settling down there and making the city her home until her death in 1948. At first she lived on the third floor of her brother's house, where she was welcomed as part of the family by his wife and two young daughters. By the 1890s, C. Hart Merriam had already become a central figure in Washington's scientific community, having founded the U.S. Biological Survey in 1885.

Florence was able to participate in a wide range of ornithological activities from the start. She helped found the Audubon Society for the District of Columbia in 1897 and by 1898 was offering bird classes for teachers. As an educator Florence Merriam was able to put into practice her contention that studying birds in the field was the best way to stop people from killing birds for sport. She believed that she could prove to schoolchildren as well as to adults that live birds were more interesting to observe than dead ones.

She backed up her educational efforts by writing instructional guides. In the June 1900 issue of *Bird-Lore* magazine, founded in 1899 and the predecessor to today's *Audubon*, she published an article entitled "How to Conduct Field Classes." And also in 1900 she wrote two chapters on "Bird Study" for the *Chautauquan*, a publication put out by the very popular adult education organization, the Chautauqua Literary and Scientific Circle Round Table.

Her teaching expanded in 1903 when the local Audubon Society started giving birding courses to the public at the National Zoo in Washington. At first her classes attracted only 15 students, but within a few years so many people had become interested in the study of birds that she organized several divisions of classes for 200 participants.

It is possible to understand her teaching method from the articles published in *Bird-Lore* magazine and reprinted by Audubon Societies as educational leaflets. Florence Bailey cleverly interweaves broader themes into specific descriptions of the habits of individual birds. In the March-April 1910 issue of *Bird-Lore*, leaflet number 43 on the red-headed woodpecker, she incorporates a wide-ranging discussion of the role birds play in the conservation of nature. She leads her readers to think for themselves by providing facts and personal anecdotes and in the case of this article adding a list of more than 30 guiding questions. She begins by praising the eating habits of woodpeckers, who "deserve the name of foresters" because "they devour enemies of the trees," and goes on to mention nesting, habitat, and physical features of the red-headed woodpecker. But she wraps much of the information in the piece around a story of how she found a nest and observed a growing family there for three weeks. In this indirect way she relays the answers to most of the questions, but also offers ideas for teachers on how to guide students to carry out their own field observations.

In her 1913 article on the tufted titmouse, educational leaflet number 71, she introduces Ralph Waldo Emerson's poem "The Titmouse" as a means to connect the behavior of birds to human psychology. She interprets the various songs of the tufted titmouse, likening them to human conversations expressive of a wide range of emotions. She enthuses about its "loud, cheery whistle," which can be enjoyed all during the winter because the bird does not migrate to southern climates, providing a moral example to humans as alluded to in Emerson's poem with which she concludes the article. Bailey's discussion focuses on the tufted titmouse that inhabits the middle and southern states rather than the related black-capped chickadee, the bird in Emerson's poem. Characteristic of Bailey's educational technique, she includes lessons in economic ornithology and the use of anecdote to describe the bird's eating and nesting habits. The tufted titmouse benefits agriculture by eating insects, in particular boll weevils and scale insects, and "one eccentric bird" built a nest out of Spanish moss in contrast to its usual nesting in a hole in a tree.

Writing about birds always remained at the center of Florence Merriam's life, and she willingly observed them in a variety of locations depending on her life's journey. At the age of 36 she married Vernon Bailey, and because the Baileys frequently observed birds together and often published works collaboratively, her descriptions assumed a new voice, that of Florence Merriam Bailey.

This marriage between fellow naturalists took place at the end of 1899. Vernon Bailey, who had grown up on a farm in Minnesota, was one of the first men hired by Dr. C. Hart Merriam when he founded the U.S. Biological Survey. Florence had known Vernon Bailey for many years, but it was not until after she moved to Washington, D.C., that their lives became linked.

The Baileys, Florence as ornithologist and Vernon as mammalogist, observed fauna of the United States together for 42 years. The childless couple traveled, studied, and wrote nature books, articles, and reports. In Kofalk's biography, she quotes from close friends of the couple who remembered that they greeted each other with a call of a songbird. The permanent home that they built on Kalorama Avenue in northwest Washington, D.C., became a central gathering place for environmentalists. They entertained often, giving large dinner parties for Washington colleagues and visiting naturalists, and Vernon's motley collection of live mammals became well known to neighbors. He fed his pet bat especially collected insects, kept a kangaroo rat in a cage on the library table and a lizard in a bowl on his desk.

The impact of the marriage on Florence Merriam Bailey's life's work was noticeable and immediate, for by summer 1900 they were already collaborating in the field. Vernon Bailey worked as a field naturalist for the U.S. Biological Survey until he retired in 1933, and his wife often accompanied him on field expeditions, observing birds wherever he was assigned to survey mammals. She was not paid, but she collected information that she later published in magazine articles or in booklets for the National Park Service. As Florence Bailey, she also authored her two most important books about birds: *Handbook of Birds of the Western United States* (1902) and *Birds of New Mexico* (1928).

For almost 40 years, the naturalist couple worked and wrote together. In the main, however, they maintained individual authorship over their writings. Florence was the expert on birds; Vernon, on mammals. In Florence's writings, Vernon's observations are often cited and in several of her larger works she mentions explicitly contributions written by her husband. Likewise, in Vernon's writings Florence's input is acknowledged and in at least one major work (*Cave Life of Kentucky Mainly in the Mammoth Cave Region*) she is listed as the author of the chapter on birds. On at least two other occasions the couple appeared as co-authors: for the book *Wild Animals of Glacier National Park: The Mammals by Vernon Bailey, The Birds by Florence Merriam Bailey*, which was published by the National Park Service in 1918, and for the article "Johnny and Paddy, Two Baby Beavers," which appeared in the January 1923 issue of *Nature Magazine*.

Florence Bailey's Writings

She used the field notes from their travels together to prepare more than 50 articles that appeared in a variety of periodicals. Some were written for children and general nature and outdoors magazines, but a majority were published in specialized birding publications, in particular *The Condor*, *Bird-Lore*, and *The Auk*. Writing in this genre, almost journalistic in tone, she was able to popularize bird watching and at the same time describe unusual birds she had observed.

An especially large number of her articles appeared in *The Condor*, a magazine of western ornithology published by the Cooper Ornithological Club of California. From 1902, when her first piece was printed, until 1919 Florence Bailey's byline could be found in almost every volume year. The articles covered a wide geographic range from Texas, New Mexico, Arizona, California, to Colorado, including even North Dakota.

Characteristic of her contributions for *The Condor* were a series of articles entitled "Meeting Spring Half Way," published in the July, September, and November 1916 issues of the magazine. These writings successfully combine astute observations about bird life with rich descriptions of the southern Texas landscape, especially plants. The three-part series offers the reader a vivid picture of a region of the country that was exotic and new to her when she traveled there with her husband in 1900. Even though the articles were printed 16 years after her visit, the tone of the writing throughout maintains an original freshness.

She starts out with an effusive description of the view out of the train window as they approach Austin in April. Spring is at least two weeks more advanced than it was in Washington, D.C., where she boarded the train. She notices this phenomenon in the songs she hears the birds chirping and in the greenness of the flora. Soon after arriving in Austin, she reports sighting the scissor-tailed flycatcher, "one of the birds that makes Texas peculiarly attractive to the bird student. To easterners, to whom the name flycatcher calls up drab birds.... Nature added splashes of salmon to the striking black and white plumage, after which she endowed her creation with the skill of an acrobat, the dash and fire of a master spirit of the air" (p. 153).

She continues with travel descriptions of the city of San Antonio, which had "the flavor of an old Spanish town," and pictorial sketches of the cattle country of mesquite and cactus that they passed through between San Antonio to Corpus Christi. "The flora was Mexican, strange thorny bushes being interspersed with brilliant flower masses. The fences were made by pitchforks with cactus pads, the pads laid along a line on the ground rooting and branching till they grow to high impenetrable fence walls that in their season become beautiful with large yellow tuni flowers. When spring comes on the prairies of Texas, even the fences burst into bloom" (p. 154).

When they arrived at the fertile coastal prairie, the author returns to her focus on bird life with her excited discovery of the cassin sparrow. "The song that dominated part of the brushy prairie was a new one to my ear and became the song of songs to me," like the "the chant of the hermit thrush in the pointed firs of the northern mountains." And she reports how she first heard the bird song. "It was on an ordinary sunny Texas morning that I walked out into the ordinary chaparral prairie in an everyday mood, ... when lo! From the brown bushes in front of me up sprang a little winged creature, a blithe spirit, an embodiment of the deepest joy of life" (p. 154).

As they headed south from Corpus Christi to the Mexican border, Florence Bailey assumes the tone of an excited traveler, reporting on everything from the "star-filled sky" they observed while sleeping on a bed of daisies beside huisache trees to Mexican-style houses and the unusual southern vegetation. She pays special attention to the "blooming cactus, splendid masses of it in fuller bloom than we had found it before.... Never again would it stand for spine-covered grotesque forms of vegetation. Does the desert bloom like a rose? No, it blooms like a cactus! Nature strews your path with thorns, it is true, but only to ensure the flowers, big generous blooms of gorgeous hues, bright lemon, soft saffron, dull orange, magenta, and glowing crimson" (p. 215).

In several of her *Bird-Lore* pieces, she writes about the family life of the birds and manages to personalize the report in such a way as to offer advice to others who would follow her example and study bird life in the field. The articles are filled with detailed information about nesting and feeding habits and she notes with almost parental interest the course of the birds' development from downy nestling to feathering and growing wing quills. In "A Family of North Dakota Marsh Hawks," she writes about how she was able to chronicle the development of five baby marsh hawks and to photograph their various stages. In this case, the story even had dramatic moments when the parent hawks became so protective of their young that when they "swooped so close to my head ... I turned my campstool upside down on my head, and walked home" (*Bird-Lore*, November 1915, p. 436).

In addition to her writings in popular birding magazines, Florence Bailey contributed more than ten scientific articles to *The Auk,* the journal published by the American Ornithologists' Union. In the 1890s she had already authored three articles in *The Auk* under her maiden name, Florence A. Merriam. One of them, "Nesting Habits of *Phainopepla Nitens* in California" (published in the January 1896 issue), was a scientific account of a study she had conducted at her uncle's ranch at Twin Oaks in San Diego County. She included a table with data that she had assembled about the number and duration of visits to the nests by male and female *phainopeplas*, popularly known as silky flycatchers. Her analysis allowed her to conclude that the males did most of the nest building. In the 1920s she returned to studies of western ornithology, reporting in *The Auk* on birds that she had studied during wintertime visits to southern Arizona. Her final journal articles were "An Arizona Feeding Table," which appeared in the October 1922 issue, and "An Arizona Valley Bottom," printed in the July 1924 issue.

The last book that Houghton Mifflin published by Florence Merriam Bailey was *Handbook of Birds of the Western United States*. Considered by many people to have been her leading contribution to the bibliography on birds, it was first published in 1902 and subsequently reissued in seventeen editions and four revisions. The book is a massive, definitive compendium of the eight orders of water birds and the eight orders of land birds found in the United States west of the one-hundredth meridian. This geographical region includes the Great Plains, Great Basin, Pacific Slope, and the lower Rio Grande Valley. For each species, Bailey provides general physical characteristics, measurements, geographical distribution, and descriptions of nests, eggs, and food. Because she wrote this book after her marriage, she made use of the Biological Survey's collections, records, charts, and illustrations, as well as the advice and services of her husband. One-third of the handbook, including the entire section on water birds, in fact, is credited to Vernon Bailey.

Nevertheless, as in her previous books, Florence Bailey maintains an individual voice and the reader can share in her enthusiasm for bird life. For instance, when she compares the voice of the western meadowlark to that of the eastern bird, she exclaims: "'There's the western meadowlark!' you cry out in eager delight, and as the train leaves him behind and you lean back on the dusty car cushions, you rest in a world of blue sky and celestial song. The lark's notes have been written down in sharps and flats, but the pure, heavenly quality of the song can never be replaced" (p. 293).

For this book, much of the field research was carried out on camping trips with Vernon Bailey, and she often includes a word picture of the place where the bird was sighted. She first heard a chorus of sparrows in the Sierra Valley in California, for example, "when we rode through the sagebrush and camped on the edge of the pines just at sunset" (p. 344). But Florence Bailey's description of the southern Texas scene where she spotted grackles (called jackdaws in Texas) was rich prose in the style of a nature writer.

> The jackdaws ... nest in the oak motts of the shin oak prairie between
> Corpus Christi and Brownsville. We found them building the last of

April at San Ignatia mott, an oasis-like grove in the middle of the prairie.
They made the noisiest blackbird colony one could wish to camp below;
and when to their squeaking clangor and hubbub was added the shrill
clatter of the scissor-tail flycatchers, the rattle of woodpeckers, the vocif-
erations of mockingbirds, the cooing of doves, the piping notes of the
vermilion flycatcher, and the voices of passing birds, it was quite like
camping in an aviary [pp. 302–03].

Florence Bailey's final book, *Birds of New Mexico*, published by the
New Mexico Department of Game and Fish in 1928, was the culmina-
tion of a lifetime's work of study and writing about birds. Not only was
the book enormous in scale, but her input rescued a manuscript that had
been started years before by an ornithologist and an illustrator, both of
whom had died before completing the project.

When the book, with more than 800 pages and 24 colored pictures,
reached the public, Florence Bailey was honored by the American
Ornithologists' Union. She was elected as the first woman fellow of the
association and received the Brewster Medal, awarded every two years to
the author of the most important book on birds of the western hemi-
sphere.

Beyond Florence Bailey's voluminous writings for magazines and her
many books, she produced several noteworthy publications for the U.S.
National Park Service. In these, she placed birds in their natural habitats,
allotting considerable space to descriptions of plants, landscape, and other
animals. The environmental settings covered in these writings ranged
from mountainous Glacier National Park to the farmlands of Kentucky
to the southwestern canyon country of Arizona.

The first publication, *Wild Animals of Glacier National Park*, was published by the National Park Service in 1918 and was authored by both Florence and Vernon Bailey, with Vernon writing the section on mammals
and Florence writing on birds. The handbook was the first to be published
for the newly established U.S. National Park Service, and theirs set the
standard, a very high one, for the succeeding decades of national park
guides. The 200-page book included detailed observations of animals they
had sighted during the summer of 1917, supplemented with notes from
park officials, photographs, and previously published drawings.

Florence Bailey's section on birds was written in her characteristic
style, filled with information but also suffused with the personal pleasure
she experienced while birding in the field. At Glacier National Park,
located in northern Montana abutting the border with Canada and noted
for deep forests and snow-clad mountains, which as she remarks is not
the most auspicious setting for bird-watching, she nonetheless mentions

that 187 species had been spotted. In the introduction to her guide she orients readers to the birds that might be seen during the summer season, when most tourists will visit the park, explaining that birds can be found at three elevations: marshes, along lakes and streams, and above the timberline. She describes common birds that visitors probably would be familiar with such as the catbird, kingbird, and the red-headed woodpecker but also gives considerable space in the handbook to unusual birds to be found only in the Arctic–Alpine slopes, namely the ptarmigan, leucosticte, and pipit.

Bailey's entry on the southern white-tailed ptarmigan or Arctic grouse, "one of the most interesting birds of the world," is an engaging story of how she spotted a mother and her family of chicks integrated into an informative description of the bird's diet and habitat. Even though she reports that "the ptarmigan is found close to the trails frequented by the tourist," it was not easy for her to locate "a round-bodied little grouse with a small head … disguised by her buffy ground color finely streaked with gray" (p. 140). She searched for the bird among "the narrow outcropping ledges and stony slopes" of Glacier National Park and came upon a terraced Alpine flower garden, "good feeding grounds for the Arctic grouse." She explained that the ptarmigan live on mountaintops among the sheep and goats, "where they, too, are nourished by the hardy, dwarf, Arctic–Alpine flora. Having had little to fear from the hand of man, these gentle birds offer one of the most delightful of all experiences to the bird lover, the opportunity to study their natural home life close at hand" (p. 144).

Above the slopes that the ptarmigan inhabits, she found the leucosticte, or rosy finch, with its gray crown, deeply notched tail and bright pink wing patch. "Where the mountains of the park reach their culminating grandeur, lofty peaks and ranges are gathered in such close conclave as to suggest a council of chiefs from north, south, east, and west. The broad seamed face of Agassiz Glacier, the rough cascaded front of Kintla Glacier, with Kintla Peak towering 4,000 feet above its lake; snow patches, glaciers, looming peaks, ridge close behind ridge, and below, a mantle of dark timber—such was the chosen home of leucosticte" (p. 174).

In her chapter on birds, Florence Bailey draws attention as well to the pipit, the smallest of the trio of birds at home in the upper reaches of Glacier Park. "He may be recognized on his Arctic–Alpine breeding grounds by his deliberate walk, his habit of tipping his tail, and occasionally nodding his head, and also by his plaintive *ke'-we* and *cheep'-ep*, uttered as he flies about, buffeted by a wind often too strong to stand against, and which sometimes blows him back against a snowbank" (p. 187).

But above all else, Florence Bailey enthuses about the songs that

birds sing and in particular the music bursting forth from two sparrows
in Glacier Park: the white-crowned and slate-colored fox sparrows.

> In the grim amphitheater of Iceberg Lake, with its high glacier debouch-
> ing into the green water, as we watched insectlike mountain goats climb-
> ing up the mountain walls above us and nutcrackers flying about over
> beds of heather, wind-bared, wide-skirted spruces, and snowbanks tinted
> with the famous pink snow of circumpolar and Alpine regions, the *High-
> up, high-up* of the white-crown seemed well attuned to the spirit of the
> place. Then suddenly, to my astonishment there rang out loud and clear
> the bright, cheery *Green, green wa'ter, see-it-there* [of the slate-colored
> fox sparrow]…. He had been singing over a spruce alcove carpeted with
> the exquisite lemon-yellow Erythronium that was filling the air with its
> fragrance at the edges of melting snowbanks. But never did I appreci-
> ate the lovely song so much as when after protracted days of following
> trails through the dark coniferous forest we came out onto the sunny
> chaparral slope of Cathedral Peak and were greeted again by the bright,
> cheering voice of our friend [p. 179].

In addition to the handbook about Glacier National Park, Vernon
Bailey wrote *Cave Life of Kentucky Mainly in the Mammoth Cave Region*
published by Notre Dame University Press in 1933. This book about animals was put together at a time when Mammoth Cave was still under
consideration for national park designation, an event that did not tran-
spire until 1941. In the report Florence Bailey focused attention once again
on birds that tourists could hope to spot in the summertime. However,
in a region of the country that she calls "a land of such ready guns," she
mentions time and again the necessity to restrict hunting seasons in order
to protect birds.

She points out the almost total absence of hawks in the area adjoining Mammoth Cave, and she credits this to "ignorance of the value of our
birds of prey … in a country where all possible help is needed to protect
the scant crops from the ravages of rodents and insects" (pp. 81–82). In
her entries on the eastern green heron, eastern bobwhite, eastern turkey,
and the American woodcock, she very directly makes pleas for their protection. Although there is no open season in Kentucky on "the handsome
green heron," she writes of the "need for educational work … if the legally
protected birds are to be saved" (p. 86).

In the description of the eastern bobwhite, she writes that "the visitor to the caves who has time to go far afield to look for birds may perhaps be assured of the presence of this delightful quail…. What a
satisfaction it is to know that this bird, whose preservation is important
not only to the sportsman and the farmer but to all those who are stirred

by its cheery voice, has so far been respected by the boy with the gun that it still remains to enrich the Mammoth Cave country" (p. 94). However, she adds that "unfortunately, the Kentucky 1933 open season does not seem planned to help the farmer" (p. 95). Similarly, in describing the American woodcock, which she names as one of our most notable birds, she regrets that "in Kentucky it is sadly in need of protection, but most unfortunately, still suffers from a month's open season" (p. 100).

Florence Bailey penned her last publication, *Among the Birds in the Grand Canyon Country*, which was published by the U.S. Government Printing Office in 1939, when she was 76 years old. Neither her enthusiasm for observing birds nor her flair for sharing this passion with the public was at all diminished. As Arno B. Cammerer, director of the National Park Service, wrote in his foreword to the book; "Mrs. Bailey has written of the canyon bird life in an intimate and friendly way." Bailey continued to emphasize domestic habits of birds: "In the bird families about us parental devotion and solicitude in their short-lived evolving forms were hinted. We happened on one family of western tanagers in the woods ... where the mule deer came to feed and, greeting them as familiar friends, grieved at the distress of the green mother of the brood, which voiced itself as she flew anxiously about, in quick repetitions of the family notes— *pit'ick, pit'ick, pit'erick*" (p. 168).

Florence Bailey's Legacy

During a full and productive life that did not end until she had reached the venerable age of 85 in 1948, Florence Bailey worked either on her own or together with her husband to popularize bird-watching. She was convinced that if people observed birds and studied their habits, then they would join the ranks of bird-lovers and work for their protection.

According to Florence Bailey, birds, no less than human beings, played a significant role in maintaining life on this planet. Birds participated in creating the human food chain, disseminating seeds, and protecting useful crops against insect damage. They beautified the environment of both town and country, and if one learned to identify birds and to appreciate their songs and diverse characteristics this knowledge would enhance the quality of one's life.

In the writing of several field guides, innumerable magazine articles, and several ornithological handbooks, she shared her passion for bird life with the American public. A lifelong study of birds surely enhanced the life of Florence Merriam Bailey.

The Next Generation

Florence Merriam Bailey was part of a multigenerational group of American women birders who made a significant contribution to the cause of wildlife conservation during the late nineteenth and early twentieth centuries. In the Introduction is a brief discussion of Olive Thorne Miller, whose writings about bird life predated and influenced Bailey's; here the life and writings of Margaret Nice, born twenty years after Bailey, are portrayed.

Margaret Morse Nice, who lived from 1883 to 1974, followed closely in the footsteps of Florence Merriam Bailey. There are striking parallels in their biographies, but many of the opportunities available to a woman conservationist in the next generation are apparent in a brief overview of Nice's life and work.

Both birders spent happy childhoods in rural northeastern United States. Margaret Morse's father was a professor of history at Amherst College, a small liberal arts college located in a rural town in western Massachusetts. The Morse family lived in a house with fruit orchards, gardens, and two acres of backyard for Margaret and her seven siblings to explore. Her love for nature was nurtured in this environment and she credits her mother for her early knowledge of wildflowers.

She began keeping a diary and making notes about what she had discovered in nature when she was nine, but her "most cherished Christmas present" arrived when she was twelve years old. It was *Bird-Craft: A Field Book of Two Hundred Song, Game, and Water Birds* by Mabel Osgood Wright, a birder of Bailey's generation. Mrs. Wright opens her book, as did Florence Bailey, with a plea to stop killing birds and hunting for eggs, encouraging a study of bird life instead. She lures the reader with colored pictures and simple descriptions of habits, migrations and songs, and for young and eager Margaret Morse the book was her companion in identification of particular bird species. The author of *Bird-Craft* was the daughter of Samuel Osgood, a well-known New York clergyman and writer, and she too belonged to the coterie of bird conservationists as founder of the Connecticut Audubon Society and of Birdcraft Sanctuary, one of the earliest bird sanctuaries in the United States.

When it came time for higher education, both Nice and Bailey attended women's colleges in western Massachusetts. In the 1880s Florence Merriam chose Smith College in Northampton and Margaret Morse, twenty years later, chose Mount Holyoke in South Hadley, which had been her mother's alma mater as well. Each prospective birder studied science at college. Nice reported in *Research Is a Passion with Me*, her posthumously published autobiography, that the five courses in zoology that she had taken provided an excellent practical and theoretical foundation for later research in ornithology. Nice also became proficient in several foreign languages, namely French, German and Italian, which made it possible for her to cultivate wide-ranging communications with ornithologists internationally.

Following college, neither woman knew precisely which course she would pursue in future life. Both considered becoming social workers, but each was drawn to further study of birds. Bailey went to the western United States and launched a career as a prolific writer, whereas Nice continued her education as a graduate student at Clark University in Worcester, Massachusetts. Her research topic was the food of the bobwhite, which she wrote up as an article published in the *Journal of Economic Entomology* in June 1910.

Her formal education ended rather abruptly in 1909, however, when she married Leonard Nice, a fellow graduate student at Clark. When he received a Ph.D. in physiology two years later, the couple moved first to the vicinity of the Harvard Medical School and then to Norman, Oklahoma, where he taught physiology at the University of Oklahoma. Mrs. Nice became a full-time wife and mother of five daughters, which caused a temporary shift in subject matter for her research and writing. Between 1915 and 1933, she published eighteen articles on child psychology and Clark University awarded her an M.A. in psychology in 1915.

But Margaret Nice laments in her autobiography that, after several years of marriage, she was "truly frustrated" and "relief came through my finding birds again." From 1919 until her death at the age of 90 in 1974, Mrs. Nice worked as an ornithologist, and, as was the case in Bailey's life, her husband assisted her career. In both women's marriages, their husbands were the breadwinners but they shared their wives' interest in birds, accompanied them on birding expeditions, and co-authored books about birds.

The first topic that attracted Nice's attention was "A Study of the Nesting of Mourning Doves," an article she published in *The Auk* in 1922. She went on to become a collaborator for the U.S. Biological Survey and wrote 35 articles about bird life in Oklahoma. Her first source was *Birds of the Western United States*, a book that Florence Bailey had written in 1902, and it was through Nice's love for birds that she became a conservationist reflecting attitudes towards nature reminiscent of those expressed previously by Bailey.

Margaret Nice chose mourning doves as the subject for her first study because of a concern for their protection awakened by a notice in a local newspaper that raised the possibility of extending the open season for dove-hunting. According to the article, there was discussion of opening the season as early as August, which Nice feared was nesting time. She immediately rushed to the campus of the University of Oklahoma to look for nests, and found several mourning doves sitting on their nests. This episode marked the beginning of both her return to ornithological research as well as to her work "to preserve some wildness on the earth," as she describes in her autobiography. Not only did she write letters to the newspapers, but she also became engrossed in a study of the nesting habits of mourning doves, the results of which she presented to a meeting of the American Ornithologists' Union.

Nice's major achievement from her years in Oklahoma was the publication in 1924 of a University of Oklahoma bulletin entitled *The Birds of Oklahoma*, which she co-authored with Leonard Nice. She introduces this book with a plea to protect all birds of Oklahoma. For four years she and her husband traveled around the state collecting information about the status and range of 361 species and subspecies of birds, thereby producing the first ornithological study for the state.

The Nice family moved to Columbus, Ohio, in 1927 where Margaret Nice undertook her most memorable studies. A two-part publication, *Studies in the Life History of the Song Sparrow*, published in 1937 and 1943, ushered in a new era in ornithology. Although she never held a paid position at a research institute, her renown as an ornithologist was well acknowledged. She served as associate editor for the journal *Bird-Banding* from 1935 until her death in 1974, with only one short break between the years 1942 and 1946. In 1939 Macmillan Company published *The Watcher at the Nest*, a birding book she wrote for a general audience.

For her work on the song sparrow, Margaret Nice was made a fellow of the American Ornithologists' Union in 1937, the second woman in the association's history to receive that honor. The first woman had been Florence Bailey for her book *Birds of New Mexico*. Nice also won the Brewster Medal in 1942, following again in Bailey's footsteps. On the other hand, as an indication of the higher level of scholarship that Margaret Nice attained during her career, she was awarded two honorary doctoral degrees from women's colleges: one from Mount Holyoke College in 1955 and the other from Elmira College in 1962.

Both Margaret Nice and Florence Bailey enjoyed long and productive lives "trying to open the eyes of the unseeing to the beauty and wonder of the earth and its wild life," as Nice wrote in her autobiography. Nice lived until the age of 90 and Bailey died at age 85.

3

Rosalie Edge
(1877–1962)

My message to those who know the meaning of conservation, the value of birds, animals, forest and soil, the joy and well-being to be had from their study—to those who feel it a sacred responsibility to pass these things on to future generations—my message to these is ... be ye implacable! ["An Implacable Widow," *unpublished autobiography, p. 231*].

Each of the women in this book shaped U.S. thinking about the natural environment, but in Rosalie Edge's case her ideas are only a part of her legacy. The style of environmental activism that she developed made her "the most vivid of the breed of radical amateurs," according to Stephen Fox, author of a book on John Muir and his followers. She wrote and spoke the words of a fighter, whether battling to save birds, wildlife, or trees, she was always campaigning for something and haranguing against an enemy. Her tactics and her persistence set precedents.

Rosalie Edge was a late-in-life convert to the cause of conservation, in contrast to Florence Merriam Bailey who had realized already in her twenties that she would devote her life to writing about birds. It was not until she had reached her fifties that her career of organizing, writing and speaking out to protect endangered flora and fauna of the United States took off. The Emergency Conservation Committee, a New York City–based advocacy group that she created in 1929, worked for more than 30 years to stop people from interfering with age-old balances set up by nature. The organization's proudest moment and climax to a four-year, hard-fought campaign was the establishment in 1938 of Olympic National

Park in the state of Washington, home to the only temperate-climate, primeval rain forest in the United States.

Childhood

Rosalie Barrow was born on November 3, 1877, as the youngest of eight children to John Barrow and Harriet Woodward. Her father, an Englishman, was first cousin to Charles Dickens and related to James Whistler. When Prince Albert sent Rosalie's father to New York City to scout out American contributions for the Crystal Palace exhibition, he stayed on Staten Island with Whistler's mother, subject of the famous painting. John Barrow immigrated to the United States in 1853 after meeting Harriet Woodward, Rosalie's mother, at a New York social function.

On her mother's side, Rosalie came from old New York lineage and was listed in the Social Register. Her grandmother told her stories of walking along unpaved trails in Manhattan when it was still largely undeveloped countryside, and her mother remembered watching carts transport soil from New Jersey to be used as garden fill for Central Park.

Her parents were married in 1857, and her father's success in the linen business guaranteed material prosperity and a privileged lifestyle for his family in New York City. Rosalie, however, was born during her parents' twentieth year of marriage, and by the time she had reached adolescence, the family's standard of living had been reduced to a state of "relative poverty." That's the authorized version of her childhood history handed down to posterity by Rosalie Edge's son.

How incongruent for a militant environmental conservationist to emerge from an upper-class childhood in late nineteenth-century New York City. Yet her fighting spirit had already revealed itself in her reputation as a troublesome student at Miss Doremus's finishing school. She went on to use her access to the upper echelon of society to aid her campaign to protect the nation's flora and fauna, and her appearance as a tall, fashionably dressed New Yorker disconcerted many a congressman, government official, lumberman, and sportsman.

Marriage

Rosalie Barrow also married an Englishman, Charles Noel Edge, in 1909 when she was 32 years old. Their marriage started out in Asia, in

Yokohama, Japan, where they were married, and for three years her husband's work as a consulting engineer took them up and down the coast of China and throughout the Malayan peninsula. They eventually moved to New York City, where Charles Edge went into the stock brokerage business and the couple took up residence on the upper east side of Manhattan. They had two children: Peter, born in 1913, and Margaret, born in 1915. But this happy family did not last long, for Rosalie Edge's fighting nature led her into championing causes that alienated her from her husband, and by 1924 the family had split up.

Her first campaign was for women's suffrage. She became corresponding secretary of the New York State Woman's Suffrage Party in 1915 and then treasurer of the New York State League of Women Voters after women won the vote in 1919. The campaign gave her experience and confidence, and many of the lessons learned in public relations she employed later when advocating for various conservation causes.

It took her many years to discover and to devote her attention to what became a lifelong passion: saving the environment. It started with birdwatching in her garden on Long Island Sound, when she and her husband bought a summer home in Rye, New York. But she did not wait until the house was built to enjoy the birds, for they camped out in tents on their lot during World War I, before they could construct a proper house.

She also mentions in her memoirs a somewhat earlier indication of what would become a future devotion to conservation. When she was about to give birth to her second child and was convinced that she was about to die, she started, as she phrased it, to "despatch donations to every organization which interested me." At that moment she joined up as a life member of the Audubon Society, but she did not activate that membership until fifteen years later.

Rosalie Edge's early bird-watching was not limited to the rural environment that surrounded her summer home. Even in the midst of New York City, she spotted birds and absorbed background knowledge that she later drew on as a conservation activist. She assembled in Central Park with a circle of fellow bird-watchers and would telephone her son at school when she sighted a new bird to add to his life-list, noting in her autobiography how "it has always been a thrill to me to find wild birds at home in the heart of New York" (p. 10). She made friends with biologists from the American Museum of Natural History, who came out into the park during lunchtime. One of these museum curators, Dr. Willard Van Name, forever changed her life when he sent her a pamphlet that he had written entitled *A Crisis in Conservation,* which accused the Audubon Society of acting in cahoots with sports organizations to support hunting of game birds.

Rosalie Edge received the publication when she was on holiday in Paris. With the dramatic flourish that characterized her writing style, she described how she reacted to first reading *A Crisis in Conservation.* "I paced up and down [my hotel room], heedless that my family was waiting to go to dinner. For what to me were dinner and the boulevards of Paris when my mind was filled with the tragedy of beautiful birds, disappearing through the neglect and indifference of those who had at their disposal wealth beyond avarice with which these creatures might be saved?" (autobiography, p. 6).

A Crisis in Conservation criticized conservation associations for reneging on their original mission of saving wild creatures, claiming that bird-protection organizations were concerned with saving songbirds only and ignored the plight of endangered species of game birds. The authors did not mention directly the name of the conservation society that they were describing, but it was impossible to hide the identity of the Audubon Society from life members.

The pamphlet so incensed Rosalie Edge that she attended the annual meeting of the Audubon Society in October 1929 and made a reputation for herself among the distinguished board of directors. She stood up again and again to ask embarrassing questions in her well-bred, New York voice that had been likened to Eleanor Roosevelt's. "What answer can a loyal member of the Audubon Society make to this pamphlet, *A Crisis in Conservation*? What are the answers? Should they stand silent in the face of accusations that the Society did little or nothing to save birds fading into extinction?" (autobiography, p. 15).

Emergency Conservation Committee

After the American Museum of Natural History attempted to restrain Dr. Van Name's pen, he proposed to Rosalie Edge that they join forces to organize a publishing concern to continue to agitate for conservation causes that needed publicity. At the age of 52, Rosalie Edge embarked on a career as a conservationist, co-founding the Emergency Conservation Committee (ECC). This organization, which lasted formally for more than thirty years but ceased its independent campaigning activities after World War II, published 94, hard-hitting pamphlets. Dr. Van Name and, gradually, others, such as journalist Irving Brant, teacher Ellsworth Lumley as well as Mrs. Edge, did the writing. Dr. Van Name paid for the printing, and Mrs. Edge assumed the role of editor and publisher. During the 1930s, the ECC testified repeatedly at congressional hearings and campaigned forcefully and successfully in support of a variety of conservation issues.

Rosalie Edge was the chairman of the Emergency Conservation Committee, and as she illustrates in her autobiography she borrowed and adapted many of the public relations tactics and skills she had learned in the suffrage campaign. She rented a small office on Lexington Avenue in Manhattan, which served as the base of operation for the Emergency Conservation Committee. There were no membership dues and no salaries, but the organization managed to raise $100,000 in donations, create a mailing list of more than one thousand names, and engage 40 scientists on a board of advisers. She was a prodigious letter-writer and addressed personal notes to every contributor and faithfully replied to all inquiries for information or publications.

Rosalie Edge was largely self-educated, although she credits Dr. Van Name with teaching her everything she learned about birds and the natural environment. In 1949, when she was seventy-two years old, Wagner College conferred upon her the degree of Doctor of Letters.

The range of issues that the ECC chose to attack varied with the political climate. When they began in the early 1930s, their primary mission was to expose the "wrongdoing of government officials and of so-called conservation organizations," according to Rosalie Edge. In 1933, with Roosevelt's New Deal ushering in a window of opportunity to active conservationists, the Emergency Conservation Committee participated in several successful efforts to expand National Park lands. When attitudes in the country shifted in 1941 with the onset of World War II, the ECC concentrated on safeguarding conservation advances already made from being overturned by military appeals to wartime need. After the war, the organization joined forces with a growing number of like-minded groups to campaign on behalf of conservation in a postwar era of reconstruction when engineers held the reins of power.

In the annual report of 1934, Rosalie Edge summarized the underlying philosophy and goals of the organization. "The tenets of faith for which they battled," as she presented them, were nothing less than a constitution of conservation principles. She eloquently highlighted the three that she considered to be fundamental:

> 1. Wild life is the heritage of all, to enjoy but not to possess.... Creatures of the wild belong to themselves alone.... Man should disturb them as little as possible.
> 2. Expanding civilization continually wrests greater areas of the earth from the domain of the wild. This interference with the age-old

balances set up by Nature causes great disturbances. The ECC vigorously opposes any unnecessary interference with the balance of nature
in the future.

3. The chief cause of the extinction of birds and animals is inten-
tional killing by man.... Because the passing of a species constitutes an
irremediable loss to science as well as to nature lovers ... the ECC fights
for the preservation of all species in sufficient numbers to prevent all
danger of their extermination, either now or in the future.

Two slogans, which Rosalie Edge printed in boldface type on the
committee's letterhead, expressed the organization's fighting spirit: "The
time to protect a species is while it is common" and "The way to prevent
the extinction of a species is never to let it become rare."

To further these principles the Emergency Conservation Committee undertook actions that protected wildlife, preserved public parkland
(in particular primeval forests), and educated the public and especially
youth about its concerns. The ECC waged its specific campaigns with the
most up-to-date methods available in the 1930s: letter writing, pamphlet
publication, and lobbying.

Fighting cruelty to animals was a major occupation of the organization. They opposed hunting and fishing for sport "except under rigid
restrictions calculated to fully protect every species." In the case of species
that were "in danger of extermination," the ECC fought for absolute pro-
hibition from killing. They rigorously attacked the poisoning policies of
the U.S. Biological Survey, naming the agency in one of its pamphlets
"U.S. Bureau of Destruction and Extermination." The organization
claimed that many of the animals poisoned by the governmental agency
were harmless and in some cases even useful to agricultural, horticultural,
or livestock industries. And in respect to birds, the ECC drew attention
to the dangers inherent in the widespread use of sprays and powders to
combat insects three decades in advance of the publication of Rachel Carson's book, *Silent Spring*.

Also years before the birth of humane societies, the Emergency Conservation Committee harangued against the fur business and especially
its use of steel traps that tortured animals before killing them. The ECC
was scrupulously attentive to proper enforcement of laws about caging wild
animals, scientific collections of rare species and the introduction of non-
native species into the United States. In every case, they wanted assur-
ances that animals were treated humanely, that permits were issued to
public institutions and that species threatened with extinction were adequately protected.

The committee encouraged the establishment of private as well as

Rosalie Edge with a red-tailed hawk, early 1940s, Hawk Mountain Sanctuary. Photograph by Maurice Brown (© Hawk Mountain Sanctuary Archives).

governmental sanctuaries "to protect every species threatened with extermination, or decline in numbers, and that these areas shall be large enough to remove all danger of extinction" (*ECC Report for 1934*, p. 6). Beginning with Florida's Pelican Island, where President Theodore Roosevelt established the first national wildlife refuge in 1903 to protect egrets and herons, the governmental system has grown to provide habitats for more than 200 endangered and threatened species.

Rosalie Edge established the first wildlife sanctuary for birds of prey: Hawk Mountain Sanctuary in eastern Pennsylvania in 1934. The Sanctuary was incorporated as a private, nonprofit organization in 1938 with Rosalie Edge as president and it is maintained today as a 2,380-acre nature preserve providing a safe haven for migrating hawks, eagles and falcons.

The impetus for founding Hawk Mountain Sanctuary was to put an end to the slaughter of thousands of raptors who migrated each fall over the rocky promontory of the southernmost Kittatinny Ridge of the Appalachian Mountains. Raptors concentrate at Hawk Mountain because the prevailing winds deflected up and over the ridges assist the birds in their long-distance journeys.

In Schuykill County, Pennsylvania, the annual sport of hawk shooting was popular and a long-held concern to conservationists. Rosalie Edge did not learn about it, however, until 1932 when a Philadelphia ornithologist described the shooting in a paper presented to the Hawk and Owl Society, an affiliate of the National Association of Audubon Societies. She traveled to Hawk Mountain with her son Peter in June 1934 and wrote in a letter to Dr. Van Name, "I could at once appreciate that it is strategically situated in regard to the hawk migration.... Outcrops of rock make ideal shooting stands and the slaughter ... is more horrible and painful to think of than as described in the Hawk and Owl report" (quoted in James J. Brett, "American Conservation's Glorious Joan of Arc," *Hawk Mountain News*, September 1984, p. 8).

She immediately leased the land and began fundraising to purchase Hawk Mountain as a safe haven for migrating birds of prey. She engaged naturalists Maurice and Irma Broun as wardens to safeguard the property from hunters to ensure that the autumn of 1934 would be the first slaughter-free season. Today, on average, 17,000 raptors are sighted there each fall, and Rosalie Edge's legacy as a conservationist continues to be appreciated by the countless visitors to the beautiful spot.

In addition to supporting efforts to protect endangered species, the committee's ire was always raised when the mass media portrayed wildlife in a negative light. The response was to send off a flurry of angry, but factual letters to the newspapers or radio stations involved. The ECC condemned motion pictures that "aroused enmity toward any wild creature" (*ECC Report for 1934*, p. 7), and Rosalie Edge was especially critical of supposedly factual newspaper stories about eagles carrying off babies or small children. She made a practice of tracking down these news articles. One Associated Press story that circulated in 1938 reported that a fifty-pound eagle swooped down and picked up a three-year-old child in Maryland; the story ended happily with a photograph of the smiling child unhurt, after a hunter fired a shot that wounded the eagle. Unbelieving Mrs. Edge informed readers that eagles cannot fly with loads of more than a few pounds, and if they do succeed to take off with an object the size of a child they would need to start from the edge of a steep cliff.

Her persistence in getting to the truth behind these "news" stories led her to the uncovering of a deliberate hoax printed in a New York newspaper in 1937. It was a picture of a golden eagle flying with an 18-month-old child held in its talons. The source for the photograph was an event staged by a Hollywood producer, who had used his own child and a semi-tame bird that had been on exhibition in a department store. To create the illusion of an eagle flying off with a baby the producer had taped the eagle's claws, strung wires around its wings from which a safety-belt and pulley carrying the baby were attached. Her unrelenting search for the origins of these eagle nightmares led her back to a horrifying story printed in McGuffey's *New Sixth Eclectic Reader* in 1857. Rosalie Edge claims that generations of Americans were educated to fear baby-snatching eagles because of myths taught to them in childhood in this widely disseminated, nineteenth-century schoolbook.

When the Emergency Conservation Committee first started its militant activism in the early 1930s, it focused its attention on efforts to reform the Audubon Society, incensed that the well-funded Society had all but abandoned the cause of wildlife protection after successfully stopping the killing and sale of bird feathers for hat decorations in the early years of the twentieth century. In particular, the ECC accused then-president Gilbert Pearson of lack of vigor in pursuit of the organization's original mission. The relentless campaign against practices of the Audubon Society, which included speaking up at annual meetings, suing for the Society's mailing list, and distributing critical pamphlets, did not subside until 1934 when Pearson was ousted from the presidency.

In addition to campaigning vigorously and persistently for wildlife protection, the Emergency Conservation Committee was a major national advocate for preserving land in a natural, unexploited state. From the committee's beginnings, it opposed the policy of the U.S. Forest Service to allow grazing of livestock in national forests. The ECC argued that grazing, especially of sheep, ruined extensive areas of public land, causing erosion, destruction of vegetation and dessication of streams.

Expanding landholdings of the National Park Service became one of the organization's main focuses. Within already designated national parkland, the ECC kept a watchful eye for signs of commercialization, opposing the construction of highways and inappropriate amusements. But by far the most significant achievement of the organization was to secure the addition to the National Park Service of large stands of old-growth forests.

From 1934 to 1941, the ECC waged three major campaigns to expand forest acreage in national parks. It was instrumental in the establishment of Kings Canyon National Park, which abuts Sequoia National Park in California; carried out an intensive four-year struggle to create Olympic National Park in Washington; and won the battle to add Jackson Hole to Grand Teton National Park in Wyoming. In addition, the committee successfully rescued 6,000 acres of primeval sugar pine forest in California from the lumberman's ax by supporting legislation to add the venerable trees to Yosemite National Park.

The third major focus of activity of the Emergency Conservation Committee was in the area of public education. The organization published a series of booklets on conservation topics that were marketed to schools, libraries, and to camps of the Civilian Conservation Corps (CCC), the New Deal's youth employment program initiated in 1933. The booklets sold for ten cents a copy, and Ellsworth Lumley, a biology teacher from the Pacific Northwest, wrote most of the teaching units from material he had prepared for his classes.

They focused on protection of wildlife, for the most part, with separate publications on hawks, eagles, owls, fish-eating birds, and waterfowl. Distinguished biologists added prefaces, and Roger Tory Peterson illustrated the booklet, *Common Hawks of North America*, which Rosalie Edge and Ellsworth Lumley co-authored. President Franklin Delano Roosevelt wrote a personal letter, which he permitted the ECC to include in the booklet, commending *The Two Eagles of North America* by Ellsworth Lumley, published in 1939. In 1938 Rosalie Edge wrote a teaching unit on forests that Harold Ickes, Secretary of the Interior, introduced.

When the United States entered World War II at the end of 1941, the ECC changed the tone in its writings to emphasize the pressing need to safeguard advances that had already been made in the conservation of wildlife and natural resources from backsliding. As Rosalie Edge wrote in the 1943 annual report, "we must strive to save our natural resources from being squandered by those who make supposed 'war necessity' an excuse for exploitation" (*Annual Report 1943*, p. 3).

At the beginning of the war, she embellished her annual reports with flowing phrases about the "passion for liberty" and how the "wonders of nature inspire and sustain our faith." She even argued that conservation-minded Americans, "those who seek to understand the laws of nature, the delicate balance that maintains harmony between wildlife of an infinite number of species and its environment, have a clearer vision of that peace and justice toward which all creation moves" (*Annual Report 1941*, preface).

However, she did not desist for one moment from her number one mission in life. "The conservation of our forests and streams, of our wildlife, and of the morale of our people to which these contribute so much, becomes of first importance" (*Annual Report 1941*, preface). She entitled the 1941 annual report *Conservation by the People*, which immediately starts off on an optimistic note with a story about a successful protest against the War Department's plans to erect an artillery range in Montana. As she reports, the people sent a barrage of letters to the Secretary of War in "an expression of democracy," encouraging him to find an alternative location for the artillery range. The site that had been selected was on Henry Lake, an important flyway or migration stop for the trumpeter swan, an endangered species.

In the next year's annual report she reminded her readers what had happened to wildlife and virgin forests during World War I, pointing out disconcerting similarities with the contemporary situation that faced conservationists in the United States in 1942. In order to secure and to guarantee adequate supplies of food during wartime, the federal government came under increased pressures from stockmen, hunters, and farmers to abandon hard-won restrictions that had been enacted to protect wildlife and their habitats. Raisers of livestock lobbied for permission to graze animals in national parks, and hunters argued that wild game could provide a valuable addition to the American diet. To ensure that yields of food crops were not needlessly ravaged by wildlife, agriculturists and horticulturists requested expansion of governmental poisoning campaigns.

During wartime it was not only the food producers who worked to turn back previously made gains in environmental conservation. Lumbermen demanded permission from the government to cut down forests that had been standing for five hundred years to meet the needs of wartime construction. Rosalie Edge responded bluntly to these sentiments in her impassioned tone of writing. "Now is the time for conservationists to make warfare against greed and selfishness, to allay hysteria, and to coordinate preservation of wildlife with projects for mass employment" (*Annual Report 1942*, p. 3).

Rosalie Edge continued throughout the duration of World War II to write about the threat of retrogressing in the protection of the natural environment of the United States, of turning the clock back on hard-won conservation battles. But by 1944 she was also turning her attention to plans for the future, preparing for the upcoming issues that conservationists would face after the war ended. The Emergency Conservation Committee was not alone and participated in several coordinated meetings of conservation organizations. The country as a whole was looking forward to massive construction projects, especially of dams, highways, airports, and houses. Much groundwork for postwar development had already been mapped out.

Conservationists and the ECC, in particular, wanted guarantees that "the beauty of the land" would be preserved and not destroyed. Rosalie Edge feared that wildlife would not be adequately protected in the midst of massive engineering projects. "And above all, now is the time to set apart more areas where the beauty of the wilderness may be preserved for posterity" (*Annual Report 1943*, p. 3).

She drew attention to how conservationists in Great Britain, whose people had suffered far more intensely from the ravages of war, were preparing for their postwar environment. They were planning to set aside reserves for communities of plants and animals, for scientific study, and for recreation. "We may well take Great Britain as our example of courage, forward thinking and patriotism," she concludes (*Annual Report 1943*, p. 3).

During the war years the Emergency Conservation Committee charged ahead with its activism on behalf of conservation causes, bolstered in the belief that "the guardianship of our country's beauty is a patriotic duty" (*Annual Report 1942*, p. 23). It battled to rescue waterfowl from overhunting, and for two winters the organization hired a lecturer to address public audiences in Montana, Idaho and Utah on the need to protect the trumpeter swan and on the value of predators, especially the coyote. The committee also actively campaigned in Michigan and Wisconsin to save Porcupine Forest on Lake Superior, in Pennsylvania to protect Cook Forest, and in the Adirondacks in New York to protect Whiteface Mountain from defacement by a ski trail.

The Campaign to Create Olympic National Park

During its lifetime of more than 30 years, the Emergency Conservation Committee claimed the establishment of Olympic National Park in Washington as its greatest achievement. As Rosalie Edge expressed in her testimony before the Congressional Committee on Public Lands in April 1936, "no words can describe that forest.... The Yosemite, even the sugar pines of the Yosemite Valley, are not more beautiful than that forest with its underlying growth…. It is like a tropical forest."

What distinguishes this park from all the other magnificent forest preserves in the United States is its characteristic of temperate rain forest. Usually, rain forests are found in tropical regions where the heat combines with the moisture to create perpetually wet and foggy conditions and profuse vegetation. In northwest Washington State on the Olympic peninsula, where more than 200 inches of rain fall per year, a temperate climate nurtures ancient forests of Douglas firs, western hemlocks, Sitka spruce, and western red cedar. "Throughout the centuries, the giant trees that have lived their thousand years fall and may still be seen entwined with the roots of trees comparatively young…. Germination takes place on top of logs and stumps, and the young trees draw sustenance from the decay of the fallen giants" (autobiography, p. 108).

The campaign lasted for four years, beginning in 1934, when the ECC published its first pamphlet, *The Proposed Olympic National Park*, and climaxing in June 1938, when President Franklin Delano Roosevelt signed the Olympic National Park legislation. The various twists and turns of the story illustrate how this victory depended upon a convergence of actions, personalities, and talents working together. It also demonstrates how Rosalie Edge assumed a central role in the making of U.S. conservation history.

After it was over, at least until the Truman administration, noted historians Charles and Mary Beard invited her to dinner to give them a firsthand account of what had taken place. Rosalie Edge summed up in her autobiography what she had reported to them: "We had told the American people the truth, told it over and over again, in pamphlet after pamphlet, that this truth had been repeated in the press, and reiterated in spontaneous letters of thousands of citizens to members of Congress" (autobiography, p. 118). How straightforward that sounds and how contrary to the shenanigans pulled by government officials and the timber industry, the tactics employed by the Emergency Conservation Committee, and the support accorded to forest protection by Franklin Roosevelt, Harold Ickes, and Henry Wallace.

Shortly after President Franklin Delano Roosevelt took office, he issued an executive order in 1934 transferring administration of 15 national monuments from the U.S. Forest Service to the National Park Service. Numbered among these national monuments was Mount Olympus National Monument in Washington State, which had been the brainchild of an earlier President Roosevelt.

In March 1909, implementing the newly enacted Antiquities Act of

1906, President Theodore Roosevelt had created Mount Olympus National Monument, guaranteeing a safe refuge for elk on forest land administered by the U.S. Forest Service. During World War I under the presidency of Woodrow Wilson, however, Mount Olympus National Monument had been stripped of half of its acreage. Because of purported wartime needs, lumber companies had lobbied the government with success for permission to harvest valuable groves of Sitka spruce.

The intention of Franklin D. Roosevelt's order to shift management of the monument's land from the Forest Service to the National Park Service was to end the devastating deforestation of Mount Olympus National Monument. Under National Park Service jurisdiction forested land was not available for timber cutting as it was under the Forest Service. But moving the administration of federally owned land from one governmental bureaucracy to another did not ensure a smooth road ahead for creation of a future Olympic National Park. The focus of controversy revolved around the size of the park-to-be, with contentious battles over which land and which trees would end up in the park and which would remain fair game for logging. Large-park advocates, including Rosalie Edge, fought against the timber industry that wanted to limit the total acreage of the national park and in any case to restrict the park's land to the highest elevations, where no valuable trees existed.

The Emergency Conservation Committee was catapulted into the center of the controversy with publication of its pamphlet, *The Proposed Olympic National Park,* written anonymously by Dr. Willard Van Name who also paid for its printing and mailing. When Congressman Mon Wallgren from the state of Washington introduced an Olympic National Park bill on March 28, 1935, the park boundaries essentially were those proposed by Van Name and not the smaller area suggested by the National Park Service.

In nine days of hearings held by the House Committee on Public Lands in April 1936, Rosalie Edge and Secretary of the Interior Harold Ickes argued forcefully for Wallgren's bill. She called for inclusion of virgin forests "as a restitution" for the land that the Forest Service had logged off.

> I really think that there is not enough made of that, that it is the right of the people of the whole United States to have given back to them the equivalent of land that was cut out in the hysteria of wartime.... No one has told you, I think, adequately of the devastation. As you drive this great highway around Mount Olympus there are miles and miles of devastation.... It is ugly to a degree, and here we are asking to save just one little compact piece of this marvelous forest of the Northwest.

Congressmen, who were advocates of the timber industry, raised cries of concern for the economic welfare of the people of Washington State. If trees could not be cut, then several towns and long-standing communities would be deprived of their economic base. Mrs. Edge countered these arguments with evidence of how creation of national parks elsewhere had provided a wide range of new employment opportunities, servicing the tourist trade.

The congressional committee passed Wallgren's bill, but it was never debated on the House floor. Instead, in February 1937 Congressman Wallgren introduced a second Olympic National Park bill. In this piece of legislation, the land area designated for the park was much smaller than it had been in the original bill. Rosalie Edge immediately dashed off a pamphlet, *Double-Crossing Mount Olympus National Park*. Her subtitle (*No Economic Need, But Only Commercial Greed, the Obstacle to the Mount Olympus Park*) encapsulates her argument.

However, the Emergency Conservation Committee did not fight the bill with pamphlets alone. Irving Brant, part of the ruling triumvirate of the organization, used every political contact he could muster up. He was a childhood friend of Secretary of Agriculture Henry Wallace, whose department was responsible for the administration of the U.S. Forest Service. He went to see Harold Ickes, Secretary of the Interior, and even met with the president. He presented the case for a large national park so passionately that Franklin Delano Roosevelt scheduled a visit to the Olympic peninsula for October 1, 1937. Brant followed up his high-level lobbying efforts with a pamphlet, *The Olympic Forests for a National Park*, beautifully illustrated with his own photographs and published by the ECC in January 1938.

The boundaries that Irving Brant proposed were widely accepted and appeared in Congressman Wallgren's third bill, which was introduced on March 25, 1938. This was the legislation that President Roosevelt signed into law in June 1938.

That was not the last word on the boundaries of the park, however. In 1947, several bills were introduced in both the Senate and the House to cut out thousands of acres of virgin forest from Olympic National Park. Rosalie Edge wrote publication number 93, *The Raid on the Nation's Olympic Forests*. In her autobiography she says that this pamphlet was the most widely distributed of any the ECC had published. Mr. Brant went to see President Truman; in the end, the acreage of Olympic National Park was not reduced.

Rosalie Edge as a Writer

In addition to her public stance as chairman of the Emergency Conservation Committee, Rosalie Edge left a noteworthy legacy as a writer. She used not only a fighting prose style, but inserted cartoons, photographs, and even an occasional original poem. Much of her writing served a purpose—mobilizing public and political opinion on behalf of a particular conservation issue. Both her first publication in 1932, *The Slaughter of the Yellowstone Park Pelicans*, and her last one in 1955, *The Wily and Wasteful Proposal for the Echo Park Dam*, as well as all the ECC annual reports fell into that category.

Yet that was not all that Rosalie Edge wrote. In 1936, her pamphlet, *Roads and More Roads in the National Parks and National Forests*, warned about an environmental problem that is still very much an issue today. As she bemoaned more than 50 years ago, "roads and more roads are dividing, shrinking and destroying the remnants of the wilderness."

Her pamphlet tried to offer some explanation for "a madness of roads—roads parallel, roads crisscross, roads elevated, roads depressed, roads circular and roads in the shape of four-leaf clovers," which today we accept as the U.S. landscape. "There is a fixed idea in the American mind, inherited from a pioneer ancestry which suffered from having no roads at all, that any additional road must be good and that one cannot have too much of a good thing" (p. 2).

Building roads, especially on federally owned land, served another purpose in the 1930s; it created jobs for Civilian Conservation Corps (CCC) workers. In the depths of the Depression, Rosalie Edge could not argue against the necessity for all roads in national parks, but instead proposed that only roads appropriate to the parks' purposes be built. Specifically, she suggested constructing one-way roads with preventive landscaping.

She aimed her most forceful prose against the national forests, which were being "honeycombed with roads." "The lumberman walks softly behind the roadmaker, computing the profit to be gained from trees which were already old when Columbus discovered America, and which cannot be replaced in a thousand years" (p. 8).

She concludes the 12-page treatise with praise for the foresight of the state of Vermont for refusing to build a skyline drive along the Green Mountains. She believed that "only trails belong to the deep forests; a road into a wild region is the prelude to its destruction."

Rosalie Edge warned in 1936 that building roads in national forests would have dire consequences. She was right.

It is time that the nation insists on the preservation of the national forests for other and greater benefits. They should guard the headwaters, equalizing the stream-flow, and preserving the lower lands from floods and erosion. They should be a haven for wildlife.... They should be laboratories for the study of ecology.... Above all, the Forests should be preserved for the recreation of those whose need impels them to withdraw from time to time from conventional life.... To all such benefits roads are inimical [p. 11].

By 1938 when the ECC published *Our Nation's Forests*, the sixth unit in its educational series, Rosalie Edge wrote in an authoritative style about a subject she not only had studied but had fought vigorously to protect. No less a figure than Harold L. Ickes introduced the 14-page pamphlet that included three appendices: questions for younger students, research topics for advanced students, and a list of general references.

In his preface, Mr. Ickes emphasized the importance of the subject matter: "The use of forests, and the ways of maintaining them, are subjects which ought to be taught in schools." He expressed his faith in the wisdom of youth, stressing that "the surest way to save what is left of our forests, and restore, through replanting, what we need for the future, is to let the young people of America know about the problem."

The publication was written in an impassioned tone embellished with illustrations to underline the message. "The few remaining areas of virgin forest of large growth timber are too precious to be destroyed. There are no forests in the world that equal those of North America in variety, size of trees, beauty and grandeur.... It is unthinkable that we should not preserve for the benefit of the world what remains of this wonder" (p. 18).

Our Nation's Forests is divided into five substantive sections. Part One, "Forests a Necessity to Man," covers the uses of cut trees, the effects of forests on climate as well as their "health-giving qualities," and "the greater value of living trees." In Part Two, "The Destruction of Our Nation's Forests," Edge includes a variety of reasons why trees have been destroyed: some people do not like forests, forest fires, insect pests, cattle grazing, and highways. The remaining three parts of the booklet ("Restoration—How Much Can Be Accomplished?" "Demands Upon Our Forests," and "Forests for the Future") concern policies for managing forests. With her instinct for public relations, the text does not look like a regulation schoolbook, but is enhanced with a poem, map, and many photographs illustrating both forest destruction as well as the beauty of living trees.

Rosalie Edge wrote expressively, using a full battery of stylistic devices to reinforce her points. Eye-catching subtitles, such as "The Lumberman's Propaganda," are interspersed with provocative photo captions:

"The forest is murdered, and erosion begins" and "The beaver, engineer and water conservationist." She concludes the publication with a rhetorical question: "What is there in all the world that surpasses the glory of the living forest?" (p. 18).

However, even though she is writing for a school audience, as a born activist she cannot resist recommending policy solutions. In the section on how to restore forests, she proposes that landowners who allow their trees to stand and not be cut down should be thanked by the government. Such property should not be taxed, she believes, for "it is an act of true patriotism to care for and replenish the forests" (p. 16).

When Rosalie Edge was 78 years old in 1955, the ECC, which by that time functioned in name only, printed Publication no. 94, *The Wily and Wasteful Proposal for the Echo Park Dam*. This pamphlet was her last, but in style, content, and passion it differed little from her first attempts to influence public opinion and to goad citizens into taking actions to protect the natural environment.

She criticized officials for contorting the facts—on this occasion for claiming to bring water to millions of people by building a dam in Dinosaur National Monument in Colorado and Utah. On the contrary, she asserts, "but the Echo Park Dam is designed purely as a power and storage dam…. Not one teacupful of water from the dam at Echo Park would reach the water-impoverished people" (p. 2). She never minced words—exclaiming that "the despoilers await like hungry wolves the opportunity to exploit our Parks" (p. 1). And her descriptions of beautiful landscapes never suffered from understatement: "The wonders of Dinosaur's lovely rivers, flowing at the base of cliffs that have no superiors in majesty" (p. 2).

But undergirding an unmistakable style was always a strong backbone. Rosalie Edge never resisted reiterating the principles of conservation that underlay her passion. In this case she supported the principle of land conservation in our national parks.

> The National Park Service, since it was established in 1916, has protected the Parks from lumber interests, stock-raising interests, and Reclamation engineers. Once let these people enter one National Park, and a precedent is set for all National Parks…. We are confident that every conservationist will act to save the greatest glory of our country, the primitive grandeur of our Parks, now immediately threatened with destruction [p. 1].

The only hint that this pamphlet was her last one, rather than her first, can be detected in the last line when she referred readers to contact another organization for fuller information. In the 1930s and 1940s, Rosalie Edge's Emergency Conservation Committee was the source for further information, but in 1955 other concerned citizens were carrying on her fight to preserve the natural environment of the United States for all the people.

Rosalie Edge's Legacy

She was an effective writer about nature, but she is remembered more for her personality, actions, and the uncompromising stance she took to protect the land, flora, and fauna of the United States. In the words of Dr. Van Name, quoted in a profile of her that appeared in the April 17, 1948, issue of *The New Yorker:* "She's the only honest, unselfish, indomitable hellcat in the history of conservation."

During the course of more than 30 years of campaigning, she made many enemies, and, as she admits in her autobiography, was "sometimes despised." But Rosalie Edge could not be ignored. Her manner, sometimes brazen, sometimes sarcastic and often called witty or even charming, got results. More often than not, Mrs. Edge was the sole woman speaking at a congressional hearing, asking an awkward question at a meeting, or championing a decidedly unladylike cause.

She was a master tactician with a penchant for public relations. She realized that outrageous acts, such as rescuing peregrine falcons from the window of a 16th-floor New York City-hotel room occupied by actress Olivia de Havilland, would make the newspapers. She also knew that her upper-class connections could lead to editorials in *The New York Times,* open doors to politicians with legislative clout, as well as provide funds for pet projects.

In the last section of her unpublished autobiography, Rosalie Edge reflected about the future of conservation and even about her own role in environmental history. She realized that the next generation was bound to approach the challenge with more training, more expertise, and more education than she had, but not necessarily with as much success.

Twelve days before her death in 1962 at the age of 85, she attended the annual meeting of the National Audubon Society in Corpus Christi, Texas. After receiving a standing ovation, she telephoned her son. "That was the last time I spoke to her," Peter Edge told an audience gathered at Hawk Mountain Sanctuary in August 1998 especially to listen to his recollections about Rosalie Edge.

His mother's life in conservation had made a full circle. It had begun with her bold questioning at the annual meeting of the National Audubon Society in 1929, and it had ended with applause and an expression of gratitude by the same organization. "My mother did not give up easily. She was active and belligerent in the field of conservation," Peter Edge remembered fondly. She had pioneered, and from her initiatives would develop a strain of citizen environmental activism that continues to impact Americans' relationship with their natural environment.

4

Marjory Stoneman Douglas (1890–1998)

Wherever fresh water runs and the saw grass starts up, that's where you have the Everglades.... 'Do you think I could get away with calling it the river of grass?' With those three words I changed everybody's knowledge and educated the world as to what the Everglades meant [Marjory Stoneman Douglas: Voice of the River, *p. 191*].

Not until Marjory Stoneman Douglas was in her fifties did she find her calling; because she died at the age of 108, that meant that she devoted half of her long life to protecting the natural environment of Florida. Before 1947, when her best-selling book *The Everglades: River of Grass* was published, she had made her living as a writer but nature was only one of a variety of topics she wrote about. She worked as a reporter and wrote editorials for the *Miami Herald* and then turned to fiction and published short stories in popular magazines.

In fact, she didn't get to Florida until 1915 when she was 25 years old, in an escape from a brief, ill-fated marriage to Kenneth Douglas. When she did arrive, the situation greeting her, as well as her innate abilities and formal education, had prepared her to be an intelligent observer and eventually a forthright voice for protecting the natural environment.

After 1947, she wrote several novels and books about Florida and from 1969, when she founded the organization Friends of the Everglades, fighting to save the Everglades became her cause célèbre. She argued forcefully that natural wetlands needed to be protected and that engineers could not and should not make the Everglades a place for human habitation. In 1993, when she was 103, President Clinton awarded her a Medal of Freedom.

Childhood

Marjory Stoneman was born on April 7, 1890, in Minneapolis, her father's hometown and the city where her parents, Frank B. Stoneman and Florence Lillian Trefethen, had met. The family stayed in Minnesota for three years only before relocating to Providence, Rhode Island. Her parent's marriage was short-lived, however, broken apart by her mother's mental illness. The couple separated when Marjory was six years old, and she spent the rest of her childhood with her mother. They went to live with her maternal grandparents in the small New England town of Taunton, Massachusetts, and Marjory's father remained an estranged parent until her move to Florida at the age of 25.

Marjory's mother, who called herself by her middle name of Lillian, and her mother's relatives were the family she knew during her impressionable school and college years. The household consisted of Aunt Fanny, the unmarried younger sister of her mother, as well as her grandmother of French ancestry and her businessman grandfather.

Even though Lillian never recovered her health, Marjory remained a deeply devoted daughter until her mother died of breast cancer at the age of 53, the same year Marjory graduated from college. "I've never been so close to anyone as I was to my mother," she wrote in her autobiography, *Marjory Stoneman Douglas: Voice of the River* (p. 30). In Marjory's eyes, Lillian was "particularly beautiful," petite and black-haired. Before her mental breakdown she had been an accomplished violinist, and when the family had lived together in Providence she had performed frequently at impromptu concerts.

The relationship between mother and daughter changed dramatically when they moved to Taunton, and Marjory remembered that her "mother gradually became more dependent on me. It was as if my mother had become my child" (p. 53). In later years, after she returned home from school she would stay with her mother, and they would take walks together and play board games.

After her parents separated in 1896, Marjory's father studied law and moved to Orlando, Florida, where he worked as an attorney. He eventually migrated south to Miami where he founded the city's first morning newspaper, the *News-Record*, which in a reorganized form emerged as the *Miami Herald* in 1910. He always maintained that Lillian had deserted him, but he did not remarry until two years after her death.

In her autobiography Marjory tries to explain why her parents' marriage might have failed but she writes about it impartially, blaming neither her mother nor father. During the seven years that they lived together, her father never managed to create a financially stable situation for the family. Because of his own father's untimely death when he was a college student, Frank Stoneman had never had the necessary financial resources either to complete his education or to establish a successful business enterprise until he arrived in Florida. On the other hand, her mother had inherited a "delicate nervous system" and was unable to cope with uncertain economic circumstances and an unpleasant familiar relationship with her mother-in-law.

For Marjory, the breakup did not affect her own feelings toward either parent. During her childhood she was emotionally supported by her mother and her mother's family, and when she was reunited with her father as an adult she enjoyed a loving relationship with him and her stepmother. Between the families, however, bitterness reigned and they never were reconciled.

Taunton, where Marjory spent most of her childhood, was an old Massachusetts town approximately 30 miles south of Boston and only 20 miles from Providence, Rhode Island. Her grandfather, who owned a brass foundry, maintained a substantial middle-class household although, as Marjory notes, by the early 1900s "the family fortunes were diminishing" (p. 51). Still, they lived in an old Victorian three-storied house with spacious gardens and indoor bathroom, and they employed a live-in maid. They were able to provide Marjory, the only child, with lessons of all types and with her own bicycle when she was eight years old. All the houses on her street had front porches, and in her autobiography she paints a word picture of what life was like on a summer evening in Taunton: "people on porches enjoying the moonlight coming through the vaulting elms and my mother and aunt would bring out the guitar and banjo and sing the kind of sentimental songs they sang in those days.... All the people on the porches would applaud" (p. 58). The family was respectable, faithful members of the Episcopal Church, and at home in this traditional New England community.

She attended public school: Barnam Street Elementary, Cohannet Grammar School, and Taunton High School. Marjory liked her schooling and praised many of her teachers. "The Massachusetts public school system was extremely good. There wasn't much that literate women could do except to teach school, and maybe that accounted for the wonderful teaching we had" (p. 49). But her most vivid memory from childhood is a love for reading. She writes about how she would frequently escape into the attic to read and reminisces about sick days, when she could stay home from school, sit in the sewing room wrapped up in a blanket, and spend all day reading.

Marjory had only words of praise for the education she received at Taunton High School. The town's high school had been established in the 1870s, with her grandfather's having played a role in its founding, so that by the time she enrolled in the early 1900s a rigorous academic curriculum had become entrenched. Although most of the teachers were women, she mentions in particular a male math teacher and a Harvard-educated teacher of classical history and German. To Marjory, however, "the greatest teacher I ever had was Mary Hamer, who gave me four years of Latin" (p. 67). Her own talent for writing was revealed for the first time when, as a senior, she was asked to write the "Parting Ode" for the graduating class of 1908.

During her teenage years in Taunton, Marjory describes herself as unattractive to boys. Because she was fat and wore glasses, she remembers that no one would ask her to dance. Her social life revolved around her several girl friends, and she recalls that the only men in her life were her grandfather and her Uncle Charlie, who lived nearby in Providence and had a summer cottage on Narragansett Bay.

She continued her education at Wellesley College, which was the "nearest good college," as she explains her choice. Many years earlier, in fact, her sixth-grade teacher, who had been a Wellesley graduate, had planted the idea of Wellesley in her mind. Later, when as an adolescent she had found herself inordinately self-conscious around men, she gravitated naturally to an all- female college, where as she put it, "I could be myself as an individual, as opposed to a young girl" (p. 72).

She flourished at Wellesley, majored in English and studied with a distinguished faculty that included Sophie Shantel Hart, head of the department; Katherine Lee Bates, Shakespeare scholar and author of the song "America the Beautiful"; poet Florence Converse; and literary scholar Vida Scudder. Before graduation in 1912 Marjory had already made initial inroads into a life as a writer, having published several pieces in the college literary magazine and having edited the college annual, *Legenda*. Perhaps most telling for her future was her first foray into nature writing. A description she wrote about the beauty of the campus elicited a big round of applause from her classmates.

College changed Marjory Stoneman in more than one sense. She moved out of her family house in Taunton when she took up residence at Wellesley and literally went out into the world on her own. Unfortunately, her mother's health deteriorated when Marjory left home. Even though Marjory wrote her a postcard every day, she returned home only for holidays; during the entire four years, only Aunt Fanny visited her at college. Neither her mother nor her grandparents managed to travel even the relatively short distance between Taunton and Wellesley.

Several Wellesley professors helped prepare her intellectually for a future life as a conservationist. In addition to professors in the English department, she mentions in her autobiography the names of Elizabeth Fisher in geography, Emily Greene Balch in economics, Mary Whiton Calkins in philosophy, and Malvina Bennett, who was the head of the Department of Expression. Especially valuable to her career as a public speaker were Bennett's lessons in voice modulation, articulation, and projection.

Marjory's college friends continued to be important to her life during the years immediately following graduation in 1912 and in at least one case throughout her entire lifetime. One friend, D.Q. Applegate, helped her find paid employment and Carolyn Percy, a lifelong friend, moved in with her at an especially critical period during those tumultuous post-college years.

She graduated from Wellesley with no clear career aspirations. Although she excelled in English composition, she did not pursue a career as a writer. In fact, she did just the opposite. She found a job in personnel at a department store in St. Louis and then moved to Newark, New Jersey, where she taught basic skills to new employees at Bamberger's department store.

During this interim in her life, she met and married Kenneth Douglas, a man thirty years her senior, who was working at the time as a reporter for the *Newark Evening News*. The marriage lasted only two years, and her husband spent six months of their time together serving a prison sentence. She eventually discovered that the man she had married was an alcoholic, who acted criminally when inebriated. By moving to Florida, she extricated herself from the relationship and later obtained a divorce.

Early Life in Miami

Her father, who was there to welcome her at the Miami train station when she disembarked in September 1915, had been an estranged parent for most of her childhood and during all of her young womanhood. She wasn't sure whether she would have recognized the tall, handsome man with a "courtly manner," if he had not approached her with open arms, eager to forget the missed nineteen years in their father/daughter relationship. "With no fuss," as she put it, he drove Marjory to his house, where she lived for several years.

Frank Stoneman had remarried and Marjory's new stepmother, Lillius Eleanor Shine, became her "first and best friend in Florida" (p. 97). Lilla, as she called herself, was a native Floridian whom Marjory's father had met in Orlando during his early years in Florida. She was a descendant of Thomas Jefferson's grandson, Francis Eppes, and was a Southern lady.

For Marjory Douglas, as well as for her father, there was something about Florida, and in particular southern Florida, that fit their temperaments. She exclaimed about the large Florida sky and the special daytime light. Biscayne Bay was magnificent. But Miami, when she first became acquainted with the city, did not impress her. It was still a small town with fewer than 5,000 inhabitants. There was not yet a public library in 1915, and she understood why. Newcomers to Miami were not interested in books but rather in making money as fast as possible. It was a frontier town.

From the start, she was able to make use of her talent for writing. As a novice reporter on the *Miami Herald*, her beat was what young women usually landed—the society pages. But in this case it offered her useful entrée into Florida life, as the state was attracting the rich and famous. She covered yacht parties, women's teas, and hotel openings and met Mr. and Mrs. William Jennings Bryan, Governor Broward's widow, and George Merrick who built Coral Gables, among many other luminaries. The newspaper maintained its offices downtown in a two-story building but employed only two or three reporters in addition to Frank Stoneman, who was editor-in-chief.

Not only did her father's newspaper offer Marjory Douglas a job, but her father also guided her reactions to the new environment. As she described in "A Personal Prologue" to her 1967 book, *Florida: The Long Frontier*, her father, "in a clear, mannerly and informed prose style," expressed his opinion "against Governor Napoleon Bonaparte Broward's immensely popular project for draining the Everglades." In fact, his editorials against dredging were so out of tune with public sentiments in 1906 that his fledgling newspaper almost went bankrupt. She assumed her father's attitudes, realizing that a land where the balance of nature had reigned relatively undisturbed for four thousand years was not the place for people to build houses, farms, and businesses. Marjory Douglas became a forceful advocate for protecting the Everglades and curtailing development.

After three years of working for the *Miami Herald*, she joined the

Navy and was the first woman to enlist when the United States entered World War I. She admits in her autobiography that the time she spent at a desk job in the Navy was "the most wasted year of my life" (p. 113). Yet she didn't give up on wartime service and managed to land an assignment in Paris working for the American Red Cross. She wrote articles and reports about Red Cross activities and continued to travel around Europe, still as an employee, several months after the war had ended.

Marjory Douglas returned to the *Miami Herald* at the beginning of 1920 and was promoted to assistant editor. In that position she took a turn writing every type of story, including editorials and poetry. She used her daily column as a platform for voicing opinions about political and social issues that she wished to highlight.

Better living conditions for Miami's Colored Town, where there was no indoor plumbing or running water, and the polluted public well was a source of rampant spreading disease, was one of her major crusades. She became so incensed about Florida's ill-treatment of vagrants, who routinely were rounded up and sent to labor camps where young men were frequently whipped to death, that she composed a ballad for the newspaper called "Martin Tabert of North Dakota Is Walking Florida Now." It was also in her newspaper column in the early 1920s that she was able to give publicity to Ernest Coe's idea for the creation of a national park in the Everglades.

Miami changed dramatically after World War I, emerging from a sleepy frontier town into a booming, vibrant city in the 1920s. Population doubled, the beaches attracted crowds, and dozens of new hotels sprung up. Even the *Miami Herald* partook in the growth with an expanded readership and list of advertisers, and Marjory Douglas became a well-known local figure.

Her life was hardly all work and no play. Even before World War I she had become ensconced in the social life of the young generation of newcomers to Miami. There were beach parties, cruises, dances, and she fell in love with a newspaper reporter who worked on the afternoon paper. This romance carried on for several years, but when the young man left her and Florida permanently, Marjory became convinced that she would never marry again.

In the midst of the real estate boom that swept through southern Florida in the 1920s, Marjory Douglas became a homeowner herself. She had always been attracted to a section of Miami called Coconut Grove. It was an older part of the city filled with exotic plants and fruit trees, and writers and painters were populating the community. She bought a small plot of land there in 1924 and hired an architect. But in typical fashion for Miami in the 1920s, her first contractor took her money and absconded, and the infamous hurricane of 1926 caused considerable damage to the outside of her house before she had moved in. Eventually by the end of 1926, a small house in Coconut Grove belonged to Marjory Douglas, where she happily dwelled for more than 70 years until her death in 1998.

After several years of working full-time as assistant editor and campaigning for controversial issues that pitted her against the publisher, the pressures of daily newspaper life took a toll on her health. In 1924, she suffered her first nervous breakdown, and, as a result, she resigned from the staff of the *Miami Herald*. During the summer of 1924, she traveled back to Taunton, Massachusetts, to visit her grandmother and Aunt Fanny. This was not her first trip back to her childhood home—she had kept in touch even though the family did not communicate with her father. When she returned from Europe in 1920, she had paid a visit to Taunton and had managed to see her grandfather for the last time before he died at the age of 94.

During the several months that she spent recuperating from her illness, Marjory Douglas discovered a new way to channel her writing talent. She started writing short stories for national magazines.

Marjory Douglas as Fiction Writer

Her knack at crafting sympathetic pieces about southern Florida's unusual casts of characters allowed her to reach a national readership and brought her a measure of success as a writer. Her story "He Man" about an airplane crash and sea drowning, published in the *Saturday Evening Post* on July 30, 1927, won an O. Henry Prize, and a number of others published in the *Saturday Evening Post* were on the same themes that she developed later into full-length books. "A Bird Dog in the Hand" (September 12, 1925) about real estate speculation led to her 1952 novel *Road to the Sun*, and "September-Remember" (December 7, 1935) about hurricane devastation was the topic for her 1958 nonfiction book *Hurricane*.

Her short stories "Plumes" and "The Road to the Horizon" were both set in the Everglades and addressed issues that she returned to throughout her writing and speaking career. As a conservationist, Marjory Douglas raised her voice and pen time and time again to save endangered species of plants and animals. In "Plumes," the species under threat is the snowy egret. The other story, "The Road to the Horizon," deals with her broader environmental concern: wetlands conservation. She demonstrates in her short story how treacherous the Everglades are to man and in a back-handed way warns her readers not to venture into this unwelcoming environment.

"Plumes," a fictional account of the killing of an Audubon Society warden, was printed in the *Saturday Evening Post* on June 14, 1930. The following year Marjory Douglas published a nonfiction piece entitled "Wings," calling attention to the fate of the snowy egret, whose numbers had been decimated by hunters. Shooting the birds to salvage their beautiful feathers, much prized by milliners, had long accorded people in this region a lucrative source of income.

In *The Everglades: River of Grass,* she describes the history of the southern Florida trade in plumes that had started up in earnest after the Civil War when "aigrettes," the French word for egrets, became fashionable adornments for women's hats. "In those days the jungles south of Okeechobee ... were covered with acres of stick nests of egret and glossy ibis and heron of every kind.... A few men with clubs or shotguns rising suddenly by those low rookeries could kill and scalp hundreds of birds in a night" (pp. 278, 279).

The short story that Douglas wrote was set in the early 1900s, when the plume business had reached scandalous proportions. Legislation to curtail the killing of Florida's egrets, however, was not enacted until 1910, and the fashion did not die out until many years later.

In "The Road to the Horizon," published in the *Saturday Evening Post* magazine on February 22, 1941, Marjory Douglas leads readers on an imaginary expedition through the Everglades. She sets the story back in time, before the 1928 opening of the Tamiami Trail, the road that now cuts across southern Florida. The two characters in the story, one a young man and the other an old dreamer, ply through miles of muck and saw grass, traveling through territory unfit for human trespassing. Their experiences defy the imagination of today's travelers whose main hurdle is keeping awake and focused on the interminable sameness of the road. In her fictional account, only Indians are able to navigate successfully through the "river of grass." The young man reaches Miami in a canoe poled by a Native American, leaving the older man behind in the care of the Seminoles.

The Everglades: River of Grass

When she described the 12-year ordeal of constructing the Tamiami Trail in *The Everglades: River of Grass,* she packed as much drama, if not more, into the nonfictional account as in the short story.

> The job was a man-killer. First a crew went forward through saw grass and water and rocky hammocks with axes and machetes, cutting a trail. They worked up to the armpits in water, tormented with mosquitoes in the season, always watchful for rattlesnakes and the uncounted dark heads of moccasins. They lived, ate and slept in muck and water.... The dredge men had their own particular hell of mired beams, and dredges sinking. Men were scarred, were drowned, battered, snakebitten, and blown up [pp. 344, 345].

This brief fragment from Douglas's book about the Everglades, which sold out the first printing of 7,500 copies by Christmas 1947, is typical. She dramatically unfolds each episode in man's confrontation with the natural environment of the Everglades, starting with an introductory chapter, which the *Reader's Digest* reprinted, to a final fifteenth chapter, "The Eleventh Hour," which warns of an uncertain future.

Yet, she insists in her 1987 autobiography, that when she got the assignment to write a book about the Everglades in the early 1940s, she knew very little about this "unique region of the earth." She told Miami writer John Rothchild, a self-confessed fan of hers, who compiled 200 hours of taped conversations into her autobiography, that "what I knew about the Everglades I've already said. That it was there, that the birds were spectacular, that it should be a national park, and that it shouldn't be drained, that there were millions of acres of it" (*Marjory Stoneman Douglas: Voice of the River*, p. 190).

This lack of expertise seems somewhat disingenuous. After all, in the 1920s she served as one of only two women on a committee spearheading the establishment of a national park. Nonetheless, the four or five years of intensive work on the book catapulted Marjory Douglas into being the Everglades' most well-known spokesperson.

The message that comes through loudly but not stridently in her best-selling book is that the Everglades are a fragile environment and man's (mostly white men's) attempts to alter its natural harmony have met with at best temporary success but more often have led to disastrous results. The first chapter, which is her crowning achievement as a nature writer, presents the reader with an all-encompassing profile of "The Nature of the Everglades." In six information-packed sections, dealing with the origin of the name, the grass, the water, the rock, the geological history, and plant and animal life, the author introduces her subject.

The region of four and one-half million acres, which begins at Lake Okeechobee, became known by its English name "Everglades" in 1819, when the United States acquired the territory of Florida from Spain. The name comes from the Anglo-Saxon word "glaed," meaning "shining" or "bright." Previously, Native Americans who lived there long before Spain or the United States claimed the territory, had called the region "Pa-hay-okee," meaning "grassy water."

The central, identifying feature of the Everglades is the saw grass, described by Marjory Douglas as "so simple, so enduring, so hostile." Yet, as she explained, botanists do not consider it to be "grass at all so much as a fierce, ancient, cutting sedge."

> The first saw grass, exactly as it grows today, sprang up and lived in the sweet water and the pouring sunlight, and died in it, and from its own dried and decaying tissues and tough fibers bright with silica sprang up more fiercely again.... The seed was dropped and worked down in the water and its own ropelike mat of roots. All that decay of leaves and seed covers and roots was packed deeper year after year by the elbowing upthrust of its own life. Year after year it laid down new layers of virgin muck under the living water. There are places now where the depth of the muck is equal to the height of the saw grass [p. 11].

The other central feature of the Everglades is the water that flows slowly as a river and whose source of supply is the rain. According to Douglas, "it is the subtle ratio between rainfall and evaporation that is the final secret of water in the Glades" (p. 24).

> [I]t is clear that rainfall alone could not have maintained the persistent fine balance between wet and dry that has created and kept the Everglades.... If Okeechobee and the lakes and marshes north that contribute to it, if rivers and swamps and ponds had not existed to hoard all that excess water in a great series of reservoirs by which the flow was constantly checked and regulated, there would have been no Everglades. The whole system was like a set of scales on which the forces of the seasons, of the sun and the rains, the winds, the hurricanes, and the dewfalls, were balanced so that the life of the vast grass and all its encompassed and neighbor forms were kept secure [p. 25].

In her introductory chapter she differentiates between various sections of the millions of acres of swampland. Of the area running approximately 60 miles south of Lake Okeechobee she writes, "This is the Everglades at their greatest concentration, a world of nothing but saw grass" (p. 31). Then further south and west she describes what are called "hammocks of the saw grass river," which are rocky outcrops covered with diverse flora and fauna. "The saw grass in its essential harshness supports little else. It repelled man. But on the rock the crowding forms made life abundant" (p. 40).

Lake jungles, pine, live oak, cabbage palmetto, cypress, each has its
region and its associated life.... The northernmost are dense with pond
apple or willow and elder and those charming border shrubs.... There
are hammocks centered about live oaks or cabbage palms, crowded and
screened with bushes. There are cypress hammocks hung with moss over
a deep brown pool where a single heron waits and the blue flag and the
water hyacinth and the green arrowy lilies catch a great shaft of light....
At the end of the saw-grass river and its bordering coasts, begins the
mangrove [pp. 52, 53].

After introducing readers to the natural environment of the Everglades, she devotes the rest of the book to an account of the breadth of
encounters between the Everglades and man, "who was among the last
of the living forms to invade its shores" (p. 39). She begins with the Native
Americans, who she contends have been the only human inhabitants to
live harmoniously with the land.

With rich detail, she relates escapades of numerous Spanish explor-
ers, government officials, and missionaries, who tried mostly in vain to
establish viable settlements. For three hundred years, either the harsh environmental conditions or the resistance of the Native Americans stymied
most Spanish ambitions. As she narrates the often dramatic history of man's
encounters with the Everglades, she seems to relish describing American
frontier settlers, the adventurers, escapees, idealists, hunters, and outlaws
who were attracted to this wilderness throughout the nineteenth century.

She ends the story with the most destructive chapter of all between
man and his environment, the saga of draining the land that has altered
the fundamental nature of the Everglades. The idea to drain the Everglades was born the same year that Florida gained statehood: 1845. Proponents always trumpeted how reclamation would lure thousands of
settlers to this land of sun, warmth, and rich muck soil. In 1905, then-
governor Napoleon Bonaparte Broward challenged his citizens to create
"The Empire of the Everglades," likening the enterprise to Holland's
reclaiming land from the sea and Britain's taming of the Nile River with
construction of the Aswan Dam in Egypt.

According to Douglas, the biggest advocates through the century—
politicians, land developers, ex-soldiers, cattlemen, men out for profit
only—never knew what they were up against. They understood neither
the nature of the land nor the water. The region had never been entirely
mapped and every survey team had faced attacks from indigenous Indian
inhabitants and had been overwhelmed by the difficult natural elements—
mud, snakes, mosquitoes. "They saw the Everglades ... as a dream, a
mirage of riches that many men would follow to their ruin.... [T]o the

intricate and subtle relation of soil, of fresh water and evaporation, and of runoff and salt intrusion, and all the consequences of disturbing the fine balance nature had set up in the past four thousand years—no one knew enough to look" (p. 286).

It was a long saga to unravel. Up to 1947, when her book was published, there had been at least four major reclamation projects in the 1880s, the early 1900s, the mid–1920s, and the early 1930s. Every time settlers had followed the dredges and started new lives in the Everglades, and every time people's dreams had been squelched.

When she began to research the book, she sought out Garald Parker, hydrologist for the state of Florida, who steered her to the files of the Internal Improvement Board in Tallahassee whose records turned out to be her most revealing source. "The Internal Improvement Board was really the governor and the cabinet wearing different hats. For decades, they'd handled all the management of the Everglades and had done a terrible job. I read all the minutes of their meetings going back for years. It was obvious to Parker, and now to me, that they didn't understand the nature of fresh water in south Florida" (*Marjory Stoneman Douglas: Voice of the River*, p. 191).

In 1882, two dredges owned by the Disston Company started out from Fort Myers with the goal of draining and improving four million acres of wetlands west of Lake Okeechobee. They dug one canal. But in 1905, when Governor Broward established a Board of Drainage Commissioners and levied a drainage tax, the dredging of "the river of grass" took off in earnest. Vegetable farmers moved onto former swampland and canals opened up transportation routes to east coast towns.

After World War I, a new era of scientific farming began with sugar and vegetable growers realizing that the rich muck soil of the drained Everglades lacked essential minerals and nutrients. So they added chemicals in a process that Marjory Douglas likened to mining: "crops take from the soil, as miners do, what the work of centuries put there" (p. 356). They sprayed against insects and, in places where the land had dried up, farmers irrigated their fields.

By the mid–1920s and especially after the destructive hurricane of 1926, "people in Florida had also wakened to the idea that all the talk about draining the Everglades was equally unreal. They had a few canals, which had cost fourteen million dollars, built for transportation as much as for drainage, which were good for neither. In high water the canals could not carry off the surplus. In low water and dry times, with no water control, they merely took away water increasingly essential" (pp. 341–342).

When Governor Martin came into office in the 1920s, he intended to return to the earlier canal-building spree of former governor Broward, but the state government had run out of money. Only with the financial backing of land developer Barron G. Collier was he able to complete the Tamiami Trail in 1928.

The next major engineering project in the Everglades was the diking of Lake Okeechobee as a response to the devastating floods that occurred in the late 1920s. Even the federal government got involved this time with the construction of canals and locks that reduced the water level of the lake by five feet. The massive flood control project extended south of the lake, saving towns, farms, and people who had settled the former Everglades region to the east and to the west along the Caloosahatchee River. Marjory Douglas continues the saga into the 1940s, detailing how fires had destroyed dried-up swampland and salt water had invaded the freshwater Everglades.

Nevertheless, in the last chapter of the book she ends on a note of hope. She can point to the establishment of the national park that President Truman dedicated on December 6, 1947, the same year her book was published. As she wrote at the time, Everglades National Park "will be the only national park in which the wildlife, the crocodiles, the trees, the orchids, will be more important than the sheer geology of the country" (*Marjory Stoneman Douglas: Voice of the River*, p. 381).

But the 1.5 million acres protected as a national park were only one part of the region of the Everglades, and demarcating the park's boundaries has always been a contentious issue. Ernest Coe, whom Douglas credits as the father of Everglades National Park, having initiated and campaigned for a park from the 1920s, refused to vote for its establishment without the inclusion of Big Cypress, north of the Tamiami Trail.

The creation of a national park, albeit one that did not encompass the entire Everglades wetlands, was not the only positive development. In the final chapter, she also expresses enthusiasm for a wartime recommendation made by the U.S. Soil Conservation Service and the U.S. Geological Survey that called for a single plan of development and water control for the entire region. If the conflicting demands for water and land use were determined on a rational basis, then the clout of powerful users would be diminished.

Yet in her final words there is more foreboding than hope: "The balance still existed between the forces of life and of death. There is a balance in man also, one which has set against his greed and his inertia and his foolishness; his courage, his will, his ability slowly and painfully to learn, and to work together. Perhaps even in this last hour, in a new relation of usefulness and beauty, the vast, magnificent, subtle and unique region of the Everglades may not be utterly lost" (p. 385).

Marjory Douglas's book *The Everglades: River of Grass* was an instant success. Rinehart and Company, who published the original edition in their Rivers of America series, reprinted the book seven times, and in the 1970s other publishers came out with paperback editions. In 1997, following up on their 1988 edition, Pineapple Press in Sarasota, Florida, publisher of several other books by Marjory Douglas, brought out a special 50th-anniversary edition. This revision included two new chapters: one written by Randy Lee Loftis and Marjory Douglas about the Everglades 40 years later, and one written by Cyril Zaneski 50 years after the first edition.

Marjory Douglas, Book Author

The original book came out when Marjory Douglas was 57 years old, and its success ushered in a new phase in her writing career as an author of books. During the succeeding 20 years, she wrote a number of full-length books, some fiction but the majority were nonfiction.

Her personal life had already experienced several upheavals. In 1938, Aunt Fanny, her last relative in Taunton, Massachusetts, died and Marjory went back to sell her childhood home. Soon after, Uncle Charlie moved down from Massachusetts to live in Douglas's house in Coconut Grove. She had always been close to this relative and she had an extra room in her house. After Uncle Charlie's wife died, he had no reason to stay up north. He and Marjory Douglas lived together amicably until he died in his eighties in the late 1950s.

The other death in the family, that of her father, occurred in 1941. He was 84 years old and Marjory was with him until the end. She had another nervous breakdown after he died. As she admits honestly in her autobiography, "undoubtedly I had a father complex. Having been brought up without him and then coming back and finding him so sympathetic had a powerful effect. It had a lot to do with my not wanting to get married again" (p. 188).

In 1948, soon after the Everglades book was published and as a celebration of sorts, Marjory Douglas traveled across the United States with several women friends. But as she disliked spending money, she was happy to return to Florida and to her more productive writing life. She had interrupted work on a novel to research and write the Everglades book. In 1952, that novel entitled *Road to the Sun*, about people lured to Florida during the land boom of the 1920s, was published.

The following year she came out with *Freedom River*, a juvenile novel about three adolescent boys: a Native American, an escaped slave and a son of Quaker abolitionists. It was set in the Everglades region in 1845, the year Florida attained statehood. Because Marjory Douglas had absorbed so much information about Florida's history while researching the Everglades book, she could include detailed scenes of Native American corn dances and the production of coontie, the staple meal made from arrowroot. She also created believable portraits of three types of communities, drawing on her own ancestral history for the Quaker abolitionist family. On her father's side, she always considered herself a direct descendant of Levi Coffin, president of the Underground Railroad. According to family tradition, Eliza and her baby, whom Harriet Beecher Stowe made famous in *Uncle Tom's Cabin*, escaped to "Uncle Levi and Aunt Katie's place in Indiana." In Douglas's imagination, the Coffin family is transferred to Florida. Her novel presented a window into three historical societies, providing several fictional examples of how people had managed to live in the natural environment of the Everglades.

More books followed during the next two decades, and she spent most of her time engaged in the research for her writing. She wrote another novel for young people entitled *Alligator Crossing*, an adventure story about the national park, before turning her focus back to nonfiction. In 1958, *Hurricane* was published, and for that book she traveled extensively, interviewing people about their experiences with hurricane damage. She went to places made famous for storm devastation, such as the Outer Banks in North Carolina, Charleston in South Carolina, Jamaica, Martinique, and Cuba.

For her next book, *Florida: The Long Frontier*, which was published in 1967 by Harper and Row, she made a number of research trips around the state. It sold very well and was her second most successful book. She also wrote a specialized book about birding in Florida and a biographical profile of the founders of the Fairchild Botanical Garden.

When Marjory Douglas reached her seventies she took on a number of new activities. She spent several years as director of the University of Miami Press and taught Florida history at Dade Junior College. But at the center of her life was her research work on the British writer/environmentalist, W. H. Hudson. For this project she received a small grant from Wellesley College and traveled three times to Argentina, where Hudson had spent his childhood. During the course of writing his biography, she also took seven trips to England. But it was during her seventies that Douglas's eyesight began to dim. She had a cataract operation when she was seventy-seven, but she was unable to continue writing. She eventually gave her manuscript on W. H. Hudson to an editor to complete.

Marjory Douglas as Environmental Activist

It was not until 1969, when she was nearly 80 years old that she started the activist phase of her life. She reports in her autobiography how she was cajoled by Joe Browder, head of the National Audubon Society in Miami, into campaigning to stop construction of a jetport in the Everglades. As she reminisces in *Marjory Stoneman Douglas: Voice of the River*:

> There was a gal working for Joe Browder by the name of Wilson. I met her one night in a grocery store and I said, 'I think you and Joe are doing great work. It's wonderful.' She looked me square in the eye and said, 'Yeah, what are you doing?' 'Oh me?' I said. 'I wrote the book.' 'That's not enough,' she countered.... I casually mumbled some platitude like 'I'll do whatever I can.... He was at my doorstep the next day and asked me to issue a ringing denunciation of the jetport to the press.... I suggested that such things are more effective if they come from organizations. Without skipping a beat, he said, 'Well, why don't you start an organization?' [p. 225].

She did establish a nonprofit organization called Friends of the Everglades, which campaigns to protect the environment of the Everglades region. Marjory Douglas was the star speaker, and every speech she gave attracted 15 or 20 new members who joined up with a contribution of one dollar. In a few years Friends of the Everglades counted 3,000 members from thirty-eight states. They won the fight against the jetport. Instead, the land was turned into Big Cypress National Preserve in 1974. Following that victory, the organization took up an ongoing list of new causes, from saving panthers to fighting sugar companies.

In the 1990s, after years of damaging engineering projects, the battle cry was to restore the Everglades to a more natural state. At ceremonies in celebration of the fiftieth anniversary of Everglades National Park held in Everglades City in December 1997, Vice President Gore announced a federal government land purchase of a 50,000-acre sugar plantation.

The U.S. Army Corps of Engineers has been developing plans to undo the damage that it has wrought upon the natural environment of the Everglades. A twenty-year undertaking that would cost more than $8 billion is under discussion to save the endangered ecosystem. The project, which requires federal and state approval as well as funding, envisions a network of large water reservoirs and underground wells to recapture 85 percent of the fresh water that is now channeled out to sea during the wet season. Hundreds of miles of canals that were constructed in the 1950s, '60s, and '70s to control floods would be destroyed, and the Tamiami Trail would be rebuilt to let water flow beneath it more naturally.

More than fifty years after Marjory Douglas, writing in the final chapter of *The Everglades: River of Grass,* warned about losing the unique region of the Everglades, we are still facing "The Eleventh Hour," as she called it.

Marjory Douglas (Florida State Archives).

Marjory Douglas's Legacy

Marjory Douglas's voice continued to be heard even after she turned 100 years old. However, more often than not she was giving a thank-you speech rather than a campaigning one. At the local, state, and national levels, Mrs. Douglas, sporting a large hat and hiding her almost blind eyes behind dark glasses, received numerous awards for her role as protector of the Everglades. Local schools and parks have been named for her, and in Key Biscayne the city has established the Marjory Stoneman Douglas Nature Center. The building that houses the Florida State Department of Natural Resources in Tallahassee bears her name, and former governor Lawton Chiles signed (in the front yard of her house in Coconut Grove) a bill to clean up the Everglades. Recognition of her contribution as an American conservationist came from the Sierra Club, which made her honorary vice president and from President Clinton, who bestowed her with the Medal of Freedom in 1993.

Her legacy lives on as an inspiration to us all even after her death in May 1998 at the age of 108. Marjory Stoneman Douglas used her talent as a writer to change people's perceptions about the wetlands of southern Florida. Wielding her pen as a newspaper reporter and storyteller, as well as a nature writer and forceful conservation campaigner, she urged us to protect endangered species of plants and animals and to live in harmony with and not to destroy the natural environment of the Everglades.

5

Helen Nearing
(1904–1995)

*Living the good life for us was practicing harmony with the earth
and all that lives in it. It was frugal living, self-subsistent, self-
sustaining. It was earning our way by the sweat of our brows,
beholden to no employer or job. It was growing our own food,
building our own buildings, cutting our own wood, and providing for our own livelihood.... Our idea was to take care of our
physical needs, housing, food, fuel, and clothing so that we could
read, write, study, teach, or make music without dependence on
the outside world* [Loving and Leaving the Good Life, *p. 100*].

Helen Nearing embarked on her environmentally sound experiment
in living when she was 28 years old, but not until she was nearly fifty did
she start writing about this way of life. In 1950, she co-authored with Scott
Nearing *The Maple Sugar Book*, in which they described both the process
and history of making maple sugar as well as some of their ideas about
self-sufficient homesteading. *Living the Good Life* by Scott and Helen
Nearing, published in 1954, not only told their personal story but also
served as a guide for others who yearned to establish a lifestyle in tune
with nature. Several books followed, most notably *Continuing the Good
Life*, which they wrote in 1979 about their self-sufficient existence on a
coastal farm in Maine. In addition, Helen Nearing wrote books on various aspects of their lifestyle, in particular *Simple Food for the Good Life*,
Our Home Made of Stone, and *Loving and Leaving the Good Life*.

She admitted that she was an unlikely farmer, having acquired homesteading skills only after her arrival in the Vermont countryside, and many
of the economic and political attitudes expressed in their co-authored
books were, in fact, Scott Nearing's beliefs that she adopted. But Helen's

philosophy of life as well as her ideas about the natural environment had earlier origins. Her childhood in suburban New Jersey growing up in a vegetarian family, followed by many years of international education in Europe, India, and Australia, set the stage for her fifty-year adventure in life with Scott Nearing.

Childhood

Helen Knothe was born in New York City on February 23, 1904. Her father, Frank Knothe, was a businessman and her mother, Maria Obreen, was a painter from Amsterdam whose uncle was the director of the Rijksmuseum. According to Helen's own writings, her parents had met in New York in 1896 at The Theosophical Society, and the teachings of this sect affected her own vision of life. Theosophy is a philosophy that proposes to establish direct contact with the divine principle through contemplation and emphasizes a spiritual underpinning for living.

While Helen was still a toddler, the family, which consisted then of an older brother and a younger sister, moved to Ridgewood, New Jersey, and lived in a substantial house with servants, extensive gardens and a tennis court. Even during her childhood Helen was never especially close to her siblings, who chose very different paths in life. Her brother, who was mechanically talented as a child, became a pilot and operated a flight school in Florida. Her sister—always stylish and social—married a businessman and lived a conventional suburban family life.

Both of Helen's parents exerted important influences on her development as a child. Whereas each contributed in his or her special ways, they both demonstrated in their own lives a strong commitment to community service. Her father chaired the Ridgewood Board of Education and her mother was president of the Women's Club. He headed the local Red Cross and she headed the local chapter of the Society for the Prevention of Cruelty to Animals. They were generously philanthropic and supported organizations in a wide range of political, social and cultural fields but all of these fell under the general heading of nonconformist in early twentieth-century United States society.

Helen's father shared with his daughter a lifelong love for books and music. When she was five, his birthday present to her was a collection of "Poems to Think About" and his large library was a constant fount of childhood reading experiences. It was there that she became acquainted with the philosophy of Emerson, the essays of Bacon, and the novels of Robert Louis Stevenson.

But it was through "musicking together," as Helen phrased it, that she remembered forming her strongest links with her father. Because he went to the office every day in New York City, he normally did not spend much time at home. Yet when Helen took up the study of the violin, "he learned to accompany me with tapes on his electric Pianola and often soothed me to sleep when I was in my adjoining room with Chopin nocturnes, Beethoven adagios, and Rubinstein melodies. I remember listening to his playing long into the night" *(Loving and Leaving the Good Life,* pp. 33–34).

Her mother provided the "harmonious heart of the family" and was deeply loved and appreciated by Helen as well as by her siblings. Because she had been born and raised in the Netherlands, her European familial connections and attitudes encouraged Helen to adopt a broader, more cosmopolitan outlook on life.

Helen's most long-lasting childhood experience involved music, and she developed a talent for playing the violin at a young age. She performed at local events and went on to study with celebrated musicians in both Holland and Austria. It was a Dutch cousin who introduced her to the violin, presenting Helen with a small-sized instrument as a gift when she came to stay with the family in New Jersey. To become a professional violinist was Helen's first serious career aspiration, but "a deep desire to contribute and to live rightly" displaced this interest in the long run *(Loving and Leaving the Good Life,* p. 31). However, her life was never without music.

Reading followed closely behind music in her personal recollections of childhood. From the age of five, she remembered becoming "addicted to books and reading," and English was her favorite subject in school. As a teenager she started filling up scrapbooks with what became a lifelong collection of "felicitous phrases and apt quotations." The last book she published just before her death in 1995 was a compendium of wise thoughts, called *Light on Aging and Dying.*

She was especially enamored of poetry and even tried her own hand at writing poems. As literary editor of the Ridgewood high school newspaper, she published a four-line verse, "Ode to Latin," and then a parody of Robert Burns's "To a Mouse, On turning up her nest with the plough, November 1785," transformed by Helen Knothe into "To a Worm, Upon cutting one in half, September 1920." But these early forays into creative writing did not develop into a career as a published writer until much later in life.

When she graduated from high school in 1921, her parents offered her three options as to where to continue her education: attending the

Boston Conservatory of Music, Vassar College, or studying the violin in Europe. She chose the latter and decided to live in Amsterdam to take violin lessons from the concertmaster of the Concertgebouw Orchestra. Her mother traveled with her to Holland and left her there to lodge at the Theosophical Headquarters building.

From 1921 to 1923 Helen's primary occupation was study of the violin. She practiced faithfully for several hours every day and attended twice-weekly concert performances of the Concertgebouw Orchestra conducted by Maestro Mengelberg. With this routine, not only did her proficiency as a violinist improve markedly but also, as she put it, "she graduated to deeper musicality" (*Loving and Leaving the Good Life*, p. 46). In February 1923 she moved to a suburb of Vienna to study with the Irish violinist, Mary Dickinson-Auner, who was then living in Austria. Under Auner's personal instruction, Helen developed professionally and began to perform in chamber music ensembles.

Nevertheless, after a period of soul searching that included a trip back home to New Jersey to confer with her parents, Helen came to the conclusion "that she had been called not to the violin, but to a higher degree…. She would like to devote herself to learning the meaning and purpose of life, then to contribute what she could to its unfolding" (*Loving and Leaving the Good Life*, p. 48). One of the leading figures in the Theosophy movement, the Englishwoman Mrs. Annie Besant, offered Helen advice in a number of personal letters, which she quoted from in her memoirs. "Do you care enough for the spiritual life and for the helping of humanity to give up everything else for that aim?" Helen's reply at that stage of her life was "yes."

It is difficult to describe Helen Knothe as a young woman in her early twenties without taking into consideration the role that Krishnamurti played in her decision-making. During her first summer in Europe, she had attended an institute where she met Krishnamurti, a young man from India who had been hand-picked to play a leadership role in the Theosophy movement. The institute was held at a castle in northern Holland owned by Baron Philip Van Pallandt, a devoted member of The Theosophical Society. The baron had invited Krishnamurti, then 26 years old, to be his guest. Helen Knothe and Krishnamurti dined together at the castle and a strong emotional attachment developed between the two young people. From the beginning, Helen, who was only seventeen at the time, assumed a supporting role to this man who was in training to become the future World Teacher of The Theosophical Society. During the following years, in meetings in Italy, Austria and in India, Helen was with him during his purification agonies when she took on a motherly posture toward him, as well as during periods of high spiritual enlightenment when he served as her priest listening to confession.

Their deeply romantic love affair lasted for six years but was never expressed sexually. She admits that they spent only a few months living in the same place, and the rest of the relationship was played out in letters, many of which she excerpts in her memoirs. Because this young man went on to have a distinguished career as an international spiritual leader, their young love was described in several biographies and even in novels, always with the purpose of belittling its importance.

By 1926 their individual paths had separated and Krishnamurti no longer felt emotionally attached to her. According to Helen, he went on to preach a "message of living in the eternal present; of being intensely aware of every moment; of seeking quality in living; of dropping petty aims; and of self-transformation through inner realization" (*Loving and Leaving the Good Life*, p. 62). Yet he never became the World Teacher of the Theosophical Society, for he eventually rejected allegiance to all organizations, rituals or creeds.

For Helen Knothe's life the period she spent living abroad was her higher education. Her own interests in this spiritual philosophy, as well as an emotional attachment to Krishnamurti, led her to attend Theosophy gatherings in Europe and India and then to live for several years at a Theosophical community in Australia. In Sydney, Australia, where she was a member of Bishop C. W. Leadbeater's Theosophy community from 1924 to 1926, she "meditated and lived on a very exalted plane," as she reflected on the two-and-a-half-year experience in her memoirs *(Loving and Leaving the Good Life*, p. 54). During that period she continued to play the violin, giving concerts in churches and on the radio, and organizing performing arts activities for children. Her outlook on society also broadened during those years in Australia, as she visited slums in Sydney and was introduced to the socialist movement, extending her vision beyond the privileged world of upper-class spirituality.

Life with Scott Nearing

It was not until she returned to the United States and to her family's house in Ridgewood, New Jersey, that she met Scott Nearing. Helen was 24 and Scott was 45 in the autumn of 1928 when they first became friends. Helen describes her reactions to meeting this "unassuming, kindly, wise husbandman" in romantic detail in *Loving and Leaving the Good Life*, the book she wrote following his death in 1983. Scott, on the other hand, wrote only one paragraph about Helen in his autobiography, *The Making of a Radical.* "I was lucky enough ... to meet a young woman about twenty years my junior.... Helen Knothe was a vigorous, lively, personable girl, a lifetime vegetarian, with a violinist's training behind her, and many years spent abroad" (p. 211).

The way it all began, according to Helen, was with a telephone call. She invited Scott Nearing to speak at a local Unitarian Church forum, of which her father was president. They chatted for a while on the phone, but even before the lecture took place Scott had asked her to accompany him on a long drive to upstate New York. There was something in his voice that had attracted her, and during the many hours of conversation in the car she discovered "a man I could trust, who knew where he was going and who was on his way, exemplifying, both in his living and in his words, conscious dedicated purpose" (*Loving and Leaving the Good Life*, p. 12).

This man, who "was to become an ideal lifetime companion," was an accomplished intellectual and notorious radical economist. By 1928 his career as a university professor had ended, after being dismissed from the University of Pennsylvania for his work against child labor and from the University of Toledo in Ohio for his writings against U.S. participation in World War I. His books were out of print, the established press had blacklisted him, and in 1919 he had been acquitted only after undergoing a trial in which he had been charged for treason because of anti-war activities.

The age difference between Helen and Scott was substantial, as were their experiences in living. Scott had been married, was the father of two teenaged sons, and was living alone in Ridgewood after separation from his family. Helen realized from the beginning that she had much to learn from him and that she would never be his intellectual equal. But in a letter from Scott that she reprinted in *Loving and Leaving the Good Life*, he clearly spelled out her special attributes: "fine musical talent; a keen sense of beauty; you easily grasp the larger truths and relate them effectively and with understanding; a facile and powerful personality, which attracts people, so that you may lead them or teach them, or sympathize with them and encourage them; a capacity for organizing and directing" (pp. 84–85).

Even with the considerable differences between the two, it did not take them more than one year to decide to live together. This happened in 1929 when they rented a room in Greenwich Village in New York City and Helen went to work as his secretarial assistant. They moved later into a three-room apartment on Fourteenth Street, supplied with cold water only and a toilet in the hall. It was from there that they masterminded their design for living the good life.

By 1932, Helen and Scott had moved onto a 65-acre farm in southern Vermont in a valley facing 4,000-foot Stratton Mountain. It was here in the township of Jamaica where they lived the "good life" made famous in their book of that name, which was published in 1954. Why did they forsake New York City for the backwoods of Vermont? They explain this in the introduction to *Living the Good Life*: "We sought to make a depression-free living.... We wanted to maintain and improve our health. We knew that the pressures of city life were exacting, and we sought a simple basis of well-being, where contact with the earth, and home-grown organic food, would play a large part.... We wanted to organize our work time so that six months of bread labor each year gave us six months of leisure, for research, travelling, writing, speaking and teaching" (pp. 5, 6). With these goals in mind, they ended up in the Green Mountains of Vermont in a place that appealed to their "reason, enthusiasms and pocketbooks." But their journey to that location was a carefully thought-out decision.

During the depths of Depression in the 1930s, Scott Nearing had been deprived of his regular avenues for making a living as a university professor, as a lecturer, or as a writer. Helen had worked for one year at factory jobs in New York and had relegated playing the violin to an avocation, rather than a money-earning profession. They needed to make a living, but they "wanted to control [their] own source of livelihood," as they wrote in *The Maple Sugar Book*. Their environmentally sound design for living was basically a way to live simply, adequately, decently, with self-respect and with nature. Even though they had chosen to settle on a farm in a cold climate, where the growing season lasted only three months, they were able to produce 75 percent of their own food requirements. They were able to earn a cash income to cover the rest of their needs with proceeds from a household maple syrup and sugar business.

They chose to leave the city because of personal bias and were drawn to country living and to Vermont, in particular, for its positive attractions. The seasonal pattern of living especially appealed to the Nearings, as they wrote in *The Maple Sugar Book*.

> If he would savor the true riches of country living he must follow the rugged path past autumn, across winter, and through spring.... Around September when the best weather of the year sets in, when the nights are snappy and the days golden and warm, when the mapled hills are a riot of burnished color, when flies and mosquitoes are a thing of past memory, the "summer people" are on the afternoon train or moving in

traffic lines along auto-littered highways toward their cliff dwellings amid the turmoil, noise, and stench of the city. They have relished the full blaze of strident summer suns. They miss, however, the rich glory that autumn alone possesses. Nor do they ever feel that gripping of the heart that accompanies the first winter storm, swept down from arctic cold by a searing north wind [*The Maple Sugar Book*, p. 211].

It was not only their predilection for the New England climate and terrain that determined the setting for the Nearings' "good life." Their innate sense of responsibility to contribute in some purposeful manner to the well-being of fellow human beings made them decide to remain in the United States. They had considered moving to Europe, where Helen had personal links, or to India or even Paraguay, where land was inexpensive and like-minded people had set up alternative communities. They chose to farm in Vermont and later in Maine because of their overriding commitment to teach and to share their discoveries about how to live with a wide audience.

Gardening was a central component to the life that Scott and Helen Nearing created together for nearly 20 years in Vermont and then for more than 30 years in Maine. Their garden was, in the words of one of Helen's anonymous sources, "a work of Art using the materials of Nature." Gardening in New England called for continuous experimenting to counter the harsh climate, to revitalize overworked soil, and "to collaborate with Mother Nature." In their garden in Maine, they could count on only three frost-free months: June, July, and August. But in colder, southern Vermont, where their garden was situated at a higher elevation and far distant from the sea, they frequently faced frost as late as mid–June, and in 1947 they reported crop damages from frost in July and August as well. What they discovered were ingenious techniques to reinvigorate the soil and select the most suitable vegetables and fruits to cultivate, and methods to extend the growing season so that they could eat fresh produce from their garden yearlong.

Their remedy for depleted soil was to fertilize with homemade compost. They readily admitted that their compost-created soil was not as natural as the soil of the forest floor, but they could not wait hundreds of years for nature to produce new, rich earth. To hurry up the process, they made use of vegetable refuse from the kitchen and garden, introduced earthworms to break down the organic matter, and kept the pile damp and warm for 60 to 90 days. As they reported, "the varied materials composing the pile will be reduced to a rich, sweet-smelling earthy mass closely resembling the black wood dirt picked up on a forest floor" (*Living the Good Life*, p. 103).

The other aspect of recreating a fertile garden out of a worn-out farm was to make use of mulching to retain moisture and to eliminate weeds. During the course of their fifty-plus years of gardening, the Nearings tried out an array of mulching materials including hay, leaves, tree branches, twigs, and sawdust.

The growing seasons in both Vermont and Maine were short; in Vermont, it lasted on average only 85 days and in Maine, 105 days. Because the Nearings were determined to eat fresh, unprocessed vegetarian food and maintain a rounded diet, they supplemented their outside garden with produce grown in a sun-heated greenhouse that they constructed for wintertime gardening. In 1977, they wrote a book entitled *Building and Using Our Sun-heated Greenhouse*, which focused entirely on this type of gardening.

They built their greenhouse out of stone and concrete and covered it with a sloping glass roof. It required no additional source of heat other than the sun, and with this facility they were able to supply themselves with green vegetables throughout the severest months of winter from November to March. They planted crops on the floor of the greenhouse, at the same level as in the outdoor garden, and left no space for walking paths between the rows. The greenhouse was useful for starting seedlings in the early spring, transplanting vegetables that still were growing outside in the late fall, and for raising winter vegetables. They were always looking for crops that would survive the winter and reported having the most success with hardy varieties of lettuce, leek, parsley, celery, chard, kale, and Chinese cabbage.

The other way that the Nearings managed to eat fresh produce throughout the year was to "eat with the seasons ... enjoying thoroughly each food as it came from the garden" (*Living the Good Life*, p. 105). This meant that when parsnips, the first vegetable to ripen in the spring, were ready for picking they would eat them continually for three or four weeks. Later, when the asparagus appeared they would eat them for one meal a day for the next eight weeks. It was not until the middle of summer that they would enjoy the corn, tomatoes, shellbeans, broccoli, cauliflower, and celery. After all the crops had been harvested, they were able to eat fresh produce, such as cabbages, winter squash, potatoes, beets, carrots, turnips, onions, pears, and apples, that would keep over winter in the storage cellar.

They managed to keep their garden growing from early in the spring to later and later in the autumn by continuously planting. As soon as they dug up one crop, they planted another. For instance, when they pulled out the peas sometimes with edible pods still on the vines, they immediately sowed spinach seeds in "the erstwhile pea row." Most of the planting for vegetables that would ripen in the fall took place during late July and August. They would harvest fresh produce into the fall as long as possible, trying to lengthen the growing season each year. "The adroit gardener can snatch a cauliflower or Chinese cabbage and a hardy chard plant here or there. He can also pick fresh spinach and lettuces and radishes, which have not yet given up their efforts to take advantage of the few hours of growing weather between frost-crusted earth in the midmorning and the onset of sunlessness in midafternoon" (*Continuing the Good Life*, p. 244).

In addition to gardening, the Nearings collaborated with nature in the production of two cash crops: maple syrup and sugar in Vermont, and blueberries in Maine. They needed to find a source of cash income to buy the additional food that they could not grow and items that they could not produce themselves and to pay expenses such as gasoline and taxes. As they described in *The Maple Sugar Book*, "we have been developing a source of livelihood from the earth.... It is hardly possible to overemphasize the importance of this relationship with the earth, its rhythms, seasons, and cycles" (p. 245).

When they first made the move from New York City to a farm in southern Vermont, they had thought that cutting trees would provide their source of supplementary cash. But when they discovered that their homestead was situated in the heart of Vermont's sugar maple country, "we accepted our destiny, tapped half a dozen trees near the house and made a few gallons of maple syrup on the kitchen stove" (p. 240).

After learning from neighbors about all the steps entailed in the process of producing maple syrup, amounting to a five-year apprenticeship, they started setting up their own business. They built a sugarhouse, bought an evaporator, and developed imaginative maple sugar products to sell. For three months in early spring for almost 20 years, the Nearings got "solid satisfaction ... from an experience that pays us while we have the joy of participating in a productive, creative, going enterprise" (p. 243). "We have earned from maple and found a means of livelihood. We have also learned from maple.... A complete syrup and sugar maker comprises in himself a woodcutter, a forester, a botanist, an ecologist, a meteorologist, an agronomist, a chemist, a cook, an economist, and a merchant" (p. 246).

For Helen, who became quite proficient at boiling sap in the sugarhouse, the task became far more than a convenient way to make a living. "There is a lordliness and a sense of power in heaving heavy logs into a blazing furnace ... and tending the huge evaporator." She described how once on a beautiful day in March when sugaring was in full swing, two men selling the *Encyclopedia Britannica* arrived at the sugarhouse and found the process so fascinating that they wanted to help. They turned out to be better salesmen than sugar boilers, however, for the Nearings bought a set of encyclopedias from them. Even though she enjoyed her labor, she had to admit that during the long days spent in "this sweet and sticky atmosphere," she would "eat only sour, vinegared, pickled, or salted food."

After nearly 20 years of "living the good life" in southern Vermont, by the beginning of the 1950s the Nearings could sense that there was a change in the air. The Green Mountains, and Stratton Mountain in particular, were being discovered and about to be transformed into a popular skiing recreational area. That was not the type of environment that they had chosen in the 1930s, and that was not the type of atmosphere in which they could live happily. Reluctantly, Helen and Scott Nearing decided to move.

The 140-acre farm they bought was located in Maine on Cape Rosier, Hancock County, in the village of Harborside overlooking Penobscot Bay. There were meadows, a cove on the beach, and 15 acres of woods. Because they used logs for both heating and cooking, the well-managed woodlot, in addition to plentiful supplies of driftwood they collected on the beach after frequent storms, provided important resources for their household.

Their Maine homestead was situated in a wild blueberry county, and blueberries, albeit cultivated bushes, became their cash crop, replacing the maple sugar business of their Vermont days. The Nearings decided to cultivate hybrid blueberries instead of burning the fields and harvesting a crop of wild berries only in alternate years, so that they could be assured of a dependable marketable crop.

They started their blueberry patch in spring 1953 by planting 228 two-year-old seedlings in twelve varieties. They harvested only five and one-half quarts of berries in 1957, but by 1965 their crop reached 655 quarts. In 1971, the "banner year," they harvested nearly 1,300 quarts, but on average the annual crop amounted to 800 quarts.

As with their first small business of maple syrup and sugar, the Nearings worked diligently and energetically at the new enterprise. They admitted that "our blueberry bushes are petted and pampered. The bushes are well pruned and well fed" (*Continuing the Good Life*, p. 288). But also as with the Vermont business, they enjoyed the work, especially the harvest. In fact, Helen relates an anecdote about a woman who arrived at the farm assuming that if she picked blueberries herself they would be less expensive. Quite the contrary, for Helen told her that "the price should be higher because you'll eat so many" (p. 290). They write in *Continuing the Good Life*, the book published in 1979 that described their life on the Maine farm, that "picking is easy and pleasant. With the birds singing and the frogs croaking and the wind blowing and the sun shining, it is nice work. With good picking conditions (berries ripe and abundant and not too much conversation), one can get ten or twelve quarts in an hour, but not everyone can move that fast" (pp. 290–291).

Helen Nearing as a Writer

Even before they left Vermont to take up the next phase in their lives together in Maine, Helen Nearing had embarked on a new career for herself. Scott was already a well-published writer when they met in 1928, so it is not surprising that it was he who encouraged her to write her first book.

After the end of World War II in the late 1940s, Scott had resumed a busy lecturing schedule during the long winters. Numerous organizations, unions, and churches invited him to speak, and Helen would usually stay at home on the Vermont farm while Scott ventured off on the lecture circuit. She spent most of the winter of 1948 working on their first co-authored publication, *The Maple Sugar Book*, which was published by the John Day Company of New York in 1950.

Helen credits Scott with the idea for the book, but her years of collecting pertinent references to the history of tapping maple trees formed the basis of the contents. They added descriptions of their own experiences with the undertaking of a maple sugar business and in a concluding chapter sketched the outlines of their experiment in living. Pearl Buck, wife of Richard Walsh, who was the Nearings' publisher at John Day, was so intrigued by their homesteading ideas that she suggested they devote an entire book to their design for living. Pearl Buck's suggestion resulted, in fact, in the publication of a number of books: *Living the Good Life*, published in 1954, *The Good Life Album of Helen and Scott Nearing*, published in 1974, and *Continuing the Good Life*, published in 1979.

For Helen Nearing, writing about living the good life in all of its dimensions opened up a new chapter in her life. Not only was she Scott Nearing's mate (as he stated in the dedication to his autobiography, "Helen, Who did half the work") but she also became an author in her own right with much to say about how to live in harmony with the New England environment. In 1977, she co-authored a book about gardening entitled *Building and Using Our Sun-heated Greenhouse*; in 1980, she wrote a book about cooking, *Simple Food for the Good Life*; and in 1983, she published a book about building, *Our Home Made of Stone.*

Whereas for Scott Nearing operating a farm gave him the independence that he sought to carry on writing and lecturing in economics and politics, for Helen Nearing living in touch with nature in Vermont and Maine gave her a vocation. She became an eloquent advocate for environmentally sound living by writing books about how she lived with Scott Nearing.

In all her solo-authored books, from the first one published in 1974 to her sixth and last one, which was published in 1995 just before her death, Helen Nearing wrote with an intensely human voice. Her sense of enjoyment with living and sincere desire to share whatever wisdom she may have acquired with her readers make these six books a significant supplement to the more famous ones that she co-authored with her husband.

One stylistic trait peculiar to Helen, which is perhaps more evident in these six books than in the "Good Life" books, is her propensity to include quotations from other authors. In a "Note to the Reader" at the beginning of her cookbook, she offers an explanation for what others might consider to be an excessive use of quotations. "I am a library inebriate; I get drunk on pithy quotations. If someone else has said it better, and earlier, why not make these sources available to you, gentle reader? Why not use their choice expressions instead of my own bald words?" (*Simple Food for the Good Life*, preface).

She wrote that she got hooked on this habit during her many years of pleasure sitting in the rare book rooms of libraries in New York, Boston and Philadelphia meticulously copying out "well-said words." However, her quotations are printed intentionally in smaller typeface so that a reader who wants to ignore them can do so with ease. In both books, *Living the Good Life* and *Continuing the Good Life*, a full page of pertinent quotations are printed opposite the first page of each chapter.

Helen's personality comes through vividly in all her books. In the first one, *The Good Life Album of Helen and Scott Nearing*, a photographic album with an introduction and captions, which New York publisher E. P. Dutton solicited and Helen wrote when she was 70 years old, the Nearings emerge as real-life people. By 1974, when the book was published, they had already become famous and young people were flocking to their Maine homestead seeking guidance on how "to live the good life."

In her book, she not only presents photographs of their joint and separate lives from 1883 to 1974, but she also introduces her parents and Scott's family with unexpected candor. "Imagine the distress of my parents when I first left music for supernal relations with Krishnamurti and then bumped to the gritty ground with Scott Nearing. However, after Scott and I were settled in Vermont, they came to see the stability and purpose of our homesteading venture, and ... became reconciled and learned to respect and to love Scott" (p. 9).

Her next book was a cookbook for vegetarians, perhaps a surprising subject for a woman who spent as little time in the kitchen as possible. *Simple Food for the Good Life* contains nearly as much philosophy of life as recipes. She had resisted writing a cookbook for years, because she had felt there was no need for yet another one to add to the thousands that had already been written. When working out the tone and format for her book, she visited public libraries in New York, Philadelphia and Boston to research how other authors throughout history had assembled their recipes. She gave up after reading hundreds of cookbooks and managing to reach only the beginning of the 1920s.

It was the French who finally convinced her to put together her own cookbook. She had been cooking for Scott and for the hordes of visitors who had dropped in for meals in Vermont or in Maine since 1932, but when they rented an apartment in the south of France during the winter of 1970, she cooked for "acquaintances of many nationalities invited in for meals" (p. 4). She served her normal fare: soups, salads, wheat berries, and desserts concocted from scraped apples and rolled oats, raisins, honey and lemon juice. "Our foreign visitors oh'd and ah'd.... You must write a cookbook and go into all the interesting details. Everything is so unusual" (p. 4).

Simple Food for the Good Life is unusual not only because of the ingredients she recommends. Helen Nearing cooked the way she lived. "The theme of my book will be: live hard not soft; eat hard not soft; seek fiber in foods and in life" (p. 8). She preferred raw foods, fresh out of the garden or pantry, nutritious rather than tasty, and simple to prepare. She liked to throw materials together, improvise as she went along, and to use ingenuity. Her specialty was vegetable soup, a knack she credits to her European-style upbringing in which a soup was on the table every day. She confessed that her successful soups were often a surprise, although beginning with a chopped onion simmered in oil would usually do the trick.

She encourages her readers to use her recipes with discretion and to "convert and invent recipes of your own, and don't be averse to sharing and passing them on" (p. 81). Somewhat surprising are the tools she recommends for the kitchen. Her "handiest" ones are an electric blender, a vegetable juicer and a French grater for nuts and seeds, although she admits that before they moved to Maine in 1952 she had cooked much more simply in a kitchen that lacked electricity.

Helen Nearing's cookbook describes an essential aspect of the healthy lifestyle that she and Scott masterminded. They ate "35 percent fruit; 50 percent vegetable (with one-third green leafy, one-third yellow, and one-third juicy); 10 percent protein; and 5 percent fat" (p. 21). In *Continuing the Good Life*, they spelled out in detail how they nourished themselves. "The basics of our diet are simple: our own herb teas and fruit for breakfast; soups and grains for lunch; salad, one cooked vegetable and some applesauce for supper.... There may be a few additions occasionally— such as sunflower seeds or nuts to the breakfast; or tofu or cottage cheese to the supper" (p. 371).

They also experimented with fasting, eating only apples, and subsisting on liquids for twenty-four hours one day a week. Their eating habits, combined with their environmentally sound way of life certainly kept them healthy. During the 20 years that they lived in Vermont they did not visit a doctor at all, and Scott Nearing decided to stop eating at the age of 100 only when his body was wearing out.

Three years after Delacorte Press published her cookbook, Helen Nearing came out with *Our Home Made of Stone: Building in Our Seventies and Nineties*, in which she enthused about a "passion for building." The book focuses mostly on construction of their stone house in Maine, but they used the same procedures and division of labor between Helen and Scott for the more than 30 structures that they successfully erected. Together, with Scott mixing the concrete and Helen laying the stone, they built houses, greenhouses, woodsheds, garages, fireplaces, outhouses, and garden walls. They chose originally to work with stone, because they "wanted a home adapted to our environment." And in New England, where they farmed, they neither quarried nor cut stone but collected granite that was lying around in abundance on the ground in Vermont and colorful stones from the beach in Maine. Helen wrote about every aspect of their lives: "Scott and I have found that each new undertaking we embarked on became an engrossing and exciting venture.... We dared to believe that ordinary untrained people could make their own homes as birds build their own nests. We were admittedly amateurs seeking an organic solution to home-conceived architecture" (p. 1).

The last book that Helen Nearing wrote, *Light on Aging and Dying*, was published in 1995, the year that she died. Even at the age of 91 she could write with a zest for living. The quotations on "good old age," "the art of dying," and "death the great good" that she assembled into this book expressed her fervent belief that "up to the last moment of life there are opportunities to make a contributory mark" (vii).

The Good Life without Scott

Scott Nearing died on August 24, 1983, at the age of 100. His death was planned and deliberate, an action in which Helen was intimately involved. Scott had sensed when he had reached his mid-nineties that his body and mind were beginning to fail. He could not keep up his part in the upkeep of the garden and his mental capabilities were also waning.

Six weeks before he died, he decided to stop eating solid foods and announced his decision at the dinner table with friends in attendance. At first he continued to drink and consumed a variety of fruit juices. Then, a week before his death he limited his liquid intake to water only. His body gradually lost all strength and he died with Helen beside him at home at Forest Farm in Harborside, Maine. However, even though he had stopped breathing, Helen felt that "I have had a sense of his continued being.... I believe in love after death as well as in life after death" (*Loving and Leaving the Good Life*, p. 185).

Even before 1983 Helen had begun to fill in for Scott Nearing. When he was asked to speak to organizations, she would go in his place and would leave him at home in the care of friends. And during the winter after his demise, she was absorbed in composing replies to the 1,000 letters and cards that she received from a variety of people whose lives Scott Nearing had impacted.

After Scott's passing, Helen, who was 79 years old, still had many years of her own life in which to live purposefully. Her intention had always been to return to the Netherlands where she had spent her early adult years before she had met Scott Nearing, but in fact she continued to live alone at Forest Farm. As she wrote in a new foreword to their book, *The Good Life*, reprinted in 1989, even though "the good life is best attempted by a couple or a group of like-minded people," nevertheless "a lone woman can live productively, fend for herself, gardening and wood-toting and housekeeping and living in nature with a sense of fulfillment and purpose."

She published several books after Scott's death and traveled abroad to attend international conferences and to present workshops on topics in which she had become expert after 50 years of living an environmentally sound life. In Maine, she carried on with the maintenance of Forest Farm and greeted continuous streams of visitors.

She includes an anecdote in the foreword to *Light on Aging and Dying*, which describes a crayon drawing that a young visitor presented to her when she was 89 years old. The child portrayed Helen Nearing surrounded by pine trees and singing birds and the words "89 ISN'T SO BAD."

Helen Nearing did not die in a planned act, but rather in a car accident on a narrow road near her home on September 17, 1995. She was 91 years old. Several years before then, when she had reached her mid-eighties, she had begun to slow down or, as she phrased it, "I realized I was coasting" (*Loving and Leaving the Good Life*, p. 190). But even the experience of old age held a fascination for Helen. "One can savor sights and sounds more deeply.... It may be the last time you see a sunset, a tree, the snow, or know winter. The sea, a lake, all become as in childhood, magical and a great wonder: then seen for the first time, now perhaps for the last. Music, birdsongs, the wind, the waves: one listens to tones with deeper delight and appreciation" (p. 191).

Helen Nearing's Legacy

Helen Nearing lived a life in tune with nature, and up to her last days shared her wisdom about how to live in an environmentally sound way with continual visitors and with countless readers of the many books she wrote alone and together with Scott Nearing. She guaranteed before she died that the Nearings' achievement in living would be remembered for posterity by arranging with The Trust for Public Land to maintain the Nearing estate.

This nonprofit land conservation organization has established The Good Life Center at Forest Farm in Harborside, Maine, "to perpetuate the philosophies and life ways of the Nearings." The homestead is operated by stewards, new people chosen every year who are funded by the Nearing Stewardship program, who live self-sufficiently and welcome visitors who come to be inspired by the Nearings' teachings. They also continue to host Monday night meetings, bringing speakers and artists together in an exchange of ideas: a cultural tradition started by the Nearings when they lived at Forest Farm. The books that the Nearings wrote are also being reissued with the aim to motivate a new generation of Americans to live responsibly and harmoniously with the natural environment.

6

Rachel Carson
(1907–1964)

For each of us, as for the robin in Michigan or the salmon in the Miramichi, this is a problem of ecology, of interrelationships, of interdependence. We poison the caddis flies in a stream and the salmon runs dwindle and die. We poison the gnats in a lake and the poison travels from link to link of the food chain and soon the birds of the lake margins become its victims. We spray our elms and the following springs are silent of robin song, not because we sprayed the robins directly but because the poison traveled, step by step, through the now familiar elm leaf–earthworm–robin cycle.... They reflect the web of life—or death—that scientists know as ecology [Silent Spring, *pp. 169–170*].

Rachel Carson ushered in the environmental movement with her treatise against chemical controls of nature. Her book *Silent Spring*, published in 1962, only two years before she died at the age of 56, empowered countless others to carry on the conservation campaign that she launched with the power of her words.

Today Carson's name is known throughout the world because of the impact of *Silent Spring*, but during her entire life she shared an intimacy with the natural world and with the sea in particular, even though she had to wait until she had graduated from college in 1929 to encounter an ocean beach for the first time. Understanding and appreciating the environment of the ocean were lifelong passions, and as a marine zoologist she brought an intuitive ecological perspective to the writing of her three books about the sea.

Childhood

Until she met the sea, Rachel Carson's world was confined to the particular plants and animals, hills and rivers that composed the natural environment of Pittsburgh, Pennsylvania. Born in Springdale, Pennsylvania, on May 27, 1907, Carson spent her childhood in this industrial community 16 miles north of Pittsburgh. At the very epicenter of industrial America with rich coal mines, belching steel mills, and congested rivers and railway hubs, Pittsburgh would seem an unlikely place for a would-be nature lover to grow up. The Carson family home, a 64-acre farm and orchard, was situated on a hill above the Allegheny River, and the town of 1,200 people depended for its livelihood on the West Penn Power Company, the major employer in Springdale.

Rachel was the third-born child of Robert Carson and Maria Frazier McLean. At the time of her birth, sister Marian was ten and brother Robert was eight. The family belonged to the Presbyterian church and ancestors on both her mother's and father's sides were of Scots-Irish background. Her father, the son of Irish immigrants, was born in the Pittsburgh area in 1864 and worked as an insurance salesman off and on throughout his lifetime. His overriding ambition to become a successful real-estate developer was thwarted, and he eventually went to work at the West Penn Power Company as did Rachel's sister and brother in the 1920s.

Of her parents, her mother exerted by far the more important influence on Rachel's life. She was a Presbyterian minister's daughter and had worked as a schoolteacher before marrying, but after the birth of her third child she channeled all of her own talents into raising Rachel. Otherwise, when Robert Carson's income proved insufficient to sustain a middle-class lifestyle, Maria Carson supplemented the family's coffers by giving piano lessons to neighborhood children.

It was her mother who almost from the day after Rachel's birth instilled a love of nature by introducing her young child to the plants and animals around the farm, transmitting a particular fondness for birds. It was her mother, as well, who encouraged Rachel's intellectual development. Rachel attended the local elementary school, School Street School, as did her older sister and brother. She was an avid reader and excellent student but spent extended periods away from the classroom, supposedly, according to her 1997 biographer, not only when ill but also because "her protective mother elected to tutor Rachel at home" (Linda Lear, *Rachel Carson: Witness for Nature*, p. 21). She was a solitary child, happiest at home and when reading or taking walks with her dogs and mother.

It was also her mother who brought *St. Nicholas* magazine into her life. This publication for children offered Rachel Carson, as it did for many other successful American authors, a first opportunity to see her name in print. Altogether the magazine published five of Carson's stories, starting in 1918 when she was 11 years old. Four of her entries were stories with war themes, several of which were suggested from letters that her brother sent home from the battlefields in World War I.

The final article, which appeared in the July 1922 issue, was her first publication about nature. Entitled "My Favorite Recreation—Going Birds'-Nesting," the piece displays a precocious talent. Not only does she make use of a mature vocabulary but she also constructs the short article with care, beginning with "that dewy May morning" and ending with "the cool of approaching night." She describes a day out walking in the woods with her dog, Pal. Her style is reminiscent of the writings of adult birders, such as Florence Bailey (see chapter 2), and in the story she demonstrates impressive knowledge about bird calls, types of nests and how to photograph them. But her intuitive sense of expression offers an early indication of what future readers could expect. She writes of her discovery of a place in the woods that "gave us a thrill of exultation. It was the sort of place that awes you by its majestic silence, interrupted only by the rustling breeze and the distant tinkle of water" (*Lost Woods*, p. 13).

After ten years at the Springdale elementary school, Rachel Carson completed her schooling at Parnassus High School, a two-mile trolley ride across the Allegheny River. There she participated in team sports and although she made a few friends, she was remembered in the high-school yearbook as a quiet, scholarly student. She graduated number one in the class of 1925 and won a scholarship to attend Pennsylvania College for Women in Pittsburgh.

Education

Rachel Carson embarked upon the next stage of life confident in her academic abilities and determined to make a contribution to the world as a writer. During the four years she spent at a small women's liberal arts college, Carson not only expanded her body of knowledge and the means of expressing her ideas, but she also matured socially and turned to science as her field of intellectual concentration. After graduating magna cum laude in 1929, Carson continued her formal education at the Marine Biological Laboratory at Woods Hole, Massachusetts, and then at Johns Hopkins University in Baltimore, Maryland, where she received a master's degree in zoology in 1932.

Pennsylvania College for Women (now called Chatham College) was only sixteen miles from her childhood home in Springdale, but during the academic year she moved into a college dormitory there. For a young woman who had grown up self-reliant with limited personal relationships beyond her immediate family, college was an introduction to a larger world of roommates, classmates who shared academic interests, and mentoring professors.

An English composition professor, Grace Croff, offered an important source of encouragement to Carson during her freshman year. She recognized Carson's talent for writing about technical subjects, praising her method of incorporating anecdotes and narrative as a way to make difficult subject matter intelligible to readers. Croff and Rachel were often seen sitting outside on campus benches engaged in out-of-class literary discussions, and Croff advised Carson to write for the college newspaper and literary magazine. "The Master of the Ship's Light," one of the stories she wrote for Croff's class, which later was printed in the college magazine, was Rachel Carson's first piece of writing about the sea.

It may have taken Rachel longer than most undergraduates to befriend fellow classmates, because during freshman year her mother continued to be her best friend. Every weekend she would either visit her daughter's dorm room or else Rachel would return to Springdale, and Mrs. Carson showed no interest in the lives of any other young women in the dormitory. By sophomore year, however, when Rachel started studying biology, she made friends with several women taking the same course. One classmate, Mary Frye, became her lab partner and worked with Rachel to establish a college-wide science club; she also accompanied Rachel to Woods Hole Marine Biological Laboratory on Cape Cod during the summer after college graduation. Never during her college years did Rachel show the slightest interest in meeting male friends. She stayed away from the college's organized social events and on the one occasion when she is known to have had a date for a dance, she showed no desire to become friends with the young man, who was a brother of a classmate.

She forged a close, intellectual and personal relationship with her biology professor, Mary Scott Skinker. Although Professor Skinker left her teaching position at Pennsylvania College for Women before Rachel's senior year, their friendship endured until Skinker's death in 1948. Skinker's relationship to Carson has been called by various names in biographies of Rachel Carson, from brilliant teacher to mentor to role model to dearest friend. One fact for sure is that they shared a love for the same subject: the natural world. Whether it was on class field trips into the north hills of Pittsburgh or while horseback riding in the Shenandoah

Mountains in Virginia, the two women felt a deep communion with one another. At the end of Skinker's life when she was approaching death in Evanston, Illinois, hospital staff contacted Rachel Carson, who was then living in Maryland, and Rachel rushed out to Illinois for a final meeting with her dear friend.

Rachel Carson never described with any enthusiasm her years at Pennsylvania College for Women and was especially critical of the science instruction she received during her senior year, after Professor Skinker had left the college. Nonetheless the four years were well spent; she discovered her field of expertise and broadened her bases of knowledge. With the exception of an education class that she detested, all the electives and required courses in subjects such as psychology, English, French, German and religion expanded her intellectual horizons. Furthermore, the experiences in dorm living as well as participation on the college's hockey and basketball teams prepared her for future departures into a world beyond the familiar one of western Pennsylvania.

After switching her major to biology during junior year, Carson devoted herself single-mindedly to acquiring the education required to become a research scientist. She took classes in zoology, physiology, anatomy, bacteriology, histology, embryology, and genetics, and complained that the level of instruction, particularly in genetics, did not prepare her adequately for graduate studies. This overdose of science courses meant that, instead of spending her time writing, Rachel increasingly viewed life through the lenses of the laboratory microscope, and for the next several years defined herself as a scientist rather than a writer.

With graduation from Pennsylvania College for Women in June 1929, Rachel Carson closed out definitively her childhood in Pennsylvania and launched immediately into a second phase of life, which would last a lifetime: a connection with the sea. She arrived at the Marine Biological Laboratory at Woods Hole on Cape Cod in August 1929 and for the first time saw the sea.

Mary Skinker, who had spent the previous summer at Woods Hole, had opened up this opportunity for Rachel, and Pennsylvania College for Women supported her financially. Her college friend, Mary Frye, shared an apartment there and the two ate dinner inexpensively at the Marine Biological Laboratory's Mess, where although there were linen tablecloths and formal waiters, all summer visitors fraternized family-style.

To Rachel Carson, exploring the Woods Hole research library was almost as exciting as walking along the beach. Biographers state categorically that the seeds for her 1951 bestseller *The Sea Around Us* were sown during that first summer at Woods Hole. For the first time in her life, the

22-year-old budding marine biologist could feast on books, journals and papers written by researchers from all over the world. Information, answers to questions, data, scientific interpretations were all available at the Marine Biological Laboratory's rich resources.

Nothing could compare, however, with the experience of being beside the ocean—a sensation that Rachel had dreamt about for 22 years. She and Mary Frye savored every moment: discovering, observing, communing with the flora and fauna, the water, the tides, the rocks, the sand and at full moon even with the mating polychete worms. In the three books that she wrote about the sea, she was able to communicate with millions of readers her sense of wonder at the mystery that she found in marine environments.

What Rachel actually did in her position as beginning investigator was to dissect cranial nerves of turtles, purportedly in preparation for research and writing a master's dissertation. In addition, she interacted with scientists at every level from recent college graduates like herself, to graduate students, to beginning professionals and well-established professors to Nobel Laureates. Everyone with a passion for marine biology was bound eventually to wash up on the beach at Woods Hole, and Carson returned at least four other summers. She visited the adjacent U.S. government's Fisheries Research Station on two different occasions as well. In 1952 she was elected a member of the Marine Biological Laboratory's Corporation.

Following quickly upon the life-changing six weeks spent on Cape Cod, by the fall of 1929 Rachel was ensconced in graduate school in Baltimore, Maryland. She was one of thirteen female graduate students at Johns Hopkins University in a combined department of zoology, botany, and plant physiology. Her course load was heavy: four classes each semester, which included organic chemistry, botany, genetics, and physiology. She did very well in the courses and laboratories and during the summer found a job as teaching assistant in an undergraduate biology course.

By the end of the first semester, Rachel had rented a house in a community 13 miles north of Baltimore. She had invited her family to live there with her, and in addition to her mother and father by summer her sister and two nieces had moved in as well.

But that was the high point in Rachel Carson's life as a graduate student. By the beginning of her second year, because of a rise in tuition, she was forced to find a part-time job and to change her status to part-time student. That meant that she took only two courses and was not able to complete her dissertation. Even though she had finished all the course work for the master of science degree by the end of the second year, Carson did not receive her degree until the following June 1932.

At the beginning of her third year, she was employed as an instructor in biology at the dental school at the University of Maryland in College Park, a teaching position that she retained for several years. Her adviser suggested a new research topic and during the course of the year she succeeded in investigating embryological development of the urinary system of catfish. Her dissertation—"The Development of the Pronephros during the Embryonic and Early Larval Life of the Catfish"—was commended more for its review of literature than for its contribution to the furtherance of scientific knowledge. Nonetheless, Rachel continued on as a doctoral student and reluctantly abandoned her research project on the salt tolerance of eels by the end of 1933, when she could no longer afford to live without a full-time job.

Employment

Rachel Carson reached adulthood just when the economy of the United States was about to usher in the most trying time in its economic history: the Great Depression. The year she graduated from college, 1929, saw the onset of what was to be a decade-long period of record high unemployment tempered somewhat only when the United States entered World War II. During the 1930s young college graduates faced very limited employment opportunities, and in the particular case of the Carson family both her father and brother faced economic difficulties as well. When Rachel determined that it was necessary for her to seek full-time employment in 1934, job prospects for marine biologists were slim.

On this occasion, as in other times in her life, she turned to Mary Skinker for help. Her former biology professor was working as a scientist in the Zoological Division of the U.S. Department of Agriculture in Washington, D.C. Skinker advised Rachel to follow her example and to prepare to take the federal civil service exams in several fields of zoology: parasitology, wildlife biology, and aquatic biology. At the same time, she arranged an interview for Rachel with her division chief, Elmer Higgins.

It worked. Higgins offered Carson a part-time job as a field aide in the U.S. Bureau of Fisheries. Her assignment was to write weekly radio scripts of seven minutes' duration on aspects of marine life, and when that job ended she was hired to work full-time as junior aquatic biologist in the bureau's Baltimore office. That was in the summer of 1936, and Rachel Carson remained in the employment of the U.S. government working in various capacities concerned with biology for the following 16 years.

At the beginning her office was situated in Baltimore in the bureau's

Division of Scientific Inquiry, and in 1939 she was transferred to the field laboratory at College Park, Maryland. By May 1942 she had been promoted to assistant aquatic biologist, the following year to associate aquatic biologist, and finally to aquatic biologist before the war had ended. Her office moved to Chicago for eight months from 1942 to 1943 during World War II, but then returned to Washington after a government reorganization to become part of the U.S. Fish and Wildlife Service within an invigorated Department of the Interior.

But Carson never really did any field or laboratory research for the government. Instead she worked throughout her 16 years in public information, by writing press releases, interpreting research and making it accessible to the public. By 1946 her formal title was information specialist, then assistant editor and finally in summer 1949 she had been promoted to chief editor of the publishing program at the Fish and Wildlife's information service. Increasingly after the war, Rachel Carson looked for ways to leave the bureaucracy to enable her to concentrate on writing. Not until June 1951, when she was awarded a Guggenheim Fellowship, did she feel financially comfortable enough to take a leave of absence. And only on June 3, 1952, after the phenomenal success of her second book *The Sea Around Us*, did she resign officially from government employment.

At first the reports she wrote for the Bureau of Fisheries concentrated on the fishes of Chesapeake Bay, but she branched out to cover marine life along the Atlantic coast and eventually authored a series of brochures that were national in scope called "Our Aquatic Food Animals." She became editor of the bureau's periodical *Progressive Fish-Culturist*, and from 1943 to 1945 wrote a number of booklets about fish resources in various regions of the United States. The intended readers for these Conservation Bulletins, entitled "Food from the Sea," were housewives struggling with meat and poultry rationing during World War II, for whom the Bureau of Fisheries was proposing cooking fish as an alternative source of protein. To some readers the publications might have appeared to have been little more than a promotion for enhancing the family diet with fish, but with Rachel Carson as author the 75 pages were crammed full of educational information about the reproduction, growth and life histories of fish. She wrote bulletin number 33, "Fish and Shellfish of New England"; number 34, "Fishes of the Middle West"; number 37, "Fish and Shellfish of the South Atlantic and Gulf Coasts"; and number 38, "Fish and Shellfish of the Middle Atlantic Coast."

The most substantial writing that Carson did for the U.S. government was a series of Conservation in Action booklets about national wildlife refuges, which were published in the early postwar years. The five illustrated booklets that Rachel Carson wrote were part of a total of twelve produced by the Fish and Wildlife Service under her editorial management. By this time Carson's subject matter had expanded beyond the world of fish because of the merger of the Bureau of Fisheries with the Biological Survey, and her editorial responsibilities encompassed all facets of the work of the newly created U.S. Fish and Wildlife Service.

To carry out the research, writing and editing of the series of conservation booklets, Carson traveled to wildlife refuges in Oregon, Utah, Montana, North Carolina, Massachusetts, and Virginia, which comprised the more than 300 sites already in existence in the late 1940s. The National Wildlife Refuge system, which today numbers more than 500 refuges, includes one along the southern Maine coast with the name Rachel Carson National Wildlife Refuge in her honor. There, the 4,800 acres of salt marshes and upland habitat, a haven for both migratory and resident birds, protect a wilderness area near to the beach resort of Wells, Maine.

The three refuges that Carson wrote about in Conservation in Action booklets published in 1947 were all located along the Atlantic flyway. Chincoteague on Assateague Island, Virginia; Parker River on the Massachusetts coast; and Mattamuskeet off the coast of North Carolina are wetlands refuges for migratory waterfowl.

In each of the publications Carson was able to inject her breadth of knowledge, not only about fish, birds and wildlife, but also about plants and geography, to offer the public a lesson in ecology. *In Chincoteague: A National Wildlife Refuge. Conservation in Action #1,* while enumerating the species of birds that visitors might be able to observe, Carson draws a vivid picture of the changing seasons, pointing out when particular waterfowl or shore birds by the thousands take up residence. Summertime, she reports, is the quietest time at Chincoteague: "the ebb between the flood tides of migration." Similarly, in *Parker River: A National Wildlife Refuge. Conservation in Action #2,* she portrays the various "zones of life" at Plum Island, which is at the heart of the refuge. For each zone, whether ocean beach, dune, thicket, salt meadow, or tidal flat of the salt marsh, Carson fully describes the ecosystem, mentioning plants and animals that can be found as well as presenting readers with an overview of the landscape.

Carson's distinctive writing style is most apparent in booklet number four, *Mattamuskeet: A National Wildlife Refuge* in which she depicts "some of the wildest country of the Atlantic coast." Filled with factual descriptions of dense woods of pine, cypress and gum and marsh grass that surround the refuge's 15-mile-long lake, the booklet includes as well perceptive portraits of whistling swans, Canadian geese and pintail ducks who spend the winter months there. As if to offer a preview of what would become her focus in the future, Rachel Carson makes an effort in this booklet to detail the ecologically correct management practiced at the refuge. The manager, who works in tune with "the great recurrent rhythms of nature moving over the marshlands as over a stage," cuts back the thickets and controls the water level in the canals that lead from the lake into the sound to maintain productive yields of food for waterfowl. She explains how fires that managers ignite in the marsh grass in early February, when most of the natural marsh food has been eaten, promote the quick growth of hundreds of acres of new green shoots of sedges, bulrushes and grass just in time to replenish the food supply for migrating geese.

Freelance Writer

During her 16 years as a civil servant, Rachel Carson was able to make use of the government's vast resources of information to write, in addition to the specific assignments undertaken on the job, freelance articles for newspapers and magazines and two full-length books. Her third book about the sea, *The Edge of the Sea*, was written and published in 1955 after she had already resigned from government service. In fact, in a somewhat ironic twist of events, it was her second assignment for the Bureau of Fisheries, the writing of a general introduction for a brochure on marine life, that launched her successful freelance writing career. Elmer Higgins, her boss, rejected the introduction that he had asked her to write but advised her to submit it to *Atlantic Monthly*. She did, and its publication as "Undersea" in September 1937 led to the Simon & Schuster contract for her first book *Under the Sea Wind*, published in 1941.

Her stint as a freelance newspaper journalist was less momentous for her ensuing career, but it helped her develop a knack for writing about science topics for the general public. Her first article, "It'll Be Shad-Time Soon," bylined R. L. Carson because she did not want to be identified as a woman, appeared in the *Baltimore Sun* on March 1, 1936, soon after she had begun writing radio scripts for the U.S. Bureau of Fisheries. Between the years 1936 and 1939 she published 15 feature articles in newspapers, not only in the *Baltimore Sun* but also in the *Charleston, S.C., News-Current* and the *Richmond Times-Dispatch*. The first seven focused on fish: shad, mackerel, oysters, but she gradually widened her range to include more general wildlife and conservation themes.

On March 10, 1938, the *Richmond Times-Dispatch Sunday Magazine* published "Fight for Wildlife Pushes Ahead" as the newspaper's way of marking National Wildlife Restoration Week. Carson's article was timely, reminding readers of the widespread impact resulting from the "Dust Bowl" and promoting programs of action that national conservation agencies were undertaking in response to the tragedy. Perhaps most noteworthy is that an article with a national perspective would be printed in a Virginia newspaper and also impressive is Carson's ability to draw upon examples remote from the Chesapeake region where she lived and worked. Furthermore, in this piece Carson already introduces two ideas that she will return to again and again in future writings: human beings' connection to wildlife devastation and an appreciation for historical changes that occur in respect to nature.

In this newspaper feature she directly links "the decline of wildlife with human destinies." Wildlife, she writes, "is dwindling because its home is being destroyed. But the home of wildlife is also our home." She goes on to recount how wild turkey, passenger pigeons, and antelope, wildlife that were once abundant in the United States, had diminished dramatically in population during the last one hundred years. She places the blame on human beings for causing these declines in animal numbers and species. "For three centuries," she asserts, "we have been busy upsetting the balance of nature by draining marshland, cutting timber, plowing under the grasses that carpeted the prairies." In a passage reminiscent of Marjory Douglas's description of draining the Florida Everglades (chapter 4), Carson criticizes the conversion of lower Klamath Lake in Oregon to agricultural use. She reports that after the lake had been drained and all the ducks had vanished, agronomists discovered that the soil did not make good farmland and people in Oregon were once again considering a plan to re-water the lake.

Even though Rachel Carson focused on fish as her wildlife of choice, she never lost interest in other animals, especially birds. She wrote two features for the *Baltimore Sun* about birdlife: one in January 1938 about ducks and the other in March 1939 about starlings. But it was a October 1938 piece about eels, "Chesapeake Eels Seek the Sargasso Sea," that broached a subject that continued to fascinate her throughout her life: the oceanic travels of eels. The last chapter of her first book, *Under the Sea Wind*, relates the life story of a common eel, and William Beebe selected this passage to reprint in a 1944 anthology of nature writing, *The Book of Naturalists*.

For Rachel Carson, writing for magazines turned out to be a much more difficult market to crack than writing for newspapers. Following the appearance of "Undersea" in *Atlantic Monthly* in 1937, Carson tried without success to interest the editors in additional contributions. Later in 1939, *Nature Magazine* did publish a piece about starlings—"How About

Citizenship Papers for the Starling?"—which was a revised version of the earlier newspaper article, but it was not until the 1940s that she was able to freelance for a number of national magazines. In 1944 she published three articles in magazines: "Ocean Wonderland" in *Transatlantic*, "Lifesaving Milkweed" in *This Week Magazine*, and "The Bat Knew It First" in *Collier's*.

She was able to educate the public about biology by writing in popular magazines, but to do so required an alteration in both tone and writing style. A report that landed on her desk at the Fish and Wildlife Service citing the news that the Peru jungle had been discovered to be the winter home of the chimney swift became the basis for "Sky Dwellers," an article she published in *Coronet* in November 1945. In the course of the article she manages to inform readers that because the small bird is the fastest in North America, "its feet have degenerated into little more than hooks" and she enthuses about the bird's unique eating, nesting and parenting characteristics in the manner of Florence Bailey (see chapter 2). But when she gets to the newsworthy part of the story—how the chimney swift's winter destination had been tracked down—she inserts a human interest angle into the article, devoting several paragraphs to amateur bird banders who helped solve "a major mystery of bird migration." Because of bandings of chimney swifts, 13 bands turned up in the jungles of Peru, were picked up by the U.S. embassy in Lima, and sent to the Department of the Interior in Washington, D.C.

In portraying the chimney swift, a bird whose entire existence is spent in the air either flying around through the sky or else nesting inside hollow trees or chimneys, Carson chose a topic altogether different from her marine subjects. But in fact it was through her popular science writings about the sea, and not about wildlife, that she was able to reach her widest audiences. In 1948 *Field and Stream* published "The Great Red Tide Mystery," an article she dashed off about the plague of microscopic sea creatures that had killed millions of Florida fish, and in 1949 the Washington, D.C., Audubon Society's magazine *The Wood Thrush* printed an early version of a piece on the birth of oceanic islands, which later appeared as a chapter in *The Sea Around Us*. The climax of her career as a magazine writer was reached in June 1951, when *The New Yorker* serialized nine of the 14 chapters from *The Sea Around Us* one month before the book's publication.

Sea Trilogy

Long before the appearance of *Silent Spring*, the book that propelled the name of Rachel Carson into world history, she already had become an internationally acclaimed writer as a biographer of the sea. The three books that she authored between 1941 and 1955 presented for the general reader both poetic and scientific explications of the mysteries of the sea.

The first one, entitled *Under the Sea Wind,* was published by Simon & Schuster in November 1941 and reissued by Oxford University Press in April 1952. The original impetus for writing this book came from Quincy Howe, the editor at Simon & Schuster who had been impressed by Carson's *Atlantic Monthly* article on the sea. He, along with author Hendrik Willem van Loon, had written letters to Carson encouraging her to expand the magazine piece into a full-length book. For several years she eked out time at nights and on weekends to write the manuscript while working full-time for the U.S. government during the day. She dedicated the book to her mother, her typist, but also the person who had been most intimately involved in its creation.

Of the three books in her sea trilogy, *Under the Sea Wind* fits most easily into the genre of nature writing, albeit into a subcategory that today may appear somewhat old-fashioned. The story of the sea is told from the perspective of non-humans, and in particular from the vantage point of a shore bird, a mackerel, and a common eel. Similar to *Salar the Salmon* and *Tarka the Otter* by Henry Williamson, books written in the 1930s, Carson gives names to her animal characters and imagines them with human-style reactions.

Carson wrote the book with two themes underlying its three parts. She wanted readers to come away with the sense of never-ending history—the ageless story of life at sea. At the same time she emphasized the universal struggle for survival that affects all living sea creatures whether large or small: the web of life and death. Throughout the book's unfolding, these ideas are ever present.

The sea world that Carson recreates in *Under the Sea Wind* has three locations: the shore, the open sea, and the deep abyss. In each, one animal becomes the focal point of the narrative. Part one describes a beach on the outer banks of North Carolina as seen through the life cycle of a shorebird, Silverbar the sanderling who migrates annually between the Arctic tundra and the outer banks. In part two, Scomber the mackerel travels from a New England harbor through the open sea, and part three follows Anguilla the eel on her life journey back and forth from the deep abyss of the Sargasso Sea. In addition, Carson fills the book with stories of countless other fish and birds who interact with these three principal characters.

Human beings also appear in *Under the Sea Wind,* usually as fishermen, and they are portrayed as a part of the total narrative of life at sea.

But because Carson has focused the book on the lives of marine animals, the story becomes especially poignant when Scomber the mackerel manages to escape from a fisherman's seine. To reinforce an ecological viewpoint, she devotes several pages to the wreck of the fishing schooner *Mary B*, described as "an oasis of life in miles of sea desert, a place where myriads of the sea's lesser fry ... found a place of attachment; and the small fish foragers found living food encrusting all the planks and spars; and larger predators and prowlers of the sea found a hiding place" (p. 240). In a particularly exciting passage she details how an octopus who made his home in the wreck's fishhold attacked an unsuspecting small cunner who had been eating mossy hydroids that were attached to the rotting timber planks. In Carson's depiction of human beings, a reader can detect a critical tone when she discusses what was at the time a relatively new industry of winter trawling in the southern ocean. The fishermen in haddock trawlers, flounder draggers, and redfish and cod boats from New England, who had discovered the wintering grounds of the shore fish, sent their nets "down through the hundred fathoms of water ... to a place of warmth and quiet, where fish herds browsed in the blue twilight, on the edge of the deep sea" (p. 253).

Critics received Rachel Carson's debut book with praise, admiring her unusual talent for writing factual scientific information with the touch of a poet. *The New York Times*, *The Christian Science Monitor*, and in particular William Beebe, renowned oceanographer and deep-sea diver, in reviewing her book for *The Saturday Review of Literature*, commented on the book's lyrical style. The problem, however, came with the reading public. One month after its publication in December 1941, Japan attacked Pearl Harbor, and Rachel Carson lost a potential market for her book. No one wanted to read about life in the ocean, and even though the book was priced at only $3 she sold fewer than 2,000 copies. Years later in 1952, when Oxford University Press republished *Under the Sea Wind*, 40,000 copies were bought up in advance of printing and part one in its entirety appeared in the April 14, 1952, issue of *Life* magazine.

The popular reception could not have been more different for Carson's next sea book, *The Sea Around Us*, when it came out in 1951. It was an instant best-seller. But not without reason, for this time her timing was propitious. Her new book viewed the sea with the eyes of an oceanographer and after World War II everyone was interested in science, eager to read about recent explorations into the lower depths of the sea and about what underwater resources might become available to man in the future. Furthermore, in the midst of the Korean War when people lived in daily fear of a nuclear holocaust and were subjected to Senator Joseph McCarthy's attacks on personal freedom, readers welcomed Rachel Carson's reassurance that the sea's natural rhythms of tides, winds, and waves would continue to impact human lives as they had in the past.

But there is much more to *The Sea Around Us* than good timing. Rachel Carson penned a real tour de force with this book, encompassing in 14 relatively brief chapters answers to questions that the general public would think of asking about the oceans plus answers to questions that most nonscientists would not even know enough to ask. It was not a book of nature writing per se and it was not primarily a book about natural history. Rather, *The Sea Around Us* was a popular science book, in which Carson described in laymen's language the most exciting discoveries made by physicists, geologists, meteorologists, and astronomers in understanding the earth's oceans. When responding to reporters' queries about her motives for writing such a book, she has been quoted as explaining that "an ocean voyage, or a trip to the shore means so much more if you know a few things about the sea" (Lear, p. 202). Her more rhetorical reply was that science was part of the reality of living in a scientific age and that knowledge of the environment was not "the prerogative of only a small number of human beings, isolated and priestlike in their laboratories" (Lear, p. 218).

Not only does she furnish the general public with fascinating scientific information, but she also says it poetically. Carson prefaces each chapter with a line or two of poetry, but what is distinguished about her writing style is her conscious care with word selection and use of alliteration and rhythm. Her mother always read aloud to Rachel what she had previously typed up, affording the author an opportunity to revise what she already had written, paying especial heed to tone and expression as well as structure and clarity.

The first part of *The Sea Around Us* is called "Mother Sea" and conjures up poetic conceptions of the oceans; after reading Carson's first paragraph one might imagine that the book would be a poet's rendering. "Beginnings are apt to be shadowy, and so it is with the beginnings of that great mother of life, the sea.... For although no man was there to witness this cosmic birth, the stars and the moon and the rocks were there, and, indeed, had much to do with the fact that there is an ocean" (pp. 3, 4). But by paragraph two she has shifted already to the hard rock of science, with lucid explanations of the geologic history of the earth. Her tone tilts toward poetry when she titles chapter six "The Long Snowfall," a metaphor for the accumulation of sediment on the floor of the sea, which she describes as "the most stupendous 'snowfall' the earth has ever seen" (p. 74). But the exposition in the rest of the chapter is filled with scientific data about the material composition of the sediment, its thickness, and pattern of distribution over the sea floor.

How was Rachel Carson able to write such a book? When *The Sea Around Us* was published, some reviewers were overwhelmed with her sweep of knowledge and her ability to explicate difficult scientific concepts in laymen's language. And they were astonished by her gender. They could not believe that the best-seller was written by a relatively young female marine biologist. But many of the same qualities that made it possible for Carson to write this book made it possible later for her to write *Silent Spring*.

She was adept at research. For *The Sea Around Us* she consulted at least 1,000 printed sources and interviewed dozens of leading scientists involved in various aspects of her story, and she was encouraged and advised by Dr. William Beebe and Harvard University oceanographer Henry Bryant Bigelow. A new edition of the book, published in 1961, was dedicated "to Henry Bryant Bigelow who by precept and example has guided all others in the exploration of the sea." She garnered invaluable source materials from her day job at the U.S. Bureau of Fisheries, where she kept abreast of classified and unclassified research findings from government departments, as well as from summers spent at Woods Hole Laboratory, during which time she took a deep-sea voyage aboard the research vessel *Albatross III*. She was an ace at digesting material, selecting core information to include, and quoting from the writings of experts: Norwegian ethnologist Thor Heyerdahl, Charles Darwin, geologist R. A. Daly, Robert Cushman Murphy of the American Museum of Natural History, and Arctic explorer Fridtjof Nansen.

The Sea Around Us made 44-year-old Rachel Carson famous. The book was translated into 32 languages, sold 250,000 copies within six months of publication, remained on the best-seller list for months, and was voted the outstanding book of 1951 by *The New York Times*. Her photograph appeared on the cover of *The Saturday Review*, and she was the recipient of the National Book Award for nonfiction and the Burroughs Medal for nature writing. Drexel, Oberlin, Smith and the Pennsylvania College for Women awarded her honorary doctorate degrees. And she rewarded herself by buying property on the coast of Maine near Boothbay Harbor on Southport Island, where from the summer of 1952 until her death in 1964 she was able to relish the natural environment she loved to write about.

The third book in the sea trilogy, *The Edge of the Sea*, followed in 1955. This time Carson wrote about biology and, as with her first book, appended a glossary for identifying plants and animals. Bob Hines, a former colleague from the Fish and Wildlife Service, illustrated the text, and she dedicated it to her neighbors in Maine, Dorothy and Stan Freeman, with whom she had developed a deep friendship. She writes in the book's dedication that they "have gone down with me into the low-tide world and have felt its beauty and its mystery."

The Edge of the Sea, in contrast to *The Sea Around Us,* was a book of luxuriant nature writing. Carson's original conception was to write a guide to shore life but eventually the idea grew into an ecological depiction of three environments along the Atlantic coast: rocky shores, sandy beaches, and the coral coast. She concentrates on descriptions of fauna and flora and allows herself to respond emotionally to what she observes, writing about tidal pools that "hold beauty within pellucid depths" (p. 115) and a "magical zone of the low water of the spring tides" (p. 3).

Her talent for sensual expression is given full play in *The Edge of the Sea.* "The pools are gardens of color composed of the delicate green and ocher-yellow of encrusting sponge, the pale pink of hydroids that stand like clusters of fragile spring flowers, the bronze and electric-blue gleams of the Irish moss, the old-rose beauty of the coralline algae. And over it all there is the smell of low tide … the sulphur smell of sponge, the iodine smell of rockweed, and the salt smell of the rime that glitters on the sun-dried rocks" (pp. 40–41).

What ties the book together is Carson's insistence on an ecological approach to nature writing. She never veers from her theme: "the cycle of life—the intricate dependence of one species upon another" (p. 151). And she reinforces her appreciation for the sea's eternal sense of time. "On all these shores there are echoes of past and future: of the flow of time, obliterating yet containing all that has gone before; of the sea's eternal rhythms—the tides, the beat of surf, the pressing rivers of the currents— shaping, changing, dominating; of the stream of life, flowing as inexorably as any ocean current, from past to unknown future" (p. 250).

The Edge of the Sea was also a success. *The New Yorker* printed a condensation of part of the book before Houghton Mifflin's edition, produced in October 1955. It made the best-seller list and remained there for months, surpassed in popularity only by *Gift from the Sea* by Anne Morrow Lindbergh, which appeared the same year.

Silent Spring

It took Rachel Carson a couple of years before embarking on the challenge that would lead her from famous writer to a world historical figure. Other people had warned about man's increasing contamination of the natural environment, but no one before 1962 had written such a powerful, succinct, scientifically argued call for public action. Rachel Carson's book *Silent Spring* ushered in the environmental movement.

In 17 hard-hitting chapters Carson presents facts, documentary evidence, research findings, and ecological analysis of man's poisoning of the total environment. She writes in the second paragraph that "chemicals are the sinister and little-recognized partners of radiation in changing the very nature of the world" (p. 16) and spells out in memorable detail throughout the book the effects of synthetic insecticides and herbicides on water, soil, plants, wildlife, fish and human beings. But in the book's final chapter she suggests alternative courses of action for mankind—a way out of this march toward death.

Rachel Carson became a muckraking writer not by choice but because she felt compelled to speak out after learning about two massive anti-insect aerial spraying campaigns undertaken by the Department of Agriculture in 1957 and 1958. In chapter 10 entitled "Indiscriminately from the Skies," she describes how gypsy moths in the northeastern states and fire ants in the south were bombarded with DDT dropped from planes left over from World War II. In each case, millions of acres were sprayed amidst public outcries about the devastating impact on animals, cropland, and human beings. And in both cases the eradication programs failed to destroy the designated insects.

Before launching into the hard facts about environmental destruction, Carson opens *Silent Spring* with "A Fable for Tomorrow," the story of an imaginary town that has experienced all the ill effects from spraying of a white granular powder that "had fallen like snow upon the roofs and the lawns, the fields and streams" (p. 14). From there, her introductory chapter provides the rationale for writing the book.

> Future historians may well be amazed by our distorted sense of proportion. How could intelligent beings seek to control a few unwanted species by a method that contaminated the entire environment and brought the threat of disease and death even to their own kind?... All this is not to say there is no insect problem and no need of control. I am saying, ... that the methods employed must be such that they do not destroy us along with the insects (p. 19).

She insists that the public has a right to decide whether or not it wants to be blanketed with pesticides, but only after the whole truth is revealed can the public express reasoned opinions.

Carson begins her presentation of the truth with a "who's who of pesticides," meticulously differentiating between chlorinated hydrocarbons and organic phosphorus insecticides. Paul Brooks, her editor at Houghton Mifflin, was critical of this chapter and tried to improve its readability by making it less formidable for the lay reader. In his biography of her, *The House of Life*, he wrote, "[n]o small literary skill is required to describe simply yet accurately such forbidding substances as DDT, chlordane, heptachlor, dieldrin, aldrin, endrin, and the rest. I always felt that if the reader could be piloted through chapter 3, the remainder would be comparatively smooth sailing" (p. 267).

In the ensuing chapters Carson guides the reader through a catalogue of pesticide-generated destruction starting with water and soil, the basic ingredients for sustaining life. She foresees the widespread contamination of groundwater because of "an appalling deluge of chemical pollution ... daily poured into the nation's waterways" (p. 45) and a poisoned supply of food grown in soil where "virtually indestructible residues continue to build up" (p. 63). When she discusses weed control with chemical herbicides that are sprayed in massive quantities on farms, ranges, lawns, golf courses, parks, and along roadsides and utility rights-of-way, she pays special attention to alternative approaches such as selective spraying, replacing monoculture cultivation with a diversity of varieties and species, and the introduction of plant-eating insects. Throughout the book Carson's refrain is to emphasize ecological methods that preserve nature's way of dealing with unwanted pests.

Her anger reaches new heights when she chronicles how wildlife and especially birds have been devastated by pesticides. She relates the results from a Michigan State University study that led to the name for her book. During the spring of 1955, ornithologists were shocked by the discovery of considerable numbers of dead robins on the university's grounds and traced the phenomenon back to the campus's spraying of elm trees in an attempt to combat Dutch elm disease. DDT was used to kill bark beetles, the culprit found to be responsible for the spread of the disease. In the autumn after the elm leaves had fallen to the ground, earthworms feasted on the sprayed elm leaves. The earthworms themselves were not affected by the insecticide but accumulated the poison in their bodies, and when migrating robins returned to the Michigan State campus in the spring to nest, they ate the earthworms. As a result, the robins "exhibited the well-known symptoms of loss of balance, followed by tremors, convulsions and death" (p. 100), and for those who avoided death there was a reported increase in sterility.

Not only ground-feeding birds but also fish-eaters, such as eagles, are subjected to indirect pesticide poisoning. When rain falls on agricultural land that has been sprayed, insecticides are washed into rivers and farm ponds causing immediate fish kills. Furthermore, river water discharged into estuaries, bays and coastal waters spreads the pollution far out to sea. Those fish that are not killed outright accumulate chemical residues in their bodies and transmit poison to birds who eat the fish. For some species, eating contaminated fish will cause immediate death but for eagles it results in infertility.

Carson devotes four chapters to the impact of pesticides on human beings, beginning with the insecticide-laden food people eat, contending that "as matters stand now, we are in little better position than the guests of the Borgias" (p. 167), an allusion to the infamous Italian Renaissance family for whom poisoning enemies was state policy. She demonstrates how chemicals "are passed on from one organism to another through all the links of the food chains" (p. 30), from alfalfa to hens to eggs or from hay to cows to milk and butter.

Rachel Carson did not write *Silent Spring* to shock readers, but rather to inform the public about new environmental health hazards caused by a "lifetime exposure to chemical and physical agents that are not part of the biological experience of man" (p. 168). She describes fully the problems people face, providing more scientific details than most readers would expect, including a full chapter on the biochemistry of enzyme destruction and genetic transformations. She alerts her audience to the special dangers to the liver and reports statistical evidence from the 1950s that shows increased incidences of hepatitis and cirrhosis.

Rachel Carson saves her strongest condemnation of pesticides until chapter 14, entitled "One in Every Four," in which she lists five or six pesticides that "in terms of evidence gained from animal experiments ... must definitely be rated as carcinogens" (p. 198). Her main source of information was Dr. Wilhelm C. Hueper of the National Cancer Institute who supplied her with data on infants with cancer who he suspected had become exposed while still inside the mother's womb. It was he who drew particular attention to DDT as a carcinogen. She also quoted Dr. Malcolm Hargraves and his associates at the Mayo Clinic, who, when trying to cure leukemia patients found that "almost without exception ... [they] have had a history of exposure to various toxic chemicals, including sprays which contain DDT, chlordane, benzene, lindane and petroleum distillates" (p. 202).

Carson wrote *Silent Spring* more than 40 years ago at a time when eliminating "those carcinogens that now contaminate our food, our water supplies, and our atmosphere" could still prevent "the threat that one in every four will develop cancer" (p. 216). Already in the 1960s, however, it was apparent that mankind was not going to reject chemical controls even though insects were "finding ways to circumspect our chemical attacks on them" (p. 217). To end her treatise on an upbeat note, she describes "a truly extraordinary variety of alternatives to the chemical control of insects" in her concluding chapter, "The Other Road" (p. 244). Under the sobriquet "biotic control of insects," she lists male sterilization techniques, bacterial insecticides, and importation of insects' natural enemies.

When *Silent Spring* reached bookstores in September 1962, readers were quick to react. It became an instantaneous best-seller and its historical significance was likened to Charles Darwin's *The Origin of Species* and to Harriet Beecher Stowe's *Uncle Tom's Cabin*. Rachel Carson was swamped with fan mail, but the chemical industry did not read the book with complacency. On the contrary, chemical corporations, professional associations, and the agricultural press mounted an enormous negative public relations campaign against *Silent Spring* and its author.

The chemical lobby spent hundreds of thousands of dollars to combat the fall in sales expected to result from Carson's presentation of the known facts and concerns about the unknown long-term impact of the unrestricted use of pesticides. Individual companies such as Monsanto Chemical Company, Velsicol Corporation and American Cyanamid employed their own scientists and communication experts to write and speak against the book. The National Agricultural Chemicals Association, the National Pest Control Association, and the Manufacturing Chemists' Association published brochures, disinformation, and parodies that they disseminated to the press. Periodicals, such as *Chemical and Engineering News*, *American Agriculturist*, and *County Agent and Vo-Ag Teacher* ran editorials, articles and "fact" sheets to refute the evidence made public in *Silent Spring*.

Perhaps more surprising than the outpouring of attacks by the chemical lobby was the vociferous condemnation of Rachel Carson by scientist members of the Nutrition Foundation, an organization of the food industry. In particular, they tried to discredit Carson's scientific credentials and criticized the book for alarming the public about the healthfulness of the food they eat. These reactions gave added credence to Carson's warning about the danger of the growing liaison between science and industry. In her address to the National Women's Press Club in December 1962, she stressed the need for public scrutiny of all sources of so-called scientific information, remarking that "research supported by pesticide manufacturers is not likely to be directed at discovering facts indicating unfavorable effects of pesticides" (*Lost Woods*, p. 208).

It was not until the following spring that the tide turned irrefutably in favor of Rachel Carson's arguments. Her April appearance on television in CBS Reports exposed an estimated ten to twelve million viewers, many of whom had not read the book, to her point of view. The CBS program made history, not money, for three out of the five commercial sponsors had canceled two days before the show's airing. After watching Carson read excerpts from six chapters of *Silent Spring*, several departments of the U.S. government "were inundated with angry letters protesting their acquiencence in programs and policies threatening to human health and animal life and decrying their lack of scientific evidence about the long-term effects of what they were doing" (Lear, p. 450).

Rachel Carson's television debut also impacted Congress. One day after the show, Senator Abraham Ribicoff, a member of the Senate Government Operations Committee, made plans to hold congressional hearings on a range of environmental hazards including pesticides. Later, on May 15, 1963, President Kennedy released the President's Science Advisory Committee's report entitled "The Uses of Pesticides," which advocated reduced applications of persistent pesticides. The report credited Rachel Carson with opening the eyes of the public to the toxicity of pesticides, and the president announced that he would put into motion measures to implement the report's recommendations.

Even though Rachel Carson died two years after *Silent Spring* was published, she played a role in initiating the first tentative steps undertaken to combat environmental pollution. On June 4, 1963, she testified for 40 minutes before the Ribicoff Committee about "the right of a citizen to be secure in his own home against the intrusion of poisons applied by other persons." She called for a reduction and eventual elimination of pesticides that leave long-lasting residues and underlined the imperative for increased research on the health hazards of pesticides. On June 6, 1963, she again presented testimony to a congressional committee, this time to the Senate Committee on Commerce. On this occasion Carson proposed the formation of a Pesticide Commission, an independent board to be set up in the executive offices with a small permanent staff whose function would be to advise the federal government on the administration of insect control programs.

Eventually the words that she wrote in *Silent Spring* encouraged citizens in the United States as well as around the world to demand that their governments take actions to reduce the use of pesticides. In the United States the most significant direct result from her book was the federal government's banning of the use of DDT in 1972, a policy whose positive impact on the welfare of wildlife was already reported later in the decade.

In the public arena, Rachel Carson's book *Silent Spring* enjoyed a long-lasting impact and on a personal level, the author was honored with a bevy of awards and requests to speak. Because of her deteriorating health, Carson was extremely selective about making public appearances but nevertheless was gratified by the reception that her book received. Her most cherished letter was from Albert Schweitzer to whom she had dedicated *Silent Spring*, and her greatest honor was induction into the American Academy of Arts and Letters on December 6, 1963.

Final Years

The seven years of Rachel Carson's life from 1957, when she began the research process for *Silent Spring*, until her death on April 14, 1964, transformed her personal biography as well as her historical legacy. In 1957 she adopted her five-year-old grandnephew, Roger Christie, after his mother's death and arranged to have a house built in Silver Spring, Maryland, while continuing to spend summers at her cottage along the coast of Maine. At the end of the following year her eighty-nine-year-old mother, with whom she had always shared a household, died.

At the same time as her family life was undergoing dramatic changes she was committing herself fully to writing an epoch-making book about the untold hazards of chemical pesticides. She attempted to explain her motivation for undertaking a project so divergent from her previous ones in a letter to her friend Dorothy Freeman: "You do know, I think, how deeply I believe in the importance of what I am doing. Knowing what I do, there would be no future peace for me if I kept silent…. [I]t is, in the deepest sense, a privilege as well as a duty to have the opportunity to speak out—to many thousands of people—on something so important" (*Always, Rachel*, p. 259). But writing *Silent Spring* required Rachel Carson "to sustain extraordinary trials," as Paul Brooks, her editor, recalled. Not only was the research involved far and above what she had done before, but "the joy in the subject itself had to be replaced by a sense of almost religious dedication and exhilaration in searching out the truth" (*The House of Life*, p. 228).

At first she tried to interest mainstream periodicals in publishing an article about the threat to human beings from highly toxic poisons, but *Reader's Digest, Ladies' Home Journal, Woman's Home Companion*, and *Good Housekeeping* refused to even consider her proposal. Only *The New Yorker*, the magazine that had previously serialized two of her sea books, was enthusiastic about this new topic and agreed to publish a three-part article even before she had signed the book contract with Houghton Mifflin in May 1958.

Carson had thought that she could complete the book in one year but the job was larger than she had imagined and at the beginning of 1960 a further impediment occurred: she was operated on for breast cancer. In fact, cancer had already metastasized into her lymph nodes and by the end of the year she began a series of debilitating radiation treatments. The illness spread throughout her body, necessitating periodic hospital stays and causing her increasing pain. She tried to conceal her health problems from the press, but by the end of 1962 she had contracted angina, a heart condition not uncommon in cancer patients undergoing massive radiation doses. This further complication restricted her mobility and added severe chest pains to her list of maladies. The cancer continued to spread and during her last year it entered her bones.

During a trip to San Francisco in October 1963, when she spoke at the Kaiser Foundation symposium "Man Against Himself," she was forced to sit while proclaiming herself an ecologist: "Humankind is affected by the same influences that control the thousands of species to which he has evolutionary ties. The pollution of the environment was a problem affecting the whole organism, in which the physical and biological environment acted on each other as a dynamic ecosystem" (Lear, p. 464). On that occasion it was also in a wheelchair that she visited the redwoods in the Muir Woods, a part of the natural landscape that she had always wanted to see.

Her deteriorating condition required additional treatments as well as blood transfusions, and in 1964 she was hospitalized in Washington, D.C., in February and underwent a hypophysectomy in a Cleveland, Ohio, clinic in March, from which she never fully recovered. After her return to Maryland on April 6, she lived only one week longer before succumbing to a coronary heart attack in her home at 11701 Berwick Road in Silver Spring on April 14. She was only 56 years old.

Her funeral at the Washington National Cathedral took place on April 17, with honorary pallbearers carrying her casket. Each man represented an aspect of Rachel Carson's life: zoologist, writer, policymaker, conservationist, birder, government employee. The six were Robert Cushman Murphy, internationally renowned ornithologist; Edwin Way Teale, nature writer; U.S. Senator Abraham Ribicoff; Stewart Udall, Secretary of the Interior; Charles Callison of the National Audubon Society; and Bob Hines, wildlife illustrator and her colleague at the Fish and Wildlife Service.

According to Carson's wishes Marie Rodell, her literary agent, was appointed executor of her literary trust, which she bequeathed to Yale

University's Beinecke Rare Book and Manuscript Library. Editor-in-chief at Houghton Mifflin, Paul Brooks, and his wife, assumed the guardianship of Roger Christie, her 11-year-old adopted son. She left financial legacies to the Sierra Club and The Nature Conservancy, and her friends established The Rachel Carson Trust for the Living Environment in December 1965 to further the causes and philosophy for which she had lived and worked.

Rachel Carson's Legacy

She was called "one of the true prophets of our time" by Reverend Duncan Howlett, who gathered with her closest friends at All Souls Unitarian Church in Washington, D.C., on April 19 to commemorate her life. But what Rachel Carson wanted most to be remembered for was her love of nature. In a posthumously published book written for children and dedicated to Roger, entitled *The Sense of Wonder,* she spelled out her philosophy. "The lasting pleasures of contact with the natural world are not reserved for scientists but are available to anyone who will place himself under the influence of earth, sea and sky and their amazing life" (*The Sense of Wonder*, p. 33). Rachel Carson, American woman conservationist, used the power of her pen to try to ensure that her generation would not be the last to be able to love the beauty of the living world.

7

Contemporary Women Conservationists

Faith McNulty, Ann Zwinger, Sue Hubbell, Anne LaBastille, Mollie Beattie, and Terry Tempest Williams

> *Night in the Cabeza restores silence to the desert, that holy, intuitive silence.... Above me is an ocean of stars, and I wonder how it is in the midst of wild serenity we as a species choose to shatter it again and again. Silence is our national security, our civil defense. By destroying silence, the legacy of our deserts, we leave no room for peace, the deep peace that elevates and stirs our souls* [*Terry Tempest Williams,* An Unspoken Hunger, *p. 124*].

After Rachel Carson published *Silent Spring* in 1962, issues of ecology, environmental pollution, and endangered species started to penetrate into public view, awakening discussion and debate. The ideas that previously only a relatively few concerned conservationists had expressed now appeared as front-page news stories, topics for prime-time television programs and endless material for magazine articles. Within a decade a popular environmental movement had begun.

The women, whose careers and writings are profiled briefly in this composite chapter, have been active in what was identified in the introduction as the third time period in U.S. conservation history, after the publication of *Silent Spring* and continuing up to the present day. Following closely in the footsteps of the six historical conservationists are six women who have voiced their beliefs and worked, as did their predecessors, to preserve this American land for future generations.

The chapter opens with the oldest of the six, wildlife reporter Faith McNulty, and then follows chronologically with Ann Zwinger, who writes about nature from her home in the Rocky Mountains of Colorado. Beekeeper Sue Hubbell, who focuses on protecting invertebrates, and Anne LaBastille, an ecologist who lives alone in the wilderness of the Adirondack Mountains, are conservationists born in the 1930s. The chapter concludes with two well-known conservationists, both born after World War II: Mollie Beattie and Terry Tempest Williams, the youngest of the six.

These contemporary women conservationists were selected because they shared fields of interest, regions of the country, or ways of living with at least one of the historical antecedents. Faith McNulty, a lover of animals from childhood, writes about saving endangered species with the same endearing commitment as Florence Bailey had when she wrote about protecting birds. Sue Hubbell, who abandoned academia in the northeastern United States to return to the land in the Ozark Mountains of Missouri, lived in a manner most akin to Helen Nearing before moving to the coast of Maine. Anne LaBastille, who built herself a log cabin in the mountains of New York State, fights for conservation causes with the forcefulness of Rosalie Edge. Ann Zwinger and Terry Tempest Williams reflect on the natural environment and their places in it, as did Mary Austin, by depicting their respective landscapes in poetic prose. Mollie Beattie's major cause was the conservation of forests as was Rosalie Edge's, but in her political role as the national spokesperson for wildlife protection she reached her public with the skill of Marjory Douglas.

Both Ann Zwinger and Sue Hubbell have written introductions for new editions of Rachel Carson's sea books. For Zwinger, *The Sea Around Us,* which she read for the first time as a young housewife living in Florida, represents her "ideal of what natural history writing should be." She writes how Carson's descriptions of the wonders of the ocean made her "acutely sensitive to the interdependence of life." In Sue Hubbell's introduction to *The Edge of the Sea,* she parallels her own life to Rachel Carson's, pointing out that both spent childhoods in the Midwest "yearning for the sea," and later in life built homes along the Maine coast. But it is Carson as an "ecological thinker" that makes the book a pleasure for Hubbell. "We feel as though a well-informed friend has taken us by the hand as we walk along the ocean's rim and explained all the bits of the world that we see, giving us an understanding of how they fit together," Hubbell notes.

Even though many similarities can be found between the historical and contemporary women conservationists featured here, still the differences are not insignificant. During the past 40 years in the United States, momentous changes have occurred in popular thinking about the environment as well as in opportunities for women.

The changes are reflected in the lives of these women conservationists. Contemporary women, for instance, have been able to take advantage of increased possibilities to study, to become experts in their fields. Mollie Beattie and Terry Tempest Williams earned master's degrees, and Anne LaBastille received not only a master's degree in wildlife management but also a doctorate in wildlife ecology. On the other hand, Rachel Carson was the only one of the historical conservationists to have pursued graduate studies.

As conservation activists, contemporary women have acquired more stature and responsibility as organizers in a mass environmental movement. In citizens' groups, as well as in governmental agencies, women have moved into the drivers' seats, leading and determining the agendas for protecting the natural environment and mobilizing public participation. Yet two of these contemporary conservationists, Anne LaBastille and Terry Tempest Williams, in starting up organizations to further their particular campaigns, are retracing the historical paths of Florence Bailey, Rosalie Edge, and Marjory Douglas, who awakened the public to their conservation interests by creating new associations for citizens concerned about the destruction of the environment. The most noticeable difference between the contemporary era and earlier decades is that today's society is more willing to pay attention to the voice of an independent woman conservationist.

Whereas Rosalie Edge wrote about causes that very few favored, her incisive opinions moved Americans to think about the role of wildlife and forests in new ways. Helen and Scott Nearing created a new way of living, producing food and shelter in an environmentally sound manner. Marjory Douglas pointed out the harmful folly of making the Florida Everglades habitable 50 years before U.S. society was willing to heed her warning. Mary Austin, who was considered to be an eccentric in her lifetime, challenged Americans to learn from Native Americans how to live in harmony with their natural surroundings. Florence Bailey invited the public to observe bird life, convinced that a population knowledgeable about the lives of birds would not find pleasure in hunting.

Contemporary conservationists are no longer ostracized as outsiders and even receive a modicum of popular support. The ideas they write about and the causes they espouse are embraced by growing segments of the American public. They are actively engaged in protecting the land they call home, whether it be mountain wilderness, arid areas, or habitats for endangered species. Faith McNulty and Sue Hubbell have reported on efforts to save endangered species before they become extinct. Anne LaBastille and Ann Zwinger make their homes in the mountains, battling to limit further human encroachment. Terry Tempest Williams campaigns for the preservation of wilderness in the canyonlands and deserts of the Southwest. And Mollie Beattie, until her untimely death at the age of 49, campaigned for the protection of wildlife as the head of the U.S. Fish and Wildlife Service within the Department of the Interior.

Faith McNulty

Carrying on in the tradition of Florence Bailey, who found a lifetime's pleasure in studying wildlife, is contemporary conservationist Faith McNulty. From the age of ten she remembers harboring a special fondness for animals and has expressed those feelings in countless articles written for *The New Yorker*, several nonfiction books about endangered species, and many creative children's books.

Faith Eugene was born in 1918 in New York City, where she lived until 1958 when she and her second husband, Richard H. Martin, bought a farm in southern Rhode Island, situated only a few miles from where her family had summered during her childhood. It is from there that she started writing about the common animals—cats, mice, woodchucks, birds—that she observes and describes with wit, curiosity, and passion. Her more serious writings, those that classify her definitively as a conservationist, are her articles and books about endangered species: desert pupfish, peregrine falcons, black-footed ferrets, whales, Indri of Madagascar, and whooping cranes.

Even though Faith McNulty's curiosity about animals was rooted in childhood, she did not choose to study animals as a scientist. Rather, as she puts it, "since I am a writer, not a scientist, ... I have learned of the new trend in the scientific study of animals with a great deal of pleasure, since it grapples with some of the ideas that intrigue me most" (*The Wildlife Stories of Faith McNulty*, prologue). These ideas are very basic: questions about "the pyramid of life" and the "central mysteries" of creation.

Although Faith McNulty had always been interested in wildlife, her career as an "animal reporter" was sanctioned officially when she was hired as a staff writer for *The New Yorker* in 1953. Her articles, some of which appeared in "Talk of the Town" columns, led to full-length books beginning in 1962, as well as assignments for other national magazines such as *Audubon, National Parks,* and *Defenders of Wildlife.*

She started writing animal books for children in 1959 and has not yet stopped. Her most recent ones—*If Dogs Ruled the World, The Silly Story of a Flea and His Dog, Playing with Dolphins,* and *How Whales Walked into the Sea*—were published by Scholastic Press in 1999. Her only child, John Joseph, was born after World War II during her first marriage to John McNulty, who died in 1956.

Altogether she has authored five nonfiction animal books for adults, beginning in 1962 with *Wholly Cats,* co-authored with her younger sister, Elisabeth Keiffer. In 1966, her book entitled *The Whooping Crane: The Bird That Defies Extinction* won the Dutton Animal Book Award. Doubleday published her following three works: *Must They Die? The Strange Case of the Prairie Dog and the Black-Footed Ferret* (1971); *The Great Whales* (1974); and *The Wildlife Stories of Faith McNulty* (1980).

Writing about animals is Faith McNulty's way to satisfy her curiosity about species unfamiliar to her. In the prologue to her last book, she described her technique: "One animal led to another.... I began to learn the ropes; how to find experts on whatever animal I was interested in at the moment and pick out from their store of knowledge the pieces that were of use to me.... On the darker side is what I have learned about the ever-widening conflict between the needs and desires of the human race and the needs of animals" (*The Wildlife Stories of Faith McNulty,* prologue).

As author of a large number of books for children, Faith McNulty has been able to propagate her knowledge of animal behavior and to profess her respect for animals and her concern for their continued right to exist. Because she wrote juvenile literature simultaneously with her *New Yorker* reporting and nonfiction writing for adults, she made double use of research carried out on a particular subject. For instance, when she visited Penny Patterson in Palo Alto, California, who raised and studied the behavior of Koko, the gorilla, McNulty included a description of Patterson's research into ape communications in her adult book, *Wildlife Stories,* as well as in *With Love from Koko,* a children's book published in 1990 by Scholastic Press. Similarly, a story detailing the habits of a woodchuck served as both an adult story and a book for children, as did her own experience raising a pet mouse.

She used the technique of recycling material to both adult and children's audiences especially successfully in recounting reactions to a late summer hurricane. In a "Talk of the Town" column in *The New Yorker,* she wrote sardonically about gearing up for a hurricane that had been forecast to bombard her Rhode Island farm but that, in fact, never hit land.

For children, and dedicated in particular "to Johnny," she uses the experience of a hurricane to spread an ecological philosophy in *Hurricane*, a children's book published by Harper & Row in 1983. "John felt that he and the gulls—the tree—even the distant ocean waves—were all linked together in a way that he had never realized before. Each was responding to the coming storm. Each would meet it in its own way" (p. 27).

When she introduces into the story the possibility that scientists in the future might discover a way to stop hurricanes from occurring, Faith McNulty voices her negative reaction: "His mother said, 'I'm not sure I want anyone to invent a way to change hurricanes and storms. People have lived with storms for millions of years. It is a part of living. We seem to think of natural things as good or bad depending on what effect they have on our own lives. But it seems to me we should think of nature as a whole. Perhaps storms make changes that are good in ways we don't know about—that are necessary to keep everything in balance'" (p. 25).

Faith McNulty's main contributions to conservation efforts in the United States have been her writings during the 1960s and 1970s about endangered species. In the introduction to *The Whooping Crane*, then–Secretary of the Interior Stewart Udall wrote that "the rescue of this bird from the brink of extinction has become the symbol of our newly developed conservation conscience.... We, the people, ... have had a shift of conscience in the last fifty years and have made the preservation of rare species of wildlife one of our national conservation purposes."

For McNulty, her motivation in writing about whooping cranes, the tallest birds in the United States, was to go beyond the symbolism and learn more about the "live creatures." She also aimed to solve a perplexing puzzle. Why, she asked, could we have been trying for almost thirty years to save the whooping crane from extinction and still have not definitely succeeded? In 1965, when she was writing her book, there existed only 44 wild whooping cranes, which in McNulty's words "very large and very grand white bird[s] with long black legs, sinuous neck[s], and thrilling, trumpetlike voice[s]" (p. 15). The cranes spent winters at Aransas Wildlife Refuge on the Gulf Coast of Texas, 75 miles north of Corpus Christi, but where they spent summers, as she put it, "was one of the most tantalizing of ornithological mysteries" (p. 16). In the book, she chronicles how scientists found the birds' migratory destination and nesting habitat in northwestern Canada.

Furthermore, she describes not only scientific information about whooping cranes' lives but introduces readers to the wildlife management debate about how best to protect endangered species. In this case, the opposing forces were the aviculturists, those who advocated breeding birds in captivity, and those who wanted to protect their wild habitats.

At the end of the 1970s, writing in *The Wildlife Stories of Faith McNulty*, she admits that her whooping crane book was the one she "learned more from and was more emotionally gripped by than any other story I have done" (p. 307). And she remained optimistic about the fate of this endangered species, because, in contrast to earlier days, more people had become concerned about its perilous state of existence and were willing to commit themselves to its protection. By 1978, the number of wild whooping cranes had increased to 69 from 44 in 1965, and there were experiments with artificial propagation that showed promise as well as the establishment of a breeding center for nonmigratory cranes.

In her second book about an endangered species, *Must They Die? The Strange Case of the Prairie Dog and the Black-Footed Ferret*, Faith McNulty confronted another debate in the forefront of conservation of wildlife policy in the United States. "Conservationists, who beg for recognition of the intangible value—scientific, ecological, and aesthetic—of wild fauna, are continually coming up against practices and ideas evolved solely from the economics of the past" (p. 8). The book describes what little is known about the black-footed ferret, a mammal that has been sighted rarely and only in prairie-dog towns in South Dakota. This endangered species, which McNulty pictures "with its brilliant markings of black and shades of brown has the grace and beauty of a tiny tiger" (p. 3), lives off prairie dogs, a rodent that is detested by ranchers. The United States government, with elaborate and large-scale "control" programs, has poisoned prairie dogs to stop them from burrowing into valuable pastures and competing with cattle and sheep for grass. In her book she details the efforts, whose impact remains unclear, to save black-footed ferrets, which scientists fear are poisoned along with prairie dogs.

At the beginning of the 1970s, Faith McNulty turned her attention to an endangered species whose continued existence is of global concern and not a conservation issue for the United States alone. Doubleday published her fourth nonfiction book entitled *The Great Whales* in 1974. Reporting this story took her to Baja California in Mexico and to Bermuda, where she interviewed scientists engaged in behavioral studies of whales. As with earlier topics, her extensive research has served dual purposes, for she not only wrote the adult book but also has authored at least three children's books on the subject of whales. The most recent one, *How Whales Walked Into the Sea*, published by Scholastic Press in 1999, depicts with splendid illustrations the history of the migration from land to sea of the world's largest mammal.

During the 1970s, she continued to write magazine articles about endangered species, several of which were collected into the 1980 book, *The Wildlife Stories of Faith McNulty*. When describing the desert pupfish, "our smallest endangered species," and peregrine falcons in California, she devotes equal space to the fauna and to their passionate human defenders.

Faith McNulty is one of many Americans who cannot imagine living in a world devoid of the wild animals that still exist today. In her writings, she expresses the voices of the many.

> It is difficult to say how people born fifty or sixty years from now into a world that is barren of almost any life except that which human beings husband or control will feel about it. Quite likely they will adapt adequately, but they may find some of the past meaningless and puzzling. What, for instance, can it mean to such a person of the future to read of the lion lying down with the lamb, or the way of the serpent upon the rock, the tiger burning bright, the sly fox, the prudent ant, the wolf at the door, or the Owl and the Pussycat going to sea? Will this future reader, leafing through an old book, experience a strange, intuitive twinge of longing as he wonders what it means to be "happy as a lark?" [*The Wildlife Stories of Faith McNulty*, Epilogue].

Ann Zwinger

Ann Zwinger writes mainly about the nature she observes from her lookout post in the Rocky Mountains of Colorado, where she has lived with her family for nearly 40 years. As a prolific author of more than a dozen books, she shares with John Muir and Mary Austin, whose lesser-known writings she recently edited, "a celebration of landscape." Her picture like depictions of flowers, trees, insects, and birds, a talent honed from an education in art history, reveal the mysteries of the natural environment to her readers.

She was born in 1925 as Ann Haymond in Muncie, Indiana, and she readily admits that in her writings she relates her exploration of the natural world in the Rocky Mountains to memories of her childhood home in the rolling hills of Indiana. "I called upon the memories of all those quieter landscapes of my youth.... You have to dip back into the reservoir of your life, and what was there, tucked away in memory, has become not mere nostalgia but a base upon which to construct" (*The Nearsighted Naturalist*, p. 6). Her most vivid recollection of a childhood spent in "the gentle Indiana countryside" is of the White River, which was located about half a mile from her family's house. Her father, who was a successful attorney, and her mother, who cultivated a beautiful garden and loved to canoe, appreciated and passed on to their daughter a strong sense of living in the natural environment of a small Midwestern city. When she writes in her first book, *Beyond the Aspen Grove,* about "a tiny burst of violets ... beneath a drift of leaves," the mention of wildflowers conjures up in her mind a memory of her mother who loved them (p. 127).

After childhood she moved away permanently from this landscape and lived in a variety of locations in the United States—Wellesley College in Massachusetts, along the coast of Florida, on a farm in Arkansas, and in the city of Colorado Springs—before buying the 40 acres of high elevation land in the Rocky Mountains. It also took her many years to begin her fruitful career as naturalist, illustrator, and prizewinning nature writer. In her first book she describes herself as a city housewife, wife to pilot Herman and mother of three daughters, whose work revolved around cooking, gardening, and raising children. In the 1960s, when Ann Zwinger was in her late thirties, the family moved part-time into the Rocky Mountains in an area to the north of Pikes Peak and exploration of the world of mountain nature moved to the front burner of her life. She began to study, observe and draw the flora and fauna she found around her at Constant Friendship, the name the family gave to their mountainous property situated at an elevation of 8,300 feet.

Ann Zwinger approaches nature with the eye of an artist, which in her case means that with the aid of a hand lens and often a microscope she studies the intricacies of the world around her. In *Beyond the Aspen Grove,* she presents an image of herself "sitting sketching in the ponderosa wood" (p. 248) and alludes often to well-known artists. She writes that the stems of Canadian reed grass "form a screen of green lines that unite the foreground flower patterns into a glowing Matisse" (p. 80) and that "on dark days the forest is a woodcut by Kirchner or Munch" (p. 279).

In an essay entitled "Drawing on Experience," which was part of a recent anthology of her writings, she "speaks of plants because they are what I enjoy drawing" (*The Nearsighted Naturalist,* p. 257). But, in fact, she has drawn a full range of flora and fauna for her many publications. She even tried to analyze her way of viewing nature through art. "When I begin in the center, as it were, and move outward, I build up a reality in which each detail relates to the one before. I wonder if this is also a way of apprehending the world, of composing it from many observations, a detail here, a detail there, creating an infinitely expandable universe" (p. 258).

Art for Ann Zwinger has been a takeoff point, offering her entrée into the field of natural history. When she arrived in Colorado she started a serious study of nature in a montane environment. She read books, took college biology courses, interviewed experts and wandered. She learned a lot, enough to inform a general public about flowers and trees, insects and birds, small animals and mushrooms, and even about the geological history of her local area. Ann Zwinger also offers advice to those who may want to follow in her footsteps, for she has come up with a technique for becoming a naturalist that worked for her. "I believe in the magic of lists," she writes in "The Art of Wandering," another essay in *The Nearsighted Naturalist*. "The naturalist in me keeps comforting lists of the important arrivals and departures that mark my natural world: when the aspen leaves flush, when they turn gold and drop; when the lake freezes and when it opens; the first hummingbird and the first pasqueflowers" (p. 275).

The combination of an artist's eye with a naturalist's knowledge has made Ann Zwinger a nature writer *par excellence*. Her list of publications is voluminous and her writing has taken her beyond her own land, into the canyons and deserts of the West and to montane environments throughout the United States. It is through her role as an author that she has become a "proselytizer," as she expresses her conservation mission. "I, as a nature writer, have an ulterior motive. If I can get people to look, they may become curious about what they see ... and in the process, they will come to be interested, and being interested is just one step from caring, and if they care they will not destroy" (*The Nearsighted Naturalist*, p. 285).

Her career as a nature writer was launched in 1970, when Random House published *Beyond the Aspen Grove*, a full-length description with drawings of the land, waters, meadows, woods, and wildlife surrounding her Rocky Mountain home. She followed up this book with three more in the 1970s: *Land Above the Trees: A Guide to American Alpine Tundra*, published in 1972 with Dr. Beatrice E. Willard, alpine ecologist; *Run, River, Run: A Naturalist's Journey Down One of the Great Rivers of the West*, about the Green River, published in 1975 and winner of a John Burroughs Memorial Association Gold Medal; and *Wind in the Rock*, about five canyons in southeastern Utah, published in 1978.

During the 1980s she continued to write books in collaboration with others, and in particular with fellow nature writer, Edwin Way Teale, with whom she co-authored *A Conscious Stillness: Two Naturalists on Thoreau's Rivers*, published by Harper & Row in 1982. Zwinger also started writing texts for photography books. In 1983, she published *Desert Country Near the Sea: A Natural History of the Cape Region of Baja California* with her photographer husband Herman H. Zwinger and, in 1987, *Colorado*

II with photographer David Muench. She also edited the papers of a nineteenth-century naturalist, *John Xantus, the Fort Tejon letters, 1857–1859*; in 1989, E. P. Dutton published her book about the desert environment, *The Mysterious Lands: A Naturalist Explores Four Great Deserts of the Southwest.*

As Ann Zwinger reached her sixties and by 1995, her seventies, her literary output did not diminish at all, and she has continued to hike, canoe, explore, and observe nature in the western regions of the United States. In 1991, *Aspen: Blazon of the High Country* with photographs by Barbara Sparks came out, and in 1995, the University of Arizona Press published *Downcanyon: A Naturalist Explores the Colorado River through the Grand Canyon.* She edited two books in the 1990s: *Writing the Western Landscape*, a collection of some of the writings of Mary Austin and John Muir, in 1994; and in 1995, together with her eldest daughter Susan Zwinger, she selected and edited *Women in Wilderness: Writings and Photographs.* She also published two more books with photographers: *Yosemite: Valley of Thunder* with photographer Kathleen Norris Cook in 1996; and *Portrait of Utah* with photographer David Muench in 1999.

Her latest books, *The Nearsighted Naturalist*, a collection of 21 essays published in 1998, and *Shaped by Wind and Water: Reflections of a Naturalist,* which appeared in 2000, are attempts to look back and take stock of her total contribution as a prolific nature writer and American conservationist. She continues to offer the lay reader almost encyclopedic descriptions of the natural world, in pictures as well as in pictorial language. Her passion for the outdoors has not waned and neither has her ability to transmit that feeling through metaphor, evocative expression, and the relating of intriguing, factual information about the natural world.

Sue Hubbell

Sue Hubbell, born in 1935, has authored books about the natural world for almost 20 years, and she has carved out a special niche: bugs. From the day in 1972 that she moved to a farm in the Ozark Mountains in Missouri, she has made her living from working with insects, at first as a beekeeper and now as a successful nature writer. From her first book, *A Country Year: Living the Questions,* published in 1986 about her life living alone on the land after her divorce, to her 1999 book *Waiting for Aphrodite: Journeys into the Time Before Bones*, she has extended public understanding to a branch of the animal world that people don't tend to accord much respect.

As she likes to report about herself, this present writing career is only the latest of many, but ever since her childhood in southern Michigan she has been fascinated by natural history and by invertebrates in particular. An interest in biology seems to have run in her family. Her father, a botanist, worked as a landscape architect in Kalamazoo until his death, when Sue Gilbert was still a young child. Her brother, Bil Gilbert, writes about vertebrates from his home in Pennsylvania and her cousin, Asher Treat, is an entomologist whose specialty is moth ear mites.

Even though Sue Hubbell lived on 105 acres in the Ozark Mountains for 25 years, it was neither the first nor the last environment that she has claimed as her home. In 1972 she and her husband, Paul Hubbell, decided to return to a simple life, growing vegetables and chopping wood on a beautiful mountain hilltop. They opposed the Vietnam War and wanted to escape from the problems infecting urban America. They abandoned their professional careers in Rhode Island, she as a librarian at Brown University and her husband as a professor of electrical engineering at the University of Rhode Island. Their only child, Brian, was sent off to boarding school in Putney, Vermont.

Soon after their arrival in southern Missouri, they took up beekeeping but within a few years their thirty-year marriage had fallen apart. Sue stayed on in the Ozarks, taking over the management of the land and the honey business and started writing a column for the *St. Louis-Post Dispatch*. Thirty-three of these early pieces, written between 1975 and 1978, were collected into a book published in 1991, entitled *On This Hilltop*.

Her life changed again in 1988 when she remarried and began dividing her time between the farm in Missouri and a house in the city of Washington, D.C. Her new husband, Arne Sieverts, who was employed in Washington, visited her in the Ozarks as she continued to earn a living as a commercial beekeeper. Not until the mid–1990s did she give up this business and move away from her hilltop farm. Before she left, she arranged for the Missouri Department of Conservation to add her land to the State of Missouri Natural Area that abutted her property. In this way she had tried to ensure that her beloved Ozark acreage would remain "forever wild."

In the late 1990s, she and Arne bought a house and five acres along the coast in Maine. She continues to divide her time between the city and the country, but she is no longer a beekeeper and has acquired a new line of invertebrate interests: marine invertebrates. Her 1999 book *Waiting for Aphrodite* is primarily about this type of bug, and in 1998 she wrote a new introduction to one of Rachel Carson's classics, *The Edge of the Sea*.

Sue Hubbell's enthusiasms have moved from land bugs to sea bugs, but her style of writing has remained true to its original form. Her first book, *A Country Year: Living the Questions* came out in the mid–1980s and although it is not limited to invertebrates only, she does devote several chapters to them, foreshadowing the themes of her later books.

A Country Year is part confession, part autobiography, and part personal reflection on nature. Throughout Sue Hubbell ingratiates herself with readers, presenting herself as a nonconformist but never as an expert. She is proud of being able to fend for herself and describes a number of newly acquired capabilities that she learned after her husband left, jobs he used to do such as chainsawing, repairing the truck, and roofing the barn.

In this book, she also introduces a wide cast of Ozarkers, and for an outsider she expresses a surprising empathy with their attitudes. Her property borders a campground owned by the local branch of Veterans of Foreign Wars and as she puts it, "None of the VFW members or their wives are close friends of mine, but I know many in the group and they often invite me to join them at their cookouts" (p. 28). She relates how when one veteran had committed suicide at the campground she had been drawn personally into sharing their grief. During the night of the tragic event, they had used her telephone to call the police and she had offered sympathetic support to the men.

In a chapter devoted to copperheads, she dismisses the Ozark attitude about snakes in one line: "Most of the snakes around are harmless, … and I have no sympathy with the local habit of killing every snake in sight" (p. 52). Instead of dwelling on differences between her views and those of Ozarkers, she packs her writing with what will become typical Hubbell trademarks: folktales about snakes, discussions of biological characteristics, and anecdotes about encounters with copperheads.

Toward the end of the book, when she writes about a campaign of local activism to stop construction of a dam, she reflects about her otherness from Ozarkers. They all love the land and can come together in "opposition to damming the river to create a recreational lake, but our sensibilities are different.... They come from families who have lived off the land from necessity.... The land, the woods and the rivers, and all that are in and on them are resources to be used for those who have the knowledge and the skills" (p. 140). In contrast to Ozarkers, she is horrified when a trapper bursts into the meeting at her house bragging about killing a bobcat whose pelt would fetch 35 dollars. "But my aesthetic is a different one, and comes from having lived in places where beauty, plants and animals are gone, so I place a different value on what remains than do my Ozark friends and neighbors" (p. 141).

As a harbinger of books that she would write in the future, *A Country Year* includes separate chapters on mites, brown recluse spiders, chiggers, cockroaches, termites, and caterpillars as well as substantial descriptions of her work as a beekeeper and honey-producer. She built up a substantial business and wrote an entire book about it, *A Book of Bees,* published in 1988.

Her eighteen million bees, divided into 300 hives, were kept at farms throughout the southern Missouri countryside. As she explained, in this way the farmers could use the bees to pollinate their crops while the same bees produced the honey that she collected, packaged and marketed. In the area she was known as the Bee Lady and in April when her shipment of new queen bees arrived, the post office would call her immediately to pick them up because her mailman was afraid that the bees might escape. She maintained a honey factory, housed on her land, with large stainless-steel tanks for storing honey and power machines for opening up the honeycombs and extracting the honey.

Her chapter on harvesting honey from the widely scattered hives vividly portrays the occupational discomforts of operating a commercial beekeeping business. To help in the harvest, she employed her nephew for one season and she reported how before beginning work, it was necessary to "desensitize Ky to bee venom" (p. 71). Even though she and he wore protective coveralls, a zippered bee veil and leather gloves, they had to expect to return home with hundreds of bee stings. If that were not discomfort enough, she mentions how the harvesting took place during the hottest part of the summer in temperatures around 100 degrees.

Afterwards, during the winter she would process the honey, putting the crystallized honey through a heating process and then packaging it into one-pound jars. The final stage was the marketing, when the Bee Lady, equipped with thousands of honey jars, would take off in her truck to urban centers and spend weeks working as a traveling saleswoman. To save money she would sleep in truck stops along interstate highways and would visit gourmet stores in Manhattan to peddle her Ozark mountain honey.

After Random House published her first book, *The New Yorker* hired her to write articles about sundry topics (not all about nature), and these pieces were collected together eventually into a 1995 book called *Far-flung Hubbell*. But at the same time Sue Hubbell geared herself up to write full-length books about bugs. What makes these books so successful is the obvious passion that Hubbell holds for her subject. She actually likes bugs, thinks writing about them is "a lot of fun," and considers entomologists her favorite people because they can't believe they can get paid for what they like to do most in life: observe the living habits of invertebrates.

Broadsides from the Other Orders: A Book of Bugs came out in 1993 and consisted of 13 chapters, each one devoted to an order of invertebrates. The chapter on the Order Odonata, dragonflies, is indicative of her approach to writing. She fills the chapter with scientific information—about the derivation of its name, eating habits, sounds it makes, its distinctive characteristic (the eye), and of course, its sex life. And yet the reader knows that this is not a textbook, for Hubbell engages the reader. She writes about her own childhood, about various countries' insect folklore, and about how psychiatrists deal with people's bug phobias, and she invariably finds a female entomologist to quote as her expert.

By the time *Waiting for Aphrodite: Journeys into the Time Before Bones* was published by Houghton Mifflin in 1999, Sue Hubbell had refined her writing about invertebrates into a fine art. She continued to tell interesting stories about obscure and not-so-obscure creatures, to find female biologists to interview, and always to focus on mating habits. But in this book she probed her subject more deeply, broaching broader scientific themes about evolution, human relationships with the natural world, and the effect of time on biological processes.

Still, a legitimate question to ask is how she decides which bugs to feature in her writings when, as she forthrightly states, invertebrates comprise "more than 95 percent of the animal species" in the world "and we have discovered only a fraction of the suspected tens of millions of them" (p. 12). Because Sue Hubbell seems to enjoy acting contrary to the norm or, as she puts it, "otherness, remoteness, and independence engage my curiosity and intellect" (p. 17), her choices do not conform to the ones that most scientists have made. The invertebrates most studied have shown some relation to human beings, either in a beneficial or else in a harmful way. They have impacted crop yields, caused diseases, or, as in the case of earthworms and bees, their behaviors have played a positive role in the human food chain.

Yet most of Hubbell's selected subjects in *Waiting for Aphrodite* do not meet those criteria. The invertebrate whose name she has enshrined in the book's title and to whom she devotes her final chapter offers a clue to her way of thinking. Aphrodite aculeata is a six-inch furry worm that lives in the mud at the bottom of the ocean. To Hubbell and to the several experts she quotes, this creature's hairy coat "shimmers with blue and green iridescence [and] is a beautiful animal" (p. 214). She even goes so far as to write about the animal's "rhythmic and graceful" pumping action that involves "the anus at the end of the body which is opened on the downstroke to allow fluid to pass through and is closed on the up-stroke" (p. 219). Liddy Hubbell drew several poses of Aphrodite for her mother-in-law's book, supposedly illustrating the true beauty of this worm.

Not all readers may be able to share the author's enthusiasm for Aphrodite's looks, but all readers will be able to understand why Sue Hubbell chose to feature Aphrodite in her book. According to theories put forth by zoologists, whom she quotes, this mud-dwelling worm may hold the secret to animal creation, the source of the generative principle that emerged from the sea's depths. "In the beginning there was the Worm," out of which evolved multicellular forms of life (p. 224).

Sue Hubbell's emphasis in *Waiting for Aphrodite* is not entirely devoted to evolutionary processes. The book addresses other fundamental ecological topics, among the most basic of which is, "Why should we pay attention to strange little animals with funny names? What are we saving them for?" (p. 186). She introduces this discussion in the chapter on sea urchins, a much-studied invertebrate because of its importance these days to fishermen in Maine. The market for sea urchin roe, a delicacy to the Japanese, blossomed in the late 1980s and early 1990s but was already waning in the late 1990s when she was writing her book. The supply of sea urchin was running out and Hubbell came across fishermen who would ask, "Why can't we kill all of the sea urchins and then find something else to fish for? Why can't every last one of them be eaten? What good are they, anyhow?" (p. 185).

Her response connects Sue Hubbell to all of the other conservationists in this book. Even though she does not express herself with the same belligerence as did Rosalie Edge, who believed in saving all creatures big and small, she makes a very strong case for protecting all living animals. "Eventually, if we continue to be profligate with the biota and all its needs, we will, of a certainty, cross some line that separates the ecosystem in which we have thrived from a new one. Crossing the line will represent a test to us, a test that the odds say we will flunk.... We can't begin to understand what it would mean to live in a new ecosystem because we don't understand the one we have. That makes me nervous" (p. 189). In other words, if we lose a species in our present ecosystem, we do not know what effect its demise will have upon the totality of the system. We can endure in this ecosystem but we may not make it in a new and different one. A conservation ethic, according to Sue Hubbell, would read like the following: "Be really, really careful with all the things in the world, particularly those that were here before we were. We may need them more than they need us. Best get to know them" (p. 190).

Anne LaBastille

Contemporary conservationist Anne LaBastille writes best-selling books about living close to nature in the Adirondack Mountains in New York. Her decision to live as an adult on 22 acres beside an isolated lake followed a childhood growing up in suburban New Jersey, where her closest green area was a local golf course. So far, Anne LaBastille sounds a lot like Helen Nearing, and in many ways they were similar. Both women, with roots in suburban New Jersey and without early exposures to wilderness or even to rural environments, consciously chose to build their own houses and to live deliberately in harmony with their surroundings in the northerly reaches of the United States.

But that is as far as the commonalities between them go. Anne LaBastille lives by herself with pet dogs, not with a like-minded companion; loves animals but is not a vegetarian; considers her self-constructed cabin a home, not a self-sufficient homestead; and earns a living as a wildlife ecologist and writer, not out of proceeds from small cash-crop businesses.

In 1965, Anne LaBastille began the life that has yielded the raw material for her many books about her life in a mountain environment. That is when she built her cabin in the woods and when she separated from her husband, Morgan Brown, an Adirondack innkeeper. But the person she was to write about was the product of an earlier history. She grew up in postwar United States, living in Montclair, a prosperous suburb of New York City, with her parents, a concert pianist and a language professor. She reiterates in every book how her mother's dictum to her—that a girl could not go camping—may have been what provoked her rebellion.

She went from Montclair, New Jersey, to attend college at first at the University of Miami and transferred to Cornell University, where she earned a B.S. degree in conservation of natural resources. She worked summers at a lodge in Big Moose, New York, and married the owner, her boss. For several years, she and her husband ran the hotel, and during winters they led tourists on natural history tours through Central America and the Caribbean islands.

After seven years, Anne's marriage broke up and she went back to her first love: the natural environment. She studied wildlife management at Colorado State University and eventually returned to Cornell, where she received a Ph.D. in wildlife ecology in 1969. Her doctoral research on the now-extinct waterbird, the giant grebe found on Lake Atitlan in Guatemala, provided the impetus for her book *Mama Poc*, published in 1990.

It was not until 1971 that Anne LaBastille launched her career as a self-employed nature writer and photographer. Her first successes were a number of articles in *National Geographic*, as well as several children's books published by the National Wildlife Federation in 1973. Her first nonfiction book for adults, *Woodswoman* published by E.P. Dutton in 1976, became a best-seller and motivated her to start a for-profit corporation called West of the Wind, which has published her most recent books: *The Wilderness World of Anne LaBastille* (1992); *Birds of the Mayas* (1993); *Woodswoman III* (1997); *Jaguar Totem* (1999); and *Woodswoman iiii* (2003). Of her five trade books about the natural environment published by commercial publishers, two describe her life in the Adirondacks and two focus on her experiences as a wildlife ecologist in Central America. The fifth book, *Women and Wilderness*, published by the Sierra Club in 1980, was her only attempt to write a book about other contemporary conservationists.

Her most popular contribution as a nature writer is an autobiographical series—*Woodswoman, Beyond Black Bear Lake* (later published as *Woodswoman II*), *Woodswoman III*, *Woodswoman iiii: Book four of the woodswoman's adventures.* These four volumes tell her story—how she took life into her own hands and determined where and how she wanted to live and how she settled in the middle of the woods beside a mountain lake five miles from the nearest neighbor. Each book chronicles distinct eras in her life (1965 to 1975, 1976 to 1986, 1987 to 1997, 1998 to 2003), portraying as well the history of environmental change on Black Bear Lake, Anne LaBastille's fictional name for "her lake."

She bought 22 acres of land that bordered the Adirondack Park, allowing her to call those six million acres her "backyard." Nearly half the land of the park was preserved in 1894 as wilderness and guaranteed to remain "forever wild" as a New York State park. The other half, where her private property is situated, is subject to land use regulations under the jurisdiction of the Adirondack Park Agency.

Although she eventually served as a commissioner of the agency, her first encounter with its rules was unnerving. The log cabin, which she constructed out of 45 spruce logs during the summer of 1965, was situated 12 feet too close to the lake. The agency demanded that she move her cabin to the required 50 feet from the shore, or else face a lawsuit. She complied.

Her home was a no-frills log cabin. She used propane gas for lighting and operating kitchen appliances, chopped wood to fire a Franklin stove for heating, and installed a water tank to assure a supply of running water. During the five months of warm weather, she took an early morning swim and waited patiently for the mail boat to deliver her communication with the outside world. She purposely and conscientiously made her life more Spartan and cut down to the essentials, choosing to forego electricity, indoor plumbing, and a telephone in order to live as close to nature and wildlife as she could manage. "I share a feeling of continuity, contentment, and oneness with the natural world, with life itself" (*Woodswoman*, p. 276).

The natural environment that Anne LaBastille continues to call home is a harsh, mountainous landscape, but to her mind they are "very comfortable mountains, deep-rooted, well preserved," and offer her a sense of continuity that she craves. After a long, cold, and snowy winter that lasts usually from November through April, this northerly region of the United States can expect only a brief spring, commonly two weeks in duration. As she described in *Woodswoman*, "three days of spring sun and the trees will leaf right out, ... into a serious, deep green, adult covering. There is very little time for immaturity in the North Country. Life is hard, rough, and sober" (p. 159).

But autumn in the Adirondacks, "a season of splendors," propels her writing style to new heights of expression, in the same way that the Vermont fall affected Helen Nearing. She focuses her attention on the wildlife: otters, white-tailed deer, beavers, and birds.

> On clear, frosty mornings, I'm awakened by the stentorian honking of Canada Geese flying low over my sleeping loft. They sound slightly hoarse, as if having just risen from their slumber on some cold and misty lake.... Their honking has the haunting quality of distant French horns. My spirit soars up beside them. I imagine the mighty Adirondack Mountains dwindling into dark humps interlaced with quicksilvered streams and moon-spangled marshes [p. 32].

Anne LaBastille counts birds as a major component of her environment, and although she does not devote full chapters to particular species of birds, they are accorded prominent space in all four books. In *Beyond Black Bear Lake*, the second book in the series, in which she describes her construction of a more remote cabin in the woods, she considers the sighting of a loon on Lilypad Pond "the perfect welcome." And her discussion of the song rendered by a young, white-throated sparrow is reminiscent of Florence Bailey's meticulous recounting of birdsongs. "Like an adolescent choirboy whose voice is changing, this sparrow cracked on high notes, skipped some low ones, and chimed a whimsical new white-throated melody" (p. 202). Coincidentally, this region of the United States was the childhood home of Florence Bailey, who devoted her entire career to writing about birds (see chapter 2).

Out of all the elements of nature that she features, "her closest friends" are the trees, linking Anne LaBastille with Rosalie Edge's brand of conservation. In particular, she describes the 300-year-old red spruces and white pines and the odorous balsam firs that populate her property. LaBastille even goes so far as to suggest that one of her veteran white pine trees has instilled in her its "all-pervading life force."

For Anne LaBastille, her life work as a conservationist does not end with writing books and articles—she campaigns with vigor for causes she supports. From the outset, when she first arranged her way of living in the Adirondacks, she had consciously made lifestyle decisions with conservation of the natural environment very much in mind. And yet she did not become engaged as an activist until the mid–1970s, assuming the responsibilities of a commissioner for the Adirondack Park Agency in 1975, a post she reluctantly resigned only in 1992. Because of a mysterious fire that caused havoc to a farm she had purchased and refurbished in the late 1980s, she became concerned that people opposed to her activism were endangering her life.

During the 1970s and 1980s, she counted the campaign to stop the spraying of herbicides on the right-of-way around the lake and the controlling of water pollution by inspecting septic systems as two significant victories. She also drew attention to a thwarted plan to locate a nuclear waste site in the Adirondacks, and, as a result of an article she wrote for *National Geographic*, she alerted her lakeside community to their problem with acid rain.

LaBastille detected the effects of acid rain around her own cabin, where she noticed several red spruce trees "turning a peculiar yellow-green color and losing needles at the crowns. For several years they bore an extra-heavy crop of cones. Then all the foliage gradually dropped off" (*Beyond Black Bear Lake*, pp. 95–96). She does not disguise her reaction.

> Meanwhile, I walk my woods and paddle my ponds, fingers to the pulse points, diagnosing, evaluating. It feels a little like watching a lover or a dear friend die a lingering death. Each year my woods and ponds seem a little worse, a little more anemic, a bit more toxified. I hope against hope that a remission is still possible. Yet I believe that the only effective therapy is to reduce sulfur dioxide and nitrous oxide emissions (with the accompanying toxic metals) and ozone by about 70 to 80 percent [p. 98].

Similarly, Anne LaBastille feels frustrated in her efforts to limit the size and number of motorboats on her lake, a problem that is "destroying neighborliness, degrading drinking water, and endangering our loons" (p. 243). Nonetheless, her commitment to conservation is as unbending as ever. She continues to teach people to respect and protect natural resources in her capacity as a registered Adirondack guide, leading hikers and campers through the wilderness.

Anne LaBastille's contributions to the cause of conservation of natural resources are international in scope, and only because of the national focus of this book has this brief profile concentrated on her U.S. writings. But she has published three books chronicling her conservation concerns in Central America: *Assignment: Wildlife* (1980); *Mama Poc* (1990); and *Jaguar Totem* (1999). Beginning in 1960, when she first spotted a giant pied-billed grebe on Lake Atitlan, Guatemala, she became absorbed in a campaign to save from extinction this flightless species of waterbird. She juxtaposed her life between summering in the Adirondack Mountains and wintering in Central America for 24 years. Unfortunately, this bird, which was twice the size of the common pied-billed grebe of the United States, was found only on Lake Atitlan and despite her concerted efforts, it no longer exists.

For her contributions to the conservation of natural resources, Anne LaBastille has received a number of honors, notably the Gold Medal for Conservationist of the Year in 1974 from the World Wildlife Fund for her work in Central America and the gold medal from the Society of Women Geographers in 1993. In 1994, Roger Tory Peterson, renowned ornithologist and nature writer, personally presented her with his National Nature Educator award. She has also been the recipient of two honorary doctorate degrees: one in science from the State University of New York at Plattsburgh and the other in letters from Ripon College, Wisconsin.

Mollie Beattie

In Mollie Beattie, who, unfortunately, died at the age of 49, we are reminded of the thoughts and actions of both Rosalie Edge and Helen Nearing. Her prominence in furthering a national conservation agenda came as a result of her appointment by President Clinton in 1993 to be director of the U.S. Fish and Wildlife Service.

Mollie Beattie was born on April 27, 1947, in Glen Cove, Long Island, and received a bachelor's degree in philosophy from Marymount College in Tarrytown, New York, in 1968. After graduation she worked in journalism and public relations in New York and Vermont for four years, but only after spending two years as a mountaineering instructor in Colorado for Outward Bound did she realize that her real calling was the study of nature and the environment. She returned to Vermont and enrolled in the forestry department at the School of Natural Resources of the University of Vermont. In 1979, with a master's degree in forestry, she was hired as a research assistant at Dartmouth College, assigned to write part of an Environmental Impact Statement for a wood-fired power plant.

From there, she went back to the University of Vermont and was employed as a project forester on a two-year Forest Demonstration Project (1980–1982). In this capacity, she taught forestry and wildlife management to private landowners and coordinated the communications of federal, state and private land management assistance organizations. From 1983 to 1985, Mollie Beattie was manager of 1,300 acres of farm and forest land of The Windham Foundation, a nonprofit educational foundation in Grafton, Vermont. She married Richard Schwolsky, who was a contractor and who owned Grafton Builders, a residential home construction company. Together, in the early 1980s, the couple built their own solar-powered house, "a mile from the last power pole, a half mile from our only neighbors, and in the winter, a half hour from our tiny village" in the middle of the Green Mountains. The moose in the driveway and the geese in the pond were their constant companions.

With Rosalie Edge, Beattie shared a commitment to protecting forests in the United States and she wrote, spoke, and created policies for the state of Vermont, as well as for the federal government, to foster the management of woodland as wildlife habitats. In Mollie Beattie's lifestyle, we find reminders as well of Helen Nearing's self-sufficiency and living a life in tune with a Vermont environment.

From 1985 to 1989, she was appointed by the governor to the position of Commissioner of the Department of Forests, Parks and Recreation, responsible for the administration of 250,000 acres of public land. As commissioner, she developed policies and legislation on forestry, land taxation, recreation, public lands, wetlands protection, and pesticide use. She created the Forest Communications Council and initiated the four-state Governor's Task Force on Northern Forest Lands, now known as the Northern Forest Council. Her next appointment was as Deputy Secretary of the Agency of Natural Resources, a post she held from 1989 to 1990. In this position she supervised the agency's three departments, and had specific authority on issues concerning fish, wildlife, forestry, public land, public trust, water quality, solid waste and energy. She also chaired a successful task force for planning to meet requirements of the federal Clean Water Act.

After earning a master's degree in public administration from the Kennedy School of Government at Harvard University, she returned to Vermont to serve as executive director from 1991 to 1993 of The Richard A. Snelling Center for Government, a public policy and service institute that she originated as a memorial to a former Vermont governor.

Mollie Beattie was the first woman to head the U.S. Fish and Wildlife Service, an agency within the Department of the Interior that enforces wildlife protection laws. It was the same governmental agency that employed Rachel Carson in the 1940s. During Beattie's tenure in this position from 1993 to 1996, she focused attention on entire ecosystems, rather than on individual species, and insisted that the Endangered Species Act does work. "It keeps species from going extinct and it has helped us stabilize and move species toward recovery," she reiterated at press conferences. Even though she admitted that the process was usually painfully slow, still she was able to claim that the Endangered Species Act of 1973 was a conservation success story. Proof of its success could be seen in the delisting from the columns of endangered species of the peregrine falcon and the bald eagle, effectively bringing them back from the brink of extinction.

Beyond saving charismatic species, she tried to educate the American public about the importance of saving species such as mussels, snails, and lichen. In an essay in the book, *Biodiversity and the Law,* published in 1996 just before her premature death, she wrote that endangered species can provide "an early warning sign of a crisis."

> [T]hese species are merely indicators of bigger ecological problems.... There is a snail in Idaho that is one of my favorite parables on this point. This snail is found in an isolated series of hot springs in a single valley. It is being pushed to extinction by overpumping of the aquifer; the springs are disappearing as the groundwater levels are lowering.... The real issue is whether we are going to continue this unsustainable use of an aquifer until ultimately no water remains for either humans or snails [p. 14].

Mollie Beattie was most proud of the impact she had on shifting thinking within the federal agency to an ecosystem approach. In managing the nation's fish and wildlife resources, she drew on her training as a forester. She had learned from Aldo Leopold and other great conservationists how "to deal with the forest as a whole, to think all at once about everything that the forest produces and everything that is seen and heard there." She explained this to members of the Senate Committee on Environment and Public Works at her nomination hearing on July 28, 1993. She transferred this way of thinking about the environment to the management of the National Wildlife Refuge System. "We want to use the refuges as anchor points for maintaining biodiversity and as keystones to demonstrate the success of the ecosystem approach" (*Biodiversity and the Law*, p. 12).

As a writer, Mollie Beattie published several pamphlets on the management of forests in Vermont, and she was the principal author of *Working with Your Woodland: A Landowner's Guide*, written in 1983 with Charles Thompson and Lynn Levine. In this book, she underlines the fundamental role that the forest plays for the whole environment, echoing the message that Rosalie Edge transmitted in her 1938 publication, *Our Nation's Forests*. "Whether the land has been logged, burned, or plowed, the forest responds with a green cover to stabilize the soil, generate oxygen, filter noise and pollutants, moderate temperatures, and provide shelter and food for animals, and beauty and woods products for people" (p. 17).

However, Mollie Beattie, the policymaker, did not stop with imparting information about the importance of forests. She guided her readers, who in this case were primarily private owners of woodland, to ways that they could practice sustainable forest management. She explained that the same forest that can produce timber can also support wildlife habitats by offering food, shelter (cover) and water that will attract and support animals. "A critical aspect of an ecologically balanced forest is the presence of tree cavities and rotten trees, which provide food, nesting, and denning opportunities for a variety of birds, mammals, and reptiles" (p. 47).

In this seemingly practical book, Mollie Beattie presents her broader ideas about the natural environment. She realized that "human use is now so widespread, intense and frequent in the forests of New England that the only realistic way to think of ourselves is as part of the forest environment" (p. 18). But in the revised edition of the book, which came out in 1993, the authors understood "the ecological meaningless of legal boundaries and the short span of a human life relative to that of a forest" (p. 230). They were not convinced that their guide provided the long-term solutions for maintaining sustainable forestland.

In contrast to most of the historical and contemporary women conservationists featured in *American Women Conservationists*, Mollie Beattie was not privileged to enjoy a long life. She was diagnosed with brain cancer and forced to resign from her position as head of the U.S. Fish and

Wildlife Service on June 6, 1996. She died on June 27, 1996, only 49 years old.

Members of the 104th Congress honored Beattie for her significant contributions to the cause of conservation in the United States by approving legislation on July 29, 1996, to rename an eight-million-acre wildlife refuge in Alaska as the Mollie Beattie Wilderness Area. She will be long remembered for her eloquent advocacy of wildlife protection and in particular for strongly supporting the return of gray wolves to Yellowstone National Park. In her obituary, which appeared in *The New York Times* on June 29, 1996, Mollie Beattie is characterized in a memorable anecdote: rubbing cold water on the belly of a wild wolf and saying, "Any day I can touch a wild wolf is a good day."

Terry Tempest Williams

Contemporary women conservationists express love for their land much more directly than did their antecedents. Terry Tempest Williams, the youngest of the writers profiled in this composite chapter, identifies herself body and soul with the earth, and in particular with her roots in the Great Basin region of Utah. In her most poignant published work, *Refuge*, written as a memoir to her mother who died from cancer at the age of 54, she equates her love for her mother to the earth: "I am reminded that what I adore, admire, and draw from Mother is inherent in the Earth. My mother's spirit can be recalled simply by placing my hands on the black humus of mountains or the lean sands of desert. Her love, her warmth, and her breath, even her arms around me—are the waves, the wind, sunlight, and water" (p. 214).

Terry Tempest was born in Salt Lake City in 1955 into a family descended from Mormon immigrants who had arrived in Utah during the 1850s. Her parents, father John Henry Tempest III, who carried on the family construction business, and her mother, Diane Dixon, were married in 1953. They had four children: three sons and Terry, the eldest child and the only daughter. Terry married Brooke Williams, a biologist, on June 2, 1975, when she was 19 years old. She decided early on in her marriage not to have children—"my ideas are my children," she explains in *Refuge*.

After graduation from the University of Utah, she was employed at the Utah Museum of Natural History in Salt Lake City, at first as curator of education and then in the mid–1980s as naturalist-in-residence. She retired from museum employment in the late 1990s to devote herself full-time to writing.

Her first book, published by Charles Scribner's Sons entitled *Pieces of White Shell: A Journey to Navajoland,* appeared in 1984 when she was still in her twenties. Williams described the book, which won the Southwest Book Award, as "a journey into one culture, Navajo, and back again to my own, Mormon" (p. 2). She organized the book into 11 chapters, structuring it around items she had collected and brought back from Navajoland in a small leather pouch: rocks, sand, seeds, turquoise, obsidian, coral, white shell, yucca, a bouquet of feathers bound by yarn, coyote fur, rabbit bone, deerskin, wool, potsherd, corn pollen, and a ceramic figurine of a storyteller. As a museum curator, Williams had become a professional collector, but in Navajoland she was employed as a teacher of seven-year-olds at an elementary school in Ramah, New Mexico.

In *Pieces of White Shell,* Williams tells stories about the artifacts—it is her way of relating a "sacred visualization" of Navajo society to her readers. As a storyteller, she introduces many themes that she has returned to and has pursued throughout her writing career. She writes about the soul of the land, its mystery, rituals associated with birds, and human connections with the land. In this early work, Terry Tempest Williams, teacher of seven-year-olds, touches the earth with her students. "On hands and knees we entered the worlds of prairie dog and burrowing owl" (p. 144), but in later writings she, as a mature woman, not only touches but fully embraces the earth.

Her writings about nature in the western region of the United States continued during the 1980s with a volume of poetry, *Between Cattails,* published in 1985, and *Coyote's Canyon,* a personal nonfiction narrative set in the desert canyons of southern Utah, published in 1989 by Peregrine Smith Books of Salt Lake City.

But, in 1991, with the publication of *Refuge: An Unnatural History of Family and Place,* a chronicle of her mother's long struggle with ovarian cancer, Terry Tempest Williams broke new ground as a nature writer. The book's dedication to her mother—"Diane Dixon Tempest who understood landscape as refuge"—tells only half the story. For not only is the book a poignant family narrative, but it also recounts the demise of birds from Bear River Migratory Bird Refuge. This wildlife reserve near Salt Lake City was closed for seven years because of severe flooding that affected the Great Salt Lake during the 1980s. Williams titles each chapter in *Refuge* after the name of a bird and relates the bird to events in her own life and to her mother's struggle with disease, because in her family "our attachment to the land was our attachment to each other" (p. 15). "The losses I encountered at the Bear River Migratory Bird Refuge as

Great Salt Lake was rising helped me to face the losses within my family" (prologue).

The Bear River Migratory Bird Refuge, located about one hour north of Salt Lake City at the delta of the Bear River in Brigham City, was the first waterfowl sanctuary established by a special act of Congress in 1928. But to Terry Tempest Williams, this place, home at various times to 208 species of birds, is her refuge as well. "Maybe it's the expanse of sky above and water below that soothes my soul. Or maybe it's the anticipation of seeing something new" (p. 21). Williams provides her own description of the refuge.

> These wetlands, emeralds around Great Salt Lake, provide a critical habitat for North American waterfowl and shorebirds, supporting hundreds of thousands, even millions of individuals during spring and autumn migrations. The long-legged birds with their eyes focused down transform a seemingly sterile world into a fecund one. It is here in the marshes with the birds that I seal my relationship to Great Salt Lake [p. 22].

Her achievement in crafting such a book is pathbreaking. *Refuge* is old-fashioned autobiography, filled with memories of childhood, special reminiscences about her mother, descriptions of her grandmother from whom she inherited a love of birds, as well as how family members, including her father and brothers, reacted to each stage of the saga. But it is also a book about 36 birds, many of whose habits she describes in as rich detail as Florence Bailey did in her bird guides. What Williams created is a book that meshed it altogether—bird life, flood, disease, love, human relationships—in a genuine, magnificent tour de force.

By the time Pantheon Books published her collection of 18 nonfiction stories, *An Unspoken Hunger: Stories from the Field*, in 1994 Terry Tempest Williams had become a powerful and respected voice for land conservation. She dedicated the book to her three nieces—Callie, Sara, and Diane—"with a prayer for their future."

Williams considers her feminism, her portrayal of nature in female terms, as central to her engagement with the land. In *An Unspoken Hunger*, two essays reinforce feminist themes: "Undressing the Bear" and "Stone Creek Woman." In another story, "The Wild Card," she summons "women wedded to wilderness" into action. "[F]lood Congress with our wild cards ... demanding that women's issues be recognized as health issues, as environmental issues, as issues centered around a quality of life that touches all of us, deeply" (p. 140). And she devotes two stories to two women heroines: artist Georgia O'Keeffe and conservationist Mardy Murie.

Terry Tempest Williams evokes her most powerful prose in passionate pleas to save the desert wilderness. In "A Eulogy for Edward Abbey," she reminds readers how his voice "lured us out of complacency again and again" (p. 76), and led her to organize a group of Utah conservationists into the Coyote Clan. The clan consists of "hundreds, maybe even thousands, of individuals who are quietly subversive on behalf of the land" (p. 78).

In "Yellowstone: The Erotics of Place," Williams attempts to combine her emotional and even sexual love of land with her political engagement. "I believe," she writes, "that out of an erotics of place, a politics of place is emerging ... a politics rooted in empathy in which we extend our notion of community, as Aldo Leopold has urged, to include all life forms—plants, animals, rivers, and soils" (pp. 86–87).

She includes at least two more explicitly political stories in *An Unspoken Hunger*: "Testimony" and "All That Is Hidden." The first one is her passionate testimony concerning the Pacific Yew Act of 1991, presented to the congressional subcommittee on fisheries and wildlife conservation and the environment. It is a straightforward plea to save the "beautiful healing trees" that contain in their bark a substance called taxol that can be used to treat ovarian and breast cancer.

"All That Is Hidden," a story that I assumed had been written to describe a hike she had taken with her husband and Gary Nabhan, an ethnobotanist, in Arizona's Cabeza Prieta National Wildlife Refuge in pursuit of bighorn sheep, in fact, castigates the United States Department of Defense for waging war on the Arizona desert. The refuge abuts the Barry M. Goldwater Air Force Range, which since the 1940s has been used for trial bombing missions.

Williams ends the piece with a powerfully written condemnation of this practice. "Night in the Cabeza restores silence to the desert, that holy, intuitive silence.... Silence is our national security, our civil defense. By destroying silence, the legacy of our deserts, we leave no room for peace, the deep peace that elevates and stirs our souls" (p. 124).

The longest piece in *An Unspoken Hunger* is "A Patriot's Journal," reflections she recorded during a two-week period, January 4 to January 17, 1991, that preceded the Gulf War. Her journal begins with a trip to a rally to protest nuclear testing in the Mojave Desert at the Nevada Nuclear Test Site. As in all her stories, she writes about real people, usually members of her family, and does not obscure the message.

In this case her uncle, a conservative Republican state senator, accompanies her to the rally and she quotes the words he uses when interviewed by a reporter.

Our family has been ravaged by cancer. Like many Utahns, I have chosen to ignore the facts surrounding radioactive fallout. I have just recently become a grandfather. I want to leave my little granddaughter, Hannah, a more peaceful world, if I possibly can. It was my generation who started this nuclear madness. Maybe it's up to my generation to stop it [p. 106].

Terry Tempest Williams, who loves life—all forms of it—cannot help but oppose the Gulf War. In another entry in her journal, on the day (January 16) commemorating her mother's death four years earlier, she writes, "Why? When we know the pain and suffering of one individual and what death means to a family, why would we purposefully choose to inflict death on all these Iraqi families through war?" (p. 113).

She ends "A Patriot's Journal" with an anecdote about her cousin who was stationed in Saudi Arabia as a linguistic specialist. She writes about telephoning her aunt on January 17, 1991, the night the war started, to ask about her cousin. Her aunt told her; "I honestly believe Scott will be fine.... But when I asked him how he was feeling, he answered, 'Mother, tell me, how does one translate madness?'" (p. 114).

Following *An Unspoken Hunger*, Pantheon Books published *Desert Quartet*, a prose poem illustrated with drawings and paintings by Mary Frank. The 58-page piece depicts Williams' conception of the desert canyon landscape of southern Utah in four sections, titled earth, water, fire, and air. Her creative rendering of the landscape is embellished with numerous poses of the naked female body.

In 1998, she edited with William B. Smart the book *New Genesis: A Mormon Reader on Land and Community*, for which she wrote only one essay. Entitled "West of Eden," her piece deals with a theology of the earth and in it she urges Mormon women "to carry the fire of Eve's desire for intimacy with all Creation and honor the humility housed within her heart that recognizes our place in wildness."

Her recent book called *Leap*, based upon her meditations on viewing the triptych "The Garden of Delights" by Hieronymous Bosch, represents a giant leap in her career as a writer. This publication defies simple categorization. It is not exclusively a nature book nor one about art, religion, or family. In fact, it combines all of these topics and more.

She described how she came to write this book to an audience gathered to hear her read at the National Museum of Women in Arts in Washington, D.C., in spring 2000. During a planned trip to Spain, when she and her husband had stopped in at the Prado Museum in Madrid, she was overwhelmed to find Bosch's painting on view. As a child growing up in a Mormon household, she had become familiar with two parts of the triptych, those that portrayed Heaven and Hell, but she had never even known about the third part, Earth, or "The Garden of Delights." She was so drawn to this painting that she returned day after day to the Prado to study it closely and eliminated the rest of the trip's itinerary.

What Terry Tempest Williams discovered in this Bosch painting was key to her own understanding of nature, life, and religion. She read passages to the audience from *Leap* that listed the names of all the birds she identified in the painting, about a conversation about life's work with a businessman she happened to sit next to on the airplane, and about her questioning of religious faith.

Beyond her writing career, Terry Tempest Williams is an activist in the spirit of Rosalie Edge and Marjory Stoneman Douglas. Not only is she part of the southern Utah Coyote Clan, campaigning to keep the redrock desert and canyon area as wilderness, but she also lectures, teaches, and gives presentations in support of her conservationist ideals. In May 2003 she was awarded an honorary Doctor of Humanities degree from the University of Utah.

Red: Passion and Patience in the Desert, her latest book, is dedicated to the Coyote Clan and America's Redrock Wilderness and contains essays, poems, congressional testimony and journal entries, some of which have been published previously. In 1995, she joined forces with fellow nature writer Stephen Trimble to fight to protect the southern Utah Redrock Wilderness. Their idea was to assemble a collection of essays from 21 writers "who have Utah's redrock sand and alkali dust in their souls." They called the book *Testimony* and released it at a press conference in front of the Capitol building in Washington, D.C.

Terry Tempest Williams's persona is linked most directly to Mary Austin, who, as Williams writes in a new introduction to Austin's *The Land of Little Rain* reissued in 1997, "believed in wild America, in all that was indigenous." Williams writes that Mary Austin "inspires us toward direct engagement with the land in life as well as on the page." Even though Austin's words were written in "Victorian diction," her "radical spirit is still with us" and voiced through the contemporary diction of Terry Tempest Williams.

8

Conclusion: Ideas for Our Time

What drove me to write this book was a central premise: these women have profoundly influenced American perceptions about their land and the flora and fauna that inhabit it, and yet most people in the United States have never even heard their names. While writing these chapters, I have focused on what each woman contributed to the cause of U.S. conservation and how each lived her life, neglecting for the most part to dwell upon gender. Yet if they had not been women, my stated reason for writing this book would not be valid.

There is a need to bring these voices back to public notice and to publicize their names only because they were women. Most of their writings have not been included in anthologies. Their thoughts and ways of expression have been lost. Their impact on the history of conservation has not been accorded the significance it deserves, except in the case of Rachel Carson. Because of the importance that Carson's writings have had on environmental thinking, in the chronicle of conservation history presented in *American Women Conservationists*, Carson's story provides the bridge that links the historical and contemporary eras.

Connecting American Women Conservationists

However distinctive her voice or disparate her cause, each of the historical conservationists whose lives and writings form the core of this book had some connection to Rachel Carson. She binds the individual stories of Mary Austin, Florence Bailey, Rosalie Edge, Marjory Douglas, and Helen Nearing together.

Marjory Douglas, Helen Nearing and Carson all are remembered as authors of seminal books that spurred changes in public attitudes about the environment and man's position in nature, but each woman was associated with a very different aspect of environmental thinking. Douglas wrote about saving the wetlands of the Florida Everglades; Nearing described living in tune with nature in New England; and Carson pleaded to stop pesticide poisoning of the total environment. And they each handled their subjects in varying manners. Douglas told the story of the destruction of the Everglades as an historical narrative; Nearing advised readers about how to live; and Carson exposed the facts and warned of resulting contamination.

Yet they all had significant impact on readers, awakening calls for action to stop man's ongoing destruction of nature. Steps have been taken to return the Everglades to its natural conditions; thousands of Americans have left urban and suburban jobs and houses to design their own ways of more natural living in rural areas throughout the country; and millions of citizens have involved themselves in a broadly based anti-pollution movement.

The six historical women conservationists featured in this book felt communion with their natural surroundings but for three—Florence Bailey, Rosalie Edge and Carson—it was their appreciation and passion for birds that opened the door to the natural environment. For each of them, observing nearby bird life offered a first access into a larger world of nature, and each retained a fascination with birds throughout the rest of her life.

Both Bailey and Carson developed an attachment to birds in childhood, learning to identify common species and becoming knowledgeable about their habits. Florence Merriam Bailey never deviated from her first path taken in nature; throughout a lifetime of writing about the environment she remained focused from beginning to end on birds. Rachel Carson did stray; when she finally saw the ocean when she was in her early twenties, her love for the flora, fauna and natural landscape of the sea coast overshadowed her passion for birds. Yet she continued to enjoy bird watching during her short life and became actively involved with the Audubon Society of Washington, D.C., as did Florence Merriam Bailey during an earlier era. Furthermore, concerns about the welfare of wildlife and especially birds prompted Carson to write *Silent Spring*, for she became determined to uncover the larger story of environmental poisoning after hearing about the deprivations of bird populations caused by pesticides.

Rosalie Edge also was attracted to birding and this interest served as her takeoff point for a late-in-life career as an environmentalist. She became an amateur birder in Central Park in New York City when she was already a mother, arousing a passion for wildlife that she would focus especially on birds of prey. Her anger at the senseless shooting of migrating hawks motivated her to protect Hawk Mountain in Kempton, Pennsylvania, and to establish a sanctuary, which became a favorite excursion destination for Rachel Carson.

Mary Austin, who wrote about arid lands, a subject that bore little relation to Carson's preoccupations with the sea and pesticide pollution, nevertheless lived a life with striking parallels to Rachel Carson's. Both women were uncommonly ambitious as children and they shared the same aspiration: to become writers. Because of this similarity, it is not surprising that both were familiar with *St. Nicholas* magazine during their respective childhoods. Mary Austin's father introduced her to this literary publication for children in the 1870s and Rachel Carson saw her name in print for the first time within the pages of *St. Nicholas* in 1918.

Both women as children had been drawn to natural history and made conscious decisions to study science as undergraduates. After college each woman moved away from the natural environment that she had known until that time and discovered not only new landscapes but also a wealth of raw material to write about. And what they wrote, *The Land of Little Rain* by Mary Austin and *The Sea Around Us* by Rachel Carson, made them famous authors.

Austin and Carson are the only historical women nature writers who have been deemed worthy of inclusion in literary anthologies, another parallel that links these two women's biographies, albeit posthumously. Even though they are featured in this book about conservationists, each made a major contribution as well to twentieth-century literature in the United States. They put their well-recognized talents as writers to use in the service of protecting the natural environment for future generations of Americans.

Rachel Carson was connected to each of the historical women conservationists in the ways mentioned above, but in addition she had affinities during her lifetime to their various attitudes about governmental policies toward the environment. Carson's position changed from participation in administering the government's agenda to criticism of specific programs and finally to advocacy for new approaches, so that at one time or another her opinions resonated with those of Austin, Bailey, Edge, Douglas, and Nearing.

Florence Bailey and Rachel Carson could be said to have been colleagues, having worked for the same federal government agency at different eras. Carson spent 16 years from 1936 to 1952 as a civil servant, employed as an aquatic biologist for the U.S. Biological Survey, which merged into the U.S. Fish and Wildlife Service in 1940. Clinton Hart Merriam, Florence Bailey's brother, created the U.S. Biological Survey in 1885 and Vernon Bailey, her husband, worked there as chief naturalist. During Vernon's more than 40 years at the U.S. Biological Survey, Florence Merriam Bailey served as an unpaid surveyor of birds, collecting information that she published in magazine articles, government publications and books.

During the 1930s Rosalie Edge was very critical of the U.S. Biological Survey, naming it the U.S. Bureau of Destruction and Extermination. In the reports that she wrote for the Emergency Conservation Committee she expressed strong opposition to the agency's policies of poisoning animals. Thirty years before Carson's attack on chemical pesticides Edge had condemned its use of sprays and powders to control pests.

Rosalie Edge was not alone among historical conservationists to criticize questionable actions taken by the U.S. government. In 1927 Mary Austin, in her capacity as representative from New Mexico to the Seven States Conference, opposed the building of Boulder Dam. Marjory Douglas criticized the U.S. Army Corps of Engineers for its destruction of the Florida Everglades with its dams and canals constructed during the first half of the twentieth century, and in 1969 she formed a citizen's group that derailed plans to build a jetport.

They all supported measures to protect wildlife, using the power of their pens. Florence Bailey wrote newspaper articles in the 1880s as part of a campaign to stop the sale of birds to milliners, and in her short story "Plume," Marjory Douglas unveils an unpleasant saga that graphically relates the demise of snowy egrets for use in the women's hat business. Rosalie Edge railed against the hunting of birds in general and protested vociferously during World War II against siting an artillery range at a lake in Montana that was known to be a flyway for trumpeter swans.

Both Rosalie Edge and Marjory Douglas, and also Rachel Carson, expended as much energy advocating for positive environmental policies as they did fighting against undesirable ones. Douglas was one of two women who served on a committee in the 1920s to create Everglades National Park, and in 1974 Big Cypress National Preserve was established on wetland that had been designated for a jetport. For Edge and her Emergency Conservation Committee the finest moment was the founding of Olympic National Park in Washington in 1938, but in addition the organization was instrumental in conserving ancient forests in both Yosemite National Park and Kings Canyon National Park in California and in Grand Teton National Park in Wyoming.

Carson and Edge spoke before congressional committees to lobby for their ideas for protecting the natural environment. In support of the proposed Olympic National Park, Edge argued for the "right of the people of the whole United States to save just one little compact piece of this marvelous forest of the Northwest." Carson testified, as well, about "the right of a citizen to be secure in his own home against the intrusion of poisons applied by other persons." But she also recommended specific measures that the government could undertake, such as focusing funds for research on health hazards of pesticides and instituting a federal commission to advise on a broad range of insect control programs.

Of all the historical women featured in this book, Helen Nearing's attitudes toward the U.S. government are the most difficult to reconcile with Carson's. The Nearings' self-sufficient way of living offered an alternative approach, an antidote to the endless polluting of the environment. In *Silent Spring*, Rachel Carson suggested alternative courses of action, other roads that society could take to avoid a future of total contamination. But her ideas were limited in scope, concerned for the most part with biological methods of pest control. Whereas the word "revolutionary" might be applied to what the Nearings wrote about and carried out during their lifetime, the word "reform" might more appropriately describe what Rachel Carson advocated.

As we embark on a new century, the ideas embodied in the writings and actions of the women conservationists featured in this book bring glimmers of hope for a brighter future for the land of the United States. In respect to wetlands maintenance, wildlife protection, preservation of forests and arid lands, sustainable living, and pollution control, what these women advocated is making a positive difference.

Wetlands Maintenance

As Marjory Stoneman Douglas asserted in 1947, swamps have value when left undrained. In the early years of the twenty-first century, citizens of rapidly growing central and south Florida, realizing that their water supply is endangered, are finally listening to her words. They also are learning that vast water management projects constructed in the past, supposedly to prevent flooding, to supply irrigation water for farming, and to drain wetlands for house building, have destroyed the natural ecosystem.

The U.S. Army Corps of Engineers has developed a $7.8 billion plan, named Everglades Restudy, to construct massive water reservoirs and underground aquifers, and to undo canals, levees, and pumping stations that it had built during the past one hundred years. The proposal, deemed to be one of the most grandiose environmental restorations in United States history, has attracted bipartisan political support in both Washington, D.C., and Florida. In the fall of 2000 both houses of Congress authorized a $1.4 billion down payment. When completed in 30 years, the plan envisages that the Everglades' "river of grass" will flow naturally once again, paying heed to the warnings of Marjory Douglas.

But many uncertainties remain. Up to now the project has embraced the disparate players in the southern Florida landscape: real-estate developers, sugar-cane growers, homeowners, national park officials, wildlife protectors, tourists, and politicians of both parties. Talking and signing agreements are one thing, and buying back the land to revert to marshland is quite another matter.

To pay for the massive restoration project a cost-sharing deal has been worked out between the state of Florida and the federal government, each pledging to cover half the total costs. Even before the Army Corps of Engineers had unveiled the details of Everglades Restudy, the federal government announced in December 1997 a $133.5 million land purchase of a 50,000-acre sugar plantation near Lake Okeechobee, in celebration of the fiftieth anniversary of the establishment of Everglades National Park.

Land acquisition by the state government has faced predictable hurdles. In an area where, during the past 50 years, population has grown from 500,000 to 6,000,000 and land values have skyrocketed, owners have not been enthusiastic about selling their property to the government to recreate marshland. The story of the state's plans to rehydrate Golden Gate, a vast area of land situated due east of the city of Naples, is indicative of the type of confrontations that loom ahead in the future.

John Rothchild, the same author who collaborated with Marjory Douglas in writing her autobiography, reported in his book *Up for Grabs* how the developer of Golden Gate had lured would-be homeowners into buying inhabitable plots of swampland during the 1960s. Customers commonly invested $2,500 an acre, paid in installments, having been duped by high-pressure sales practices that were eventually branded as unethical in Florida courtrooms. Although developer Leonard Rosen's company Gulf American Land Corporation was sold in 1974 and Rosen himself died in 1987, the 183 miles of canals and 880 miles of roads he constructed still exist. Houses were built in the northern section of Golden Gate because property there was situated on somewhat higher and drier land, but the southern section of Golden Gate looks much like it did 30 years ago—a grid of streets and canals with few houses.

Still, the landowners, and in some cases the descendants of the original owners, are resisting selling their land to the state. The state government started buying back nearly 20,000 parcels of Golden Gate South in 1985, and by the late 1990s had managed to purchase only one-third of the lots. The price the state is willing to pay for the land, $300 an acre, is admittedly low, but beyond the price is the finality of selling. Building a house in Golden Gate South represented a lifetime dream for many winter-weary Michigan residents.

Land purchase certainly stands as a formidable barrier to the realization of the Everglades water restoration plan, but other concerns are appearing on the horizon as well. Several scientists and outspoken environmentalists are beginning to question the fundamental logic of the plan. Why must the U.S. Army Corps of Engineers erect new elaborate structures when the aim is to recreate a natural flow of water? Why can't old structures be torn down, full stop, without investing additional capital on questionable, new engineering projects?

The challenge in the end may be one of resolving conflicting philosophies. Can engineers and ecologists now agree about how to save the Everglades? Can environmentalists trust the same organization that mismanaged the distribution of water in the Everglades for more than one hundred years to transform itself into an institution that permits water to flow naturally in central and southern Florida? And when it comes to protecting endangered species of animals, is it reasonable to expect acceptance of a regional natural habitat approach when environmentalists and real-estate developers have battled in the courts for decades over land to be set aside as habitats for a single endangered species of bird or fish?

Saving the Florida Everglades is only one aspect of the larger story of the conservation of wetlands' areas in the United States. The public has become conscious of the importance of wetlands for water filtration, regulation of the water cycle, soil erosion prevention, wildlife habitat, and flood control. In regions throughout the country, where long ago marshes have been filled in and replaced with buildings or where permits for new reclamation projects are in process, residents have begun pressuring local authorities to restore wetlands as a vital part of the nation's ecosystem.

One successful initiative is taking place in Cambridge, Massachusetts, in the immediate neighborhood of the Massachusetts Bay Transportation Authority's (MBTA) red line T station at Alewife. Ellen Mass founded The Friends of Alewife Reservation in September 1999 and during a few years the group of concerned citizens has worked hard to clean up the 115-acre site in the Mystic River Watershed, counteracting one hundred years of neglect. Mass, who has lived only a few miles from the reservation for more than 30 years, became a dedicated environmentalist after returning home in 1999 from a five-month solo car journey that took her through 45 national and state parks as far west as Arizona. During her 13,000-mile drive, she saw unspoiled natural wonders but also neglected and mismanaged waterways much like Alewife. She returned to Cambridge with an environmental mission to restore the local wetlands. According to a recent article in *The Cambridge Chronicle*, "Mass has come to embody the very spirit of the place ... whether scrambling down a bank overgrown with invasive plant species to confirm a beaver sighting or leading a group of schoolchildren on a nature walk" (February 13, 2002). The Metropolitan District Commission, owner of the Alewife Reservation, has welcomed citizen participation in its restoration planning to improve wildlife natural habitats, water quality, and flood storage of the extensive wetlands system.

Wildlife Protection

Florence Bailey wrote in the 1890s and early years of the twentieth century that feathers were more beautiful on live birds than atop a woman's hat and believed that people would not want to kill wildlife if they gained an understanding of the habits of live animals. Since her time, the U.S. public has voiced continual concerns about the extinction or near extinction of countless species of animals, and as a reaction to this awakened interest in safeguarding wildlife, Congress enacted the Endangered Species Conservation Act in the late 1960s, a predecessor to the Endangered Species Act of 1973, which is still in effect.

Protecting endangered species has created a flurry of widely publicized legal controversies and there have been recurring attempts to restrict the funding necessary to implement the legislation, and yet there have been some notable successes in the recovery of species once doomed to extinction. Recently, the peregrine falcon and the golden eagle have been removed from the federal government's list of endangered species. Their regained health is credited largely to governmental action in 1972 that banned the use of DDT.

In 1995 Mollie H. Beattie, director of the U.S. Fish and Wildlife Service, which is the successor governmental institution to the U.S. Biological Survey, reported that out of the 909 threatened and endangered species that have been protected under the act's jurisdiction, only seven have since become extinct. On the other hand, critics of the legislation argue that once a plant or animal is added to the list of endangered species, very few species recover fully enough to be delisted. In fact, fewer than two dozen species have been removed since 1973.

The path to delisting is an arduous one, often requiring the protection of the species' natural habitat and usually necessitating a concerted effort by wildlife experts to raise the species in captivity for eventual release into the wild. Conservationists have protected entire ecosystems by saving the natural habitats of the spotted owl and the snail darter, have reintroduced the wolf into Yellowstone National Park and have blocked housing projects and water skiing on lakes in the Pacific Northwest to protect the fragile migration routes of salmon.

In recent years women often have taken a lead in actions to protect wildlife in the United States. They have headed organizations, such as Kathryn S. Fuller, president of the World Wildlife Fund–US, or founded new ones such as Joyce Tischler, who started the Animal Legal Defense Fund in 1979. Her organization sued the Navy in what proved to be a futile attempt to prevent the military's use of dolphins but the fund has had more success defending animals used in scientific research.

Margaret Owings, who was called California's "tiger for conservation," was one of the nation's most prominent wildlife conservationists. In 1968 she established a nonprofit trust called Friends of the Sea Otter to protect the keystone species and its marine habitat. The sea otter, whose numbers had been decimated in the nineteenth and early years of the twentieth centuries in a lucrative fur trade, had been protected by the state of California's designation of a one-hundred-mile coastline refuge. That was not good enough for Owings, however, who demanded a complete ban on the hunting of otters, not only within the boundaries of the refuge; because of the success of the Friends of the Sea Otter organization, the once-threatened sea otter is now totally protected. But Margaret Owings was known to many people who cannot recognize a sea otter, for she devoted most of her 85 years to defending the entire intricate web of life on the California coast. Until her death in 1999 she had championed the cause of sea lions, mountain lions, and redwood trees, and as both an accomplished artist and writer Margaret Owings expressed an intuitive sense of stewardship for the natural environment.

Around the United States an increasing number of local wildlife protectors have become active as well. Mary Bradshaw has spearheaded efforts to conserve sandhill cranes in Montana. In the 1940s only 400 sandhill cranes could be counted in the western United States. Since then, due mainly to large-scale campaigns to poison the coyote, which is the bird's natural enemy, numbers of sandhill cranes have recovered to such an extent that by 1973 the tall, graceful bird was removed from the endangered species list. By the late 1990s, birders estimated that its population had climbed to 19,000 in the Rocky Mountain Flyway with additional thousands counted in California and Arizona.

Mary Bradshaw is trying to create a refuge for sandhill cranes on her ranch in western Montana, but she faces opposition. Because farmers complain that the birds eat their grain crops, hunters have been permitted to shoot an ever-increasing number of the once rarely seen species. On the other hand, Bradshaw contends that sandhill cranes can exert a beneficial economic impact on the region, arguing that the attractive birds can lure birders to visit, helping to transform the area into a tourist destination from which local businesses would certainly profit.

Other efforts to reintroduce wildlife elsewhere in the country have met with a comparable mixture of reactions. Grizzly bears have not been welcomed enthusiastically by ranchers who fear that wild animals will prey on their livestock. Newly introduced mountain lions have killed people in California and Colorado, and in Florida, once-endangered alligators are encroaching into populated areas.

In the case of the California condor, this bird when raised in captivity has become so tame that it has torn through screen doors and entered people's bedrooms in communities to the north of Los Angeles. In 1987, when only 27 California condors existed in the wild, officials captured the last remaining huge birds and started a breeding program. The program succeeded, and at last count the number of California condors had climbed to 162. But instead of securing a natural habitat for this large bird with a wingspan of nine feet, the breeders have raised them in man-made environments without predators and subject them to injury from electrical lines when the birds are released into the wild.

Reintroducing wildlife into the United States, even into such areas that have been especially maintained as wilderness preserves such as Yellowstone National Park, has raised new problems for human interaction with the natural environment. The recovery program for wolves has aroused not only the ire of ranchers, but it has resulted in the killing of many of the animals that have been raised so carefully in the breeding program. With wolves preying on cattle, sheep and even horses, stockmen, whose livelihoods depend upon raising livestock, have suggested only somewhat sarcastically that the family ranch may become the next endangered species.

Preservation of Forests

Rosalie Edge wrote that the price index for timber is not the sole gauge of a tree's worth and criticized road-building projects in national forests. In the 1990s, the federal government removed thousands of miles of roads from national forests, and public outcries against clear-cutting have made some impact on curtailing this especially destructive logging practice.

In October 1999 President Clinton preserved nearly sixty million acres of National Forests, placing them off limits for construction of new roads and banning most commercial logging on the forested land. The timberlands included 49.2 million acres in the lower forty-eight states and 9.3 million acres in Alaska. Environmental groups have pointed out that more than half of the national forests in the United States have already been logged, mined or drilled into for oil, but they commended Clinton's historical initiatives as essential for preserving the remaining forests for recreation, wildlife habitat, and resources of clean water. Clinton has been compared to Theodore Roosevelt, who, as president, originated many of this nation's conservation policies, which, during the course of the twentieth century, have been subjected to continual reversals with changing administrations.

Privately owned forests have not fared so well, and activists on both the east and west coasts have engaged timber companies in often long, drawn-out legal battles. One campaign in Humboldt County, California, has featured women environmentalists and has introduced a new genre of activism called tree-sitting. Julia "Butterfly" Hill lived in a redwood tree, which she named Luna, for two years from December 1997 to December 1999, and her campaign led to eight additional tree-sits in California, Oregon, and Washington. When she climbed down out of Luna, the timber company agreed to spare the tree as well as a nearly three-acre buffer zone around the giant redwood. For her part, Hill and her supporters pledged to pay $50,000 to the company as compensation for lost revenue, and in the end, the company chose to donate the funds to Humboldt State University to further forestry studies.

Legal hassles brought a prominent female politician into this controversy as well. Dianne Feinstein, a U.S. senator from California, brokered an agreement between the Pacific Lumber Company and conservationists to protect old-growth redwood trees and habitat areas for the marbled murrelet. The Headwaters Agreement allowed for the continued sustainable harvesting of redwoods while at the same time protecting the oldest trees for a minimum of fifty years.

At the other side of the country, in the Maine woods, vast expanses of northern timberlands are being sold off by paper companies, who have owned and managed the forests for at least one hundred years. There are efforts afoot to establish a national park on these lands, but local Maine residents are not enthusiastic about federal control. They prefer the status quo that had been worked out with the commercial logging companies over many years, which had allowed hunters, fishermen, boaters, and snowmobilers public access to the forested land. With 15 percent of the land in the state of Maine up for sale, conservationists are concerned that uncut forests are ripe for tourism, recreation and country-house development.

Today, a growing number of citizen environmental groups are planting trees throughout the United States on eroded land, along waterways, and even in urban areas, bringing to fruition ideas that Rosalie Edge advocated during the 1930s. The public is learning about the medical potential of forest plants, and they are becoming aware of the invaluable role that forests play in the absorption of carbon gases that create global warming.

Preservation of Arid Lands

When Mary Austin wrote in 1903 about the rich ecosystem of the Mojave Desert, most people considered this dry land to be worthless, and to accentuate the situation the city of Los Angeles drained Owens Lake, which lies 225 miles north of Los Angeles, to help supply water for the city's population. Today, dust storms from the dry lake bed cause the worst air pollution in the United States, and the municipal government of Los Angeles finally has agreed to cover at least part of the dry bed with vegetation, gravel, and water.

Environmentalists have had some success in conserving vast acreages of desert lands as national parks, in particular the 1994 California Desert Protection Act, which protected more than nine million acres of the Mojave Desert. At the same time, the U.S. military also has been successful in securing vast acreages of California desert for field-testing weapons. Together, the 1.1 million–acre China Lake Naval Weapons Center and the 643,000-acre National Training Center are deemed to be inadequate as training grounds for future types of warfare needs.

Because 21st-century tank warfare tactics involve large brigades rather than smaller battalions, the army says that it requires more territory in which to prepare. New tanks shoot 50 percent further and new supporting helicopter gunships shoot three times the distance of the older helicopters. Therefore, even though an environmental impact report in 1997 argued that the army's planned expansion further into the desert would "harm significantly, if not destroy, pristine desert land," additional land acquisitions for military training are forging ahead.

Recently, however, environmentalists defeated a plan to site a high-tech dump on land abutting Joshua Tree National Park near Palm Springs in southern California, claiming further support for Mary Austin's perception that preserving the desert is important to the continuation of the natural web of life. Minerva Hoyt, who is called the mother of Joshua Tree National Park, campaigned for nearly twenty years to see the proclamation of Joshua Tree National Monument in August 1936. When she was already in her fifties, after the death of her husband and infant son in 1918, she used her membership and leadership in the Garden Club of California to arouse fellow gardeners' interest in desert landscapes.

By the end of the 1920s she had developed a spectacular publicity and educational forum—exhibits of desert habitats. In 1928, she mounted her first exhibition, complete with animals, plants, and depictions of mountain scenery, at the International Flower Show in New York City and afterwards donated the exhibit to the New York Botanical Garden. This exhibition was followed by one for the Massachusetts Horticultural Society in Boston and another for the Royal Horticultural Society in London. At the World's Botanical Congress in Cambridge, England, she formed the International Deserts Conservation League.

Although these exhibitions educated the public about desert flora and fauna, it was, in fact, her persistent lobbying to save a desert habitat in a natural state in California that resulted in the preservation of 825,340 acres as Joshua Tree National Monument. She presented a proposal for a desert national park to the National Park Service for the first time in 1930, but had to wait until Franklin D. Roosevelt's presidency for the federal government to take action on her idea. The national monument lost some of its land to mining interests in 1950, but in 1994 the monument was redesignated Joshua Tree National Park and as such Minerva Hoyt's lifelong aim—to protect a desert in its natural state—was at last fulfilled.

Protection of arid lands remains a pressing concern to conservationists and, as such, disputes about conflicting land uses frequently find their way into courtrooms. Near to Joshua Tree National Park in Palm Springs, the fashionable desert resort only 100 miles from Los Angeles, environmentalists are battling with land developers in a heated dispute over the construction of a new golf course on land claimed as habitat for bighorn sheep. Because much of the desert floor accommodates hotels and shopping malls, developers of golf courses, which already number more than 100 in the Coachella Valley of southern California, are eyeing the mountain slopes that surround Palm Springs. This creates problems for bighorn sheep, accustomed to grazing on these hillsides. The pesticides and fertilizers, necessary to maintain manicured golf courses, have decimated the numbers of bighorn sheep, and encroachment on their natural habitat has led to the animal's recent designation as an endangered species.

Sustainable Living

When Helen and Scott Nearing moved onto a mountain slope in Vermont in 1932, they created a sustainable homestead and a way of living in tune with New England's natural surroundings. They abandoned the Green Mountains of Vermont in 1952 because their mountain slope had been turned into a popular ski run, they wrote sadly in *Living the Good Life*. But today their ideas about natural living—producing food organically, building simple housing, and using renewable sources of energy—have transformed people's ways of living not only in mountainous regions but also in marginal rural areas throughout the country.

The Nearings were vegetarians and their farming techniques led to the growth of an organic gardening movement. Followers have improved upon many of their methods for building soil, breeding plants, managing pests, extending the season to year-round production, and even composting human manure.

The contemporary generation of organic food producers has not restricted itself to vegetable growing. Now farmers also manage livestock organically, raising small herds of cattle, operating dairies, and pasturing poultry. Organic apple growers, using physical and biological pest controls and no artificial fertilizers, can stock orchards with antique varieties and return to many of the practices of last century before fruit growers had ever heard of artificial fungicides and pesticides.

The newest trend, however, called permaculture, is a food production method that encourages perennial cultivation and minimal management. A natural woodland offers the optimal location for this type of farming, for a temperate-climate forest garden with its self-seeding vegetables, herbs, mushrooms, shrubs, and trees can supply year-round human nutritional needs.

Succeeding generations of people with sustainable living habits also have carried on the Nearings' tradition of wholesome eating and publishing compendiums of natural food sources that list hundreds of fruits, vegetables, legumes, grains, nuts, seeds, oils, and herbs. Entire books have been written that feature dandelions and daylilies as useful additions to healthy diets, and several authors have come up with updated versions of Helen Nearing's cookbook, *Simple Food for the Good Life*. A Vermont doctor who recently wrote a family cookbook has even touted psychological benefits from wholesome cooking, purporting that preparing daily meals can be a joyful activity filled with opportunities for family communion.

Another essential aspect of sustainable living from the Nearings' "good life" model is independent homebuilding. Today people are making use of a variety of natural materials to construct houses out of earth, mud, and straw. The rammed earth method involves mixing earth, water, and a little cement into wooden frames to create thick masonry walls. Another popular earth-building technique is based on a material called cob, defined as a lump, which is an old-fashioned concrete made from natural unprocessed materials and is mixed together with sand, clay and straw.

In addition to building houses made from earth, construction with straw bales has spread in popularity because the material's inherent qualities make it seismically stable, fire resistant and a potent thermal insulator. Building structures with straw bales is especially practical for farmers who can annually replenish their renewable resource.

An important objective is the creation of energy-efficient buildings, and solar design, earthen walls, and wind energy have become central elements in this type of architecture. Environmentally friendly construction can make use of earthen walls for insulation, passive solar energy for strategic site and window placement, and small-sized wind turbines for harvesting wind energy. Even the backyard can serve a useful function, for innovative builders have come up with energy-efficient landscaping to reduce utility bills.

Pollution Control

In 1962 Rachel Carson warned about the already-known as well as the potential dangers inherent in the overuse of synthetic pesticides, predicting dire consequences for the environment, wildlife, water, soil, and human health. After *Silent Spring* was published some regulation of the application of pesticides did occur, but Payal Sampat, writing in *Deep Trouble: The Hidden Threat of Groundwater Pollution*, a report published in December 2000 by the Washington-based Worldwatch Institute, reveals that "pesticide use grew 10-fold between the 1940s and the 1990s" (p. 28).

What Carson did set off with her disturbing exposure of the facts about chemical pollutants was a worldwide environmental movement. Since 1962 informed citizens have pressured governments to create laws, institutions, and research facilities to acknowledge, analyze and control pollution. In the United States the Environmental Protection Agency (EPA) was established in 1970 and in 1972 Congress passed the Federal Environmental Pesticide Control Act, which banned the use of DDT. In 1980 the U.S. government went a step further in its efforts to clean up an environment dirtied by chemical wastes with the creation of a superfund for toxic waste abatement.

Yet, at the beginning of the 21st century, environmental pollution caused by chemicals still poses an enormous threat to the continuation of life as we have known it. Banning organochlorines, the type of highly persistent pesticide that includes DDT, did have some positive impact, but some of the organochlorines were not outlawed until many years after the 1972 ban on DDT. Soil fumigant dibromochloropropane, for example, continued to be applied widely in fruit orchards in the San Joaquin Valley in California until 1977, and termite exterminators were using dieldrin in metropolitan Atlanta until 1987 (*Deep Trouble*, p. 25). And the next generation of pesticides is by no means free of toxins for human beings. Already, carbamate insecticides have been shown to damage the nervous system, several herbicides can cause reproductive problems, and other commonly used chemicals have been found to be carcinogens or disruptive to the body's immune systems.

When Rachel Carson collected evidence to support the devastating scenario she presented in *Silent Spring,* she concluded that "there is probably nothing more disturbing than the threat of widespread contamination of groundwater" (*Silent Spring*, p. 47). In the 1990s the U.S. Geological Survey found that the threat had become the reality. They reported the detection of "two or more pesticides in groundwater in nearly a quarter of the sites sampled across the United States" (*Deep Trouble*, p. 26). The new pesticides that scientists believed had shorter lives and therefore would be less dangerous to human health were found to break down relatively quickly in soil but to persist far longer in groundwater. Furthermore, as Carson had warned, unpredictable interactions occur among the many chemicals that come together in water. They degrade, mix, change, and react. As Carson stated in her inimitable prose, in chemically polluted waters "are mingled chemicals that no responsible chemist would think of combining in his laboratory" (*Silent Spring*, p. 49), and that is what is happening in our aquifers today.

Pollution of drinking water supplies is one of a host of new types of environmental concerns that analysts have described as affecting populations, communities and ecosystems. In *Beyond Silent Spring,* a 1996 United Nations Environment Programme publication written by Helmut Emden and David Peakall, the authors contend that in Carson's era the problems "tended to be acute and local," whereas now with acid rain, global warming and the ozone hole the impact is more widespread (p. 6).

The battle against harmful insects, microbes, and weeds has not been a success according to anyone's calculations. Not only have 85–90 percent of the pesticides used for agriculture never reached their target organisms (*Deep Trouble*, p. 40), but during the many decades of intensive application, hundreds of species of insects and weeds have evolved that are resistant to the poisons. Carson had forecast such an "Age of Resistance" because of her knowledge of the population dynamics in the insect world, and she had warned against control programs that upset the balance that nature has created.

In *Silent Spring* she suggested various biological programs that were based on nature's own systems of control as alternatives to chemical pesticides. She recommended planting diversified crops and varieties to replace monoculture agriculture, horticulture or forestry, introducing plants that repel specific pests, and making use of pests' natural enemies: parasites and predators. Progress toward the adoption of these alternatives has been slow, but in recent years along with the promotion internationally of sustainable development policies a strategy known as Integrated Pest Management (IPM) has been making some headway. IPM programs usually involve modified spray programs that encourage a reduction in the overall dependence on pesticides and at the same time lead to the introduction of biological control tactics.

Environmental and human health problems have not diminished since Rachel Carson issued the alert in *Silent Spring*, but progress has been made in helping people to cope with the ill effects of living in a chemically saturated environment. Medical doctors, environmental scientists, entomologists, biologists, plant pathologists, and geneticists have been working on methods for treating flora, fauna and humans.

In Buffalo, New York, pediatrician Dr. Doris Rapp, who is past president of the American Academy of Environmental Medicine, has been providing treatment for children suffering from allergies and chemical sensitivities for more than thirty years. In her book *Is This Your Child's World?* she identifies substances that cause changes in behavioral patterns and she exposes cleaning chemicals and insecticides whose applications inside school buildings can directly impact children's academic achievement. Rapp shows parents how to track down the common food or chemical that may be the culprit, causing their child to be hyperactive or a slow learner. Exposures to chemicals can be responsible for fatigue, headaches, intestinal problems, muscle aches, recurrent infections, bed wetting, hay fever, asthma, hives and learning and behavioral problems, according to

Rapp. By demystifying environmental illness, Dr. Rapp's book goes beyond analysis and offers parents effective approaches to handle "problem" children.

At the governmental level, several countries and cities have enacted legislation that has had the effect of decreasing the total quantity of pesticides in use. In Sweden, Denmark, Finland, and Norway, pesticide sales have been subjected to taxation, and Montreal recently proposed a bylaw to ban pesticide use outdoors on all private or public property with only limited exceptions.

But regulation and restrictions may not be enough. In the opinion of one contemporary environmentalist, "protecting our water in time requires the same fundamental restructuring of the global economy as does the stabilizing of the climate and biosphere as a whole—the transition from a resource-depleting, oil- and coal-fueled, high-input industrial and agricultural economy to one that is based on renewable energy, compact cities, and a light human footprint" (*Deep Trouble*, p. 46).

Conservation in the Future

In order for the conservation ideas embodied in this book to continue to exert a positive impact on the ways we live on our U.S. land, the American public will have to be vigilant and constantly find new approaches to land conservation. With the population of the United States forever increasing and bringing with it new confrontations over conflicting land uses between humans and wildlife and between humans and humans, it will be a continual challenge to preserve some semblance of a natural environment in the United States during the twenty-first century.

All the women featured in this book shared a passion for the environment of the United States and devoted their lives to preserving it. They were concerned about future generations of Americans, the inheritors of the land, and at some time during each of their lives, they addressed the next generation directly.

Many of these best-selling writers wrote works about nature especially for children. Mary Austin, Marjory Douglas, Rosalie Edge, Rachel Carson, Faith McNulty, Anne LaBastille and Terry Tempest Williams each wrote at least one children's book, and several of these authors devoted a major proportion of their total output to children's literature. Others taught classes or led groups into the natural environment so that they could pass on their knowledge to the following generations. Florence Bailey gave birding courses in Rock Creek Park in Washington, D.C., and

Helen Nearing offered seminars at her homestead in Harborside, Maine. Ann Zwinger and Sue Hubbell not only shared with their own children their conservationist ways of thinking but have collaborated in publishing projects with their offspring. Anne LaBastille and Terry Tempest Williams educated young people directly in their capacities respectively as Adirondack Park guide and naturalist-in-residence at the Utah Museum of Natural History.

Perhaps this concern about the next generation is part and parcel of being a woman, with a natural instinct to mother the young. The conservationists featured in this book belong to a long tradition of U.S. women who have taught about the environment.

Anna Comstock, whose book *Handbook of Nature-Study for Teachers and Parents* was published in 1911, usually is credited with launching a nature-study movement in the United States. The large book of nearly 1,000 pages, divided into sections on animals, plants, earth, and sky, was used as a curricular text in U.S. public schools up through the 1930s. It was published in eight languages and reissued in 24 editions. Nature study as a new school subject assumed the aura of an educational fad, responsible for introducing fieldwork in the real world outside the traditional classroom and encouraging children to carry on their own investigations.

For Anna Comstock, writing this book was her means of opening the window to the "working units of this wonderful universe" and spreading her love of nature to future generations. In the book's propagation of an ecological outlook, it appears philosophically akin to contemporary attitudes toward environmental education. As the publisher explained in the preface to the 1939 edition, printed after Comstock's death, the subject matter of the handbook is "the study of the organism in its environment, its relation to the world about it, and the features which enable it to function in its surroundings."

By extending the science classroom to include the real world of nature, Anna Comstock's nature-study movement led the way for succeeding generations of educators to establish outdoor science laboratories. In Arlington, Virginia, for example, the county's female science supervisor founded the Phoebe Hall Knipling Outdoor Laboratory on two hundred acres of land in the foothills of Virginia in 1967, and each year 8,000 Arlington schoolchildren take school field trips there to study principles of conservation.

Women are continuing to pass on to future generations their understandings about the natural environment, making use of the latest teaching methods. Colleen DeLong, education coordinator at Cornell University's

Lab of Ornithology in Ithaca, New York, maintains a website where visitors of all ages can exchange knowledge about nature. By means of the Internet, birders can record their own sightings of birds and study nesting habits through the eyes of a camera that is mounted in the birdhouse.

Margaret Murie, born in 1902, is perhaps the best-known and longest-living American conservationist to encourage new generations to defend and protect the wilderness. Terry Tempest Williams, who referred to her as "a spiritual grandmother," is only one of a list of contemporary conservationists who claim Margaret Murie as their mentor. Murie herself has been identified most closely with the wilderness of Alaska; she campaigned with her husband, Olaus Murie, to establish The Arctic National Wildlife Refuge in the 1950s, testified at congressional hearings for passage of the Alaska Lands Act of 1980, and published two books about Alaska. She grew up in Fairbanks in the early years of the twentieth century and was the first woman to graduate from the University of Alaska in 1924.

Her first book, *Two in the Far North*, published in 1962, described living in the Alaska wilderness with her husband in the 1920s when he was employed by the U.S. Biological Survey. Afterwards, when the family moved to the Teton Mountains in Wyoming, where she still lives, he became an expert on elk in North America and together they wrote *Wapiti Wilderness*. Olaus Murie resigned from the U.S. government in the 1930s and helped to form the Wilderness Society, which he directed, beginning in 1946. Margaret Murie worked alongside her husband at the Wilderness Society, and when he died in 1963 she carried on passionate campaigning for conservation causes in which she believed. Not only did she champion land protection in Alaska, but she worked to establish North Cascades National Park, an area of high mountains, glaciers, and waterfalls in the state of Washington, and to block construction of dam projects in Wyoming, Montana, Idaho, California, and Oregon. For her lifelong achievements as a conservationist, President Clinton awarded the Medal of Freedom to Margaret Murie in 1998, who was at that time 96 years old.

Whether as educators, writers, or activists, the words, the passions, and the stories of the lives of these women conservationists hopefully will inspire following generations to share their convictions. These women, in the words of the popular anthem "This Land is Our Land," were committed to preserve this American land "from the redwood forest to the gulf stream waters."

Appendix
List of Published Writings
of Twelve Women Conservationists

Chapter 1: Mary Austin

The Land of Little Rain. Boston: Houghton Mifflin, 1903.
The Basket Woman. Boston: Houghton Mifflin, 1904.
Isidro. Boston: Houghton Mifflin, 1905.
The Flock. Boston: Houghton Mifflin, 1906.
Santa Lucia. New York: Harper and Brothers, 1908.
Lost Borders. New York: Harper and Brothers, 1909.
Outland. (Gordon Stairs, pseud.) London: John Murray, 1910.
The Arrow Maker. New York: Duffield, 1911.
Christ in Italy. New York: Duffield, 1912.
A Woman of Genius. New York: Doubleday, Page, 1912.
The Green Bough. New York: Doubleday, Page, 1913.
The Lovely Lady. New York: Doubleday, Page, 1913.
California: Land of the Sun. London: A. and C. Black, 1914.
Love and the Soul Maker. New York: Appleton, 1914.
The Man Jesus. New York: Harper and Brothers, 1915.
The Ford. Boston: Houghton Mifflin, 1917.
The Trail Book. Boston: Houghton Mifflin, 1918.
The Young Woman Citizen. New York: Woman's Press, 1918.
No. 26 Jayne Street. Boston: Houghton Mifflin, 1920.
The American Rhythm. New York: Harcourt, Brace, 1923.
The Land of Journeys' Ending. New York: The Century Co., 1924.
The Children Sing in the Far West. Boston: Houghton Mifflin, 1928.
Taos Pueblo. San Francisco: Grabhorn Press, 1930.
Everyman's Genius. Indianapolis: Bobbs-Merrill, 1931.
Starry Adventure. Boston: Houghton Mifflin, 1931.

Earth Horizon: An Autobiography. Boston: Houghton Mifflin, 1932.
Can Prayer Be Answered? New York: Farrar and Rinehart, 1934.
Indian Pottery of the Rio Grande. Pasadena, CA: Esto, 1934.
One Smoke Stories. Boston: Houghton Mifflin, 1934.

Chapter 2: Florence Merriam Bailey

Birds Through an Opera Glass. Boston: Houghton Mifflin, 1890.
My Summer in a Mormon Village. Boston: Houghton Mifflin, 1894.
A-Birding on a Bronco. Boston: Houghton Mifflin, 1896.
Birds of Village and Field. Boston: Houghton Mifflin, 1898.
Handbook of Birds of the Western United States. Boston: Houghton Mifflin, 1902.
Wild Animals of Glacier National Park: The Mammals by Vernon Bailey, The Birds by Florence Merriam Bailey. Washington, DC: Government Printing Office, 1918.
Birds of New Mexico. Santa Fe, NM: New Mexico Department of Game and Fish, 1928.
Among the Birds in the Grand Canyon Country. Washington, DC: Government Printing Office, 1939.

Chapter 3: Rosalie Edge

"The Slaughter of the Yellowstone Park Pelicans." New York: Emergency Conservation Committee, 1932. Publication No. 20.
"Twelve Immediately Important Problems of the National Parks and of Wild Life Conservation." New York: Emergency Conservation Committee, 1935. Publication No. 48.
"Roads and More Roads in the National Parks and National Forests." New York: Emergency Conservation Committee, 1936. Publication No. 54.
"Double-Crossing the Project for the Proposed Mount Olympus National Park." New York: Emergency Conservation Committee, 1937. Publication No. 63.
Our Nation's Forests. New York: Emergency Conservation Committee, 1938. Publication No. 73. Conservation Series Unit VI.
"The Ducks and the Democracy." New York: Emergency Conservation Committee, 1942. Publication No. 87.
"The Duck Hawk and the Falconers." New York: Emergency Conservation Committee, 1944. Publication No. 90.
"The Raid on the Nation's Olympic Forests." New York: Emergency Conservation Committee, 1947. Publication No. 93.
"The Wily and Wasteful Proposal for the Echo Park Dam." New York: Emergency Conservation Committee, 1955. Publication No. 94.

Chapter 4: Marjory Stoneman Douglas

The Everglades: River of Grass. New York: Rinehart and Company, 1947.
Road to the Sun. New York: Rinehart and Company, 1952.

Freedom River. New York: Charles Scribner's Sons, 1953.

Hurricane. New York: Rinehart and Company, 1958.

Alligator Crossing. New York: John Day and Company, 1959.

The Key to Paris. Philadelphia: Lippincott, 1961.

Florida: The Long Frontier. New York: Harper & Row, 1967.

The Joys of Bird Watching in Florida. Miami, FL: Hurricane House, 1969.

Adventures in a Green World: David Fairchild and Barbour Lathrop. Coconut Grove, FL: Field Research Projects, 1973.

Marjory Stoneman Douglas: Voice of the River. (Autobiography with John Rothchild.) Englewood, FL: Pineapple Press, 1987.

McCarthy, Kevin, ed. *Nine Florida Stories*. Gainesville, FL: University Press of Florida, 1990.

McCarthy, Kevin, ed. *A River in Flood and Other Florida Stories*. Gainesville, FL: University Press of Florida, 1998.

Chapter 5: Helen Nearing

Nearing, Helen and Scott Nearing. *The Maple Sugar Book*. New York: John Day, 1950.

Nearing, Helen and Scott Nearing. *Living the Good Life*. New York: Schocken, 1954.

Nearing, Helen and Scott Nearing. *USA Today*. Harborside, ME: Social Science Institute, 1955.

Nearing, Helen and Scott Nearing. *The Brave New World*. Harborside, ME: Social Science Institute, 1958.

Nearing, Helen and Scott Nearing. *Socialists around the World*. Harborside, ME: Social Science Institute, 1958.

Nearing, Helen and Scott Nearing. *Our Right to Travel*. Harborside, ME: Social Science Institute, 1959.

The Good Life Album of Helen and Scott Nearing. New York: E. P. Dutton, 1974.

Nearing, Helen and Scott Nearing. *Building and Using Our Sun-heated Greenhouse*. Charlotte, VT: Garden Way, 1977.

Nearing, Helen and Scott Nearing. *Continuing the Good Life*. New York: Schocken, 1979.

Simple Food for the Good Life. New York: Delacorte, 1980.

Wise Words on the Good Life. New York: Schocken, 1980.

Our Home Made of Stone. Camden, ME: Down East Books, 1983.

Loving and Leaving the Good Life. Post Mills, VT: Chelsea Green Publishing Company, 1992.

Light on Aging and Dying. Gardiner, ME: Tilbury House, 1995.

Chapter 6: Rachel Carson

Under the Sea-Wind. New York: Simon & Schuster, 1941.

The Sea Around Us. New York: Oxford University Press, 1951.

The Edge of the Sea. Boston: Houghton Mifflin, 1955.

Silent Spring. Boston: Houghton Mifflin, 1962.
The Sense of Wonder. New York: Harper & Row, 1965.

Chapter 7: Contemporary Women Conservationists

FAITH MCNULTY

The Funny Mixed-up Story. Los Angeles: Wonder Books, 1959.
Arty the Smarty. Los Angeles: Wonder Books, 1962.
McNulty, Faith and Elisabeth Keiffer. *Wholly Cats.* Indianapolis: Bobbs-Merrill, 1962.
When a Boy Gets Up in the Morning. New York: Knopf, 1962.
When a Boy Goes to Bed at Night. New York: Knopf, 1963.
The Whooping Crane: The Bird That Defies Extinction. New York: E. P. Dutton, 1966.
Must They Die? The Strange Case of the Prairie Dog and the Black-footed Ferret. Garden City, NY: Doubleday, 1971.
Prairie Dog Summer. New York: Coward, McCann & Geoghegan, 1972.
The Great Whales. Garden City, NY: Doubleday, 1974.
Woodchuck. New York: Harper & Row, 1974.
Whales, Their Life in the Sea. New York: Harper & Row, 1975.
Mouse and Tim. New York: Harper & Row, 1978.
How to Dig a Hole to the Other Side of the World. New York: Harper & Row, 1979.
The Burning Bed. New York: Harcourt Brace Jovanovich, 1980.
The Elephant Who Couldn't Forget. New York: Harper & Row, 1980.
The Wildlife Stories of Faith McNulty. Garden City, NY: Doubleday, 1980.
Hurricane. New York: Harper & Row, 1983.
The Lady and the Spider. New York: Harper & Row, 1986.
Peeping in the Shell. New York: Harper & Row, 1986.
With Love from Koko. New York: Scholastic Press, 1990.
Orphan. New York: Scholastic Press, 1992.
Dancing with Manatees. New York: Scholastic Press, 1994.
A Snake in the House. New York: Scholastic Press, 1994.
Listening to Whales Sing. New York: Scholastic Press, 1995.
Endangered Animals. New York: Scholastic Press, 1996.
When I Lived with Bats. New York: Scholastic Press, 1998.
How Whales Walked into the Sea. New York: Scholastic Press, 1999.
If Dogs Ruled the World. New York: Scholastic Press, 1999.
Playing with Dolphins. New York: Scholastic Press, 1999.
The Silly Story of the Flea and His Dog. New York: Scholastic Press, 1999.

ANN ZWINGER

Beyond the Aspen Grove. New York: Random House, 1970.
Zwinger, Ann and Beatrice E. Willard. *Land Above the Trees: A Guide to American Alpine Tundra.* New York: Harper & Row, 1972.

Run, River, Run: A Naturalist's Journey Down One of the Great Rivers of the West. New York: Harper & Row, 1975.

Wind in the Rock: The Canyonlands of Southeastern Utah. New York: Harper & Row, 1978.

Zwinger, Ann and Edwin Way Teale. *A Conscious Stillness: Two Naturalists on Thoreau's Rivers.* New York: Harper & Row, 1982.

A Desert Country Near the Sea. New York: Harper & Row, 1983.

Zwinger, Ann and David Muench (photographs). *Colorado II.* Portland, OR: Graphic Arts Center Publishing Co., 1987.

The Mysterious Lands: A Naturalist Explores the Four Great Deserts of the Southwest. New York: Dutton, 1989.

Aspen: Blazon of the High Country. Salt Lake City, UT: Peregrine Smith Books, 1991.

Zwinger, Ann, ed. *Writing the Western Landscape: Mary Austin and John Muir.* Boston: Beacon Press, 1994.

Downcanyon: A Naturalist Explores the Colorado River Through the Grand Canyon. Tucson, AZ: University of Arizona Press, 1995.

Zwinger, Ann and Susan Zwinger, eds. *Women in Wilderness: Writings and Photographs.* San Diego, CA: Harcourt Brace, 1995.

Yosemite: Valley of Thunder. San Francisco: HarperCollins, 1996.

The Nearsighted Naturalist. Tucson, AZ: University of Arizona Press, 1998.

Zwinger, Ann and David Muench (photographs). *Portrait of Utah.* Portland, OR: Graphic Arts Center Publishing Co., 1999.

Shaped by Wind and Water: Reflections of a Naturalist. Minneapolis, MN: Milkweed Editions, 2000.

Zwinger, Ann and David Muench (photographs). *Colorado.* Portland, OR: Graphic Arts Center Publishing Co., 2001.

SUE HUBBELL

Country Year: Living the Questions. New York: Random House, 1986.

Book of Bees—And How to Keep Them. New York: Random House, 1988.

On This Hilltop. New York: Ballantine Books, 1991.

Broadsides from the Other Orders: A Book of Bugs. New York: Random House, 1993.

Far-flung Hubbell. New York: Random House, 1995.

Waiting for Aphrodite: Journeys into the Time Before Bones. Boston: Houghton Mifflin, 1999.

Shrinking the Cat: Genetic Engineering Before We Knew About Genes. Boston: Houghton Mifflin, 2001.

ANNE LaBASTILLE

Bird Kingdom of the Mayas. New York: Van Nostrand, 1967.

The Opossums. Washington, DC: National Wildlife Federation, 1973.

The Seal Family. Washington, DC: National Wildlife Federation, 1973.

White-tailed Deer. Washington, DC: National Wildlife Federation, 1973.

Wild Bobcats. Washington, DC: National Wildlife Federation, 1973.

Woodswoman. New York: E. P. Dutton, 1976.

Assignment: Wildlife. New York: E. P. Dutton, 1980.

Women and Wilderness. San Francisco: Sierra Club Books, 1980.

Beyond Black Bear Lake. New York: W.W. Norton, 1987. [Later published as *Woodswoman II.*]

Mama Poc. New York: W.W. Norton, 1990.

The Wilderness World of Anne LaBastille. Westport, NY: West of the Wind Publications, 1992.

Birds of the Mayas: Maya Folk Tales: Field Guide to Birds of the Maya World. Westport, NY: West of the Wind Publications, 1993.

Woodswoman III. Westport, NY: West of the Wind Publications, 1997.

Jaguar Totem: The Woodswoman Explores New Wildlands and Wildlife. Westport, NY: West of the Wind Publications, 1999.

Woodswoman IV: Book Four of the Woodswoman's Adventures. Westport, NY: West of the Wind Publications, 2003.

MOLLIE BEATTIE

Forest Management Information and Services: A Guide for Vermont Woodland Owners. Burlington, VT: University of Vermont Extension Service, 1981.

Investment Potential of Timber Management in Vermont. Burlington, VT: University of Vermont Extension Service, 1982.

Beattie, Mollie, Charles Thompson, and Lynn Levine. *Working with Your Woodland: A Landowner's Guide*. Hanover, NH: University Press of New England, 1983. Revised edition, 1993.

"Biodiversity Policy and Ecosystem Management." In *Biodiversity and the Law*, William J. Snape, ed. Washington, DC: Island Press, 1996.

TERRY TEMPEST WILLIAMS

Fancy Free. London: Evans, 1974.

Magic Lights & Streets of Shining Jet. New York: Greenwillow Books, 1977.

Pieces of White Shell: A Journey to Navajoland. New York: Charles Scribner's Sons, 1984.

Williams, Terry Tempest and Ted Major. *The Secret Language of Snow*. San Francisco: Sierra Club/Pantheon Books, 1984.

Between Cattails. New York: Charles Scribner's Sons, 1985.

Coyote's Canyon. Salt Lake City, UT: Peregrine Smith Books, 1989.

Refuge: An Unnatural History of Family and Place. New York: Pantheon Books, 1991.

An Unspoken Hunger: Stories from the Field. New York: Pantheon Books, 1994.

Desert Quartet. New York: Pantheon Books, 1995.

Williams, Terry Tempest and Thomas Lyon, eds. *Great and Peculiar Beauty: A Utah Reader*. Salt Lake City, UT: Gibbs Smith, 1995.

Williams, Terry Tempest and Stephen Trimble, eds. *Testimony*. Minneapolis, MN: Milkweed Editions, 1996.

Williams, Terry Tempest, William B. Smart, and Gibb M. Smith, eds. *New Genesis: A Mormon Reader on Land and Community*. Salt Lake City, UT: Gibbs Smith, 1998.

Leap. New York: Pantheon Books, 2000.

Red: Passion and Patience in the Desert. New York: Pantheon Books, 2001.

Index